Ronald L. Jacobs

Work Analysis in the Knowledge Economy

Documenting What People Do in the Workplace for Human Resource Development

D1569233

palgrave
macmillan

Ronald L. Jacobs
University of Illinois at Urbana Champaign
Champaign, IL, USA

ISBN 978-3-319-94447-0   ISBN 978-3-319-94448-7   (eBook)
https://doi.org/10.1007/978-3-319-94448-7

Library of Congress Control Number: 2018965502

Cover credit @ Arijit Mondal
Cover design by Oscar Spigolon

This Palgrave Macmillan imprint is published by the registered company Springer Nature Switzerland AG
The registered company address is: Gewerbestrasse 11, 6330 Cham, Switzerland

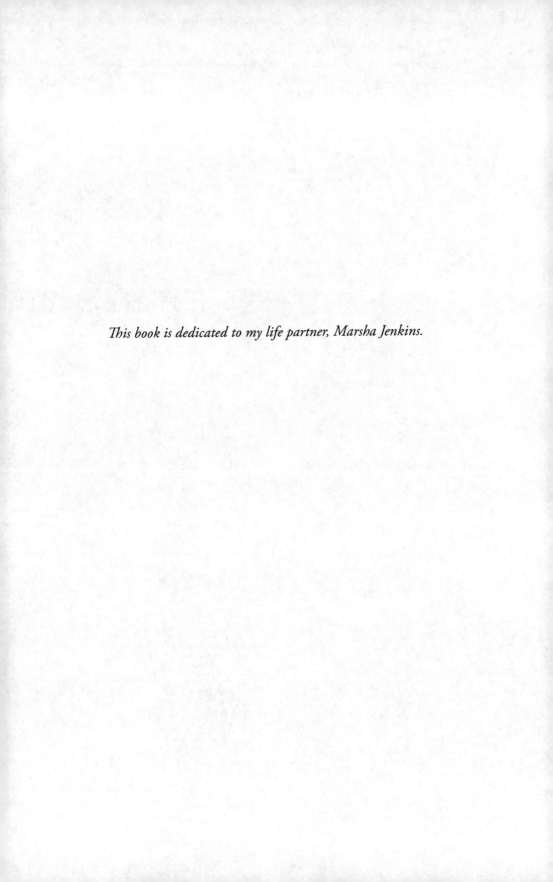

This book is dedicated to my life partner, Marsha Jenkins.

Preface

This book is about the group of techniques used to address two broad questions of importance in organizations: What is the work that people do? And what are the characteristics of the people who successfully do the work? Together, the techniques comprise what is known as work analysis, a process that is indisputably a foundational part of human resource development (HRD) practice. The primary audience of the book comprises current and future HRD and human resource (HR) professionals. Being able to understand work analysis and conduct one or more of the several work analysis techniques described in this book is often a major job expectation of these individuals. The book also seeks to inform and guide technical and vocational educators, organization managers, quality and safety staff members, and workforce and economic development policy makers as well.

Work analysis provides information that has a wide range of uses to support HRD professional practice, including designing training and education programs, designing performance support systems, implementing performance improvement and organization development initiatives, and planning career development efforts. No other professional activity makes available the same extensive set of information as does work analysis. There can be no doubt that work analysis represents a foundational set of knowledge and skills for those involved in improving workplace performance and learning.

The need to understand work analysis appears even more critical given the increasing prevalence of knowledge work in organizations globally. Organizations now face the daunting challenge of documenting these new instances of work, often involving higher-level problem solving, decision making, and critical analysis skills, and then using the information to support efforts to develop individuals to perform the work on a reliable basis. As a result, the book recognizes that work continues to undergo change toward greater complexity, often using information and communications technology as a primary resource, and that the process of work analysis should be responsive to those changes. Those readers who have preconceived notions about work analysis, based on how aspects of it were used in industrial settings in the early part of the twentieth century, should be pleasantly surprised by the more responsive perspective of this book.

Unfortunately, in spite of its recognized importance, work analysis typically receives only limited attention in most undergraduate and graduate curricula. A cursory review of graduate programs of HRD and HR management at several major universities suggests that few, if any, of them offer coursework that goes beyond stating the general importance of the topic. As a result, most HRD and HR management graduates enter practice lacking an understanding of one of the most fundamental activities related to their professions. How many HRD graduates can actually conduct a job analysis, which is a commonly needed activity in many organizations? Indeed, many practitioners and faculty members, as well, often defer becoming involved in such projects, simply because they lack the experience necessary to carry out such a useful project. In presenting both conceptual and practical information, this book seeks to help address this situation.

As stated, the perspective of this book is that work analysis constitutes a set of knowledge and skills that is essential for effective HRD professional practice, and the need is even more pronounced given the emergence of the knowledge economy. The book seeks to address both major questions that relate to understanding work analysis. Some readers may be surprised by this more inclusive perspective, given that few other resources include them as part of a single set of understanding. In spite of their inherent theoretical differences, the two questions in fact represent the needs of contemporary organizations and societies, making it nearly impossible to separate them in practice.

Thus, decisions about how to define work analysis for HRD and, by extension, which techniques to include in the text were founded on both an understanding of the literature and reflections drawn from my own experiences in organizations. Even so, the book recognizes the inherent limitations of prescribing how others should view work analysis and how to carry out the various techniques. Finding the one best way that will fit equally well across all situations is a fool's errand. Frederich Nietzshe, the German philosopher and poet, is famously quoted as saying "You have your way. I have my way. As for the right way, the correct way, and the only way, it does not exist" (Brobjer, 2008). That is, perfection cannot be accomplished with certainty. The book represents a beginning point for readers in terms of work analysis, not an end point.

To move forward in their learning, readers might consider using the following learning process. Readers should seriously consider the information presented in the text, try out using the techniques as much as possible in practice, whether in real or simulated work situations, reflect on the results and the feedback they achieve, and then finally adapt what they have learned to find their own best ways to achieve their own desired results. Astute practitioners will recognize that what has been described represents the elements of sound reflective practice.

Plan of the Book

The book has been designed to present the content clearly and logically. In this way, the book can be used as a text to accompany undergraduate- or graduate-level courses, as a resource for individuals seeking to conduct a project in their organization, school, or agency setting, or to support professional development workshops on the topic. The sequence of the chapters parallels my own approach for presenting the content in the university courses I have taught, and it may be helpful to other instructors as well.

The chapters of the book are grouped into four parts. The four chapters in Part I provide an introduction to work analysis with a focus on understanding work analysis in the context of the HRD field. Part II introduces and discusses in depth how to conduct several techniques that comprise work analysis. Part III shows how to make use of work analysis information to support the design of a range of HRD programs. Finally, Part IV presents two concluding chapters that discuss work analysis in the context of the emerging digital workplace and recommendations for future considerations related to work analysis in the knowledge economy.

Each chapter of the book has been organized in the following way:

- Each chapter title is clear and logically builds from the previous chapters.
- The subject headings are explanatory.
- The chapters in Part II have the same basic format: Description of the Technique, How to Conduct the Technique, and Comment sections.
- The chapters in Part III present information on how to use work analysis information to design various HRD programs, with a specific process presented to guide these actions.
- The chapters in Part IV provide a synthesis of the information in regard to knowledge work and the future practice of work analysis.
- Relevant case study examples and comments from practice are embedded throughout the chapters as appropriate.

- A comment section is included at the end of each chapter that provides a synthesis of the information presented in the chapter.
- Reflection questions are provided at the end of each chapter.
- The appendix presents four examples of S-OJT modules based on knowledge-based tasks.

Final Comments

This book represents nearly 40 years of research and development related to work analysis. Clearly, such an accumulation of scholarship and experience could never have occurred without having opportunities to organize and reflect on the information over time. As a result, all of the tables and figures in the book are original and most all of them represent examples drawn from actual case studies, not simulated ones.

To that end, I wish to acknowledge the two major universities in which I have served during my career—the Ohio State University and the University of Illinois—for affording me the platform from which to engage as a researcher and at times also a consultant across a wide range of organizations. It is difficult to conceive how a book such as this one could be written without such engagements in the field. I also wish to acknowledge that the universities provided me the opportunity to teach undergraduate and graduate courses on work analysis, interacting with literally several hundred students over the years. I can attest that there may be no better way to deeply learn about a topic than the opportunity to teach it to others, blending the theory and the practice.

My experiences as a practitioner could never have been as beneficial without having valued clients as partners. Over the years, many of my clients have since become colleagues and friends as well. For me, there can be no greater personal satisfaction than to build a trusting and respectful professional relationship to achieve the project goals, and then to develop lasting personal relationships with those same individuals along the way.

It should be noted that few of my consulting opportunities have actually been framed as work analysis projects *per se*. That is, having a client request that a work analysis be the sole focus of the project. More often, work analysis was embedded in a broader project effort used to help the client address challenging goals, such as implementing safety and quality improvement programs, facilitating organizational change efforts, meeting regulatory requirements, designing classroom-based and structured on-the-job training programs, identifying areas of individual need through a competency development program, and documenting the nature of occupations for national standards. Such is the supporting role of work analysis. Work analysis provides the information necessary to ensure the success of these and many other HRD projects.

Finally, I wish to specifically acknowledge individuals who have supported my work and influenced my thinking on work analysis throughout the years. Recognizing individuals by name is fraught with risk because of the possibility of omitting those who deserve to be included. But I shall try to the best of my ability, hoping that I have not slighted anyone. For over 30 years, no single individual has influenced my thinking on the topic more than Mike Jones. First as a student, then as a client and friend, Mike has served as a trusted sounding board about work analysis concepts and practices. Perhaps most importantly, Mike has continually reminded me about the inherent dignity of work, regardless of the level of the employee or the nature of the work being done. Even workers who perform what may seem to others to be the most menial kinds of work, in fact, take much pride in what they do and deserve our respect for doing it.

Also influencing my thinking about work analysis has been Richard Swanson, a long-time friend and colleague. My first exposure to the topic came in the 1970s through Dick, while I was a staff member at Bowling Green State University. Others who have influenced my thinking, both directly and indirectly, include Dave Gedeon, Ivor Davies, Bob Heinich, Bruce McDonald, Terry McGiffin, Tom Sands, Fred Nichols, Tom Gilbert, Jan De Jong, Chan Lee, Aahad Osman-Gani, Himank Priyadarshi, Roger Kaufman, Bob Norton, Jeff Flesher, Mohammad Bu-Rahmah and Yacoub Al-Tarrah, Justin Li, Cui Lianbin, and Gemechu Waktola, to name just a few. Finally, also worthy of mention and thanks is the group of current graduate students at the University of Illinois who have both inspired and assisted me in the final preparation of the manuscript.

To those named, and to all others who I have been in contact and perhaps I should have acknowledged by name, I extend my sincerest thanks and gratitude.

Champaign, IL, USA   Ronald L. Jacobs
October 2018

Reference

Brobjer, T. H. (2008). *Nietzsche's philosophical context: An intellectual biography* (p. 149). Urbana, IL: University of Illinois Press.

Contents

List of Figures

List of Tables

Part I

Introduction to Work Analysis

Part I provides an introduction to work analysis in the context of the emerging knowledge economy. Many readers may find that the perspective presented here differs from their own preconceived notion about this area of human resource development (HRD) practice. Today, HRD professionals are being challenged to make contributions in a far more complex environment, requiring a more comprehensive perspective of work analysis.

Part I

1

Defining Work Analysis

The vice president of human resources (HR) from a global telecommunications company decided it was time to find out what are the responsibilities of several key engineer job titles across the company's various global locations. The information would be used to help design a corporate-wide training program for new hire engineers, a strategic goal for the organization. The vice president received back information from several human resource development (HRD) and HR managers, and he immediately realized that the responses submitted were much too broad, inconsistent, and often inaccurate, making the information practically useless for training purposes.

One regional HRD manager even apologized for not sending more specific information, explaining that these jobs were simply too complex to document with any accuracy. The vice president was clearly frustrated when reviewing the unhelpful responses he received, and he began to wonder how the planned training program could be effectively designed without the information he had requested.

The situation described is not unique. Today, many HRD professionals find it difficult to analyze the work in their organizations, and the challenge is made even more daunting when analyzing the work of higher-level technical and professional staff, such as engineers, information technology specialists, and senior managers, among others. The following questions might be asked: Are there limits to what kinds of work can be analyzed? Is work analysis restricted only to work that is relatively simple to perform and easily observed? If these questions were answered in the affirmative, the boundaries of HRD practice in organizations would ultimately be limited, which would not be acceptable.

© The Author(s) 2019
R. L. Jacobs, *Work Analysis in the Knowledge Economy*,
https://doi.org/10.1007/978-3-319-94448-7_1

Perspective of Work Analysis

The underlying assumption of work analysis is that all work, regardless of its complexity, can be documented—that is, made explicit for all to examine—and that information about the work can be made useful for designing an array of HRD programs. Some may disagree with this assumption, suggesting that work today has somehow evolved beyond our ability to analyze it. In this sense, work analysis may be the most misunderstood, if not the most under-utilized, aspect of HRD professional practice.

This book focuses both on understanding work analysis and acquiring the skills to use the various techniques related to this area of practice, regardless of the nature of the work. So the book provides more than just a conceptual under-standing of the topic. It seeks to describe in depth how to actually conduct a work analysis and use the resulting information to design an array of HRD programs. The book focuses specifically on those work analysis techniques that seem most appropriate in today's dynamic, knowledge-based work context.

Work analysis is an area of practice carried out largely by HRD professionals, which explains the primary focus of the book. Other practitioners may also engage in various aspects of work analysis, addressing questions relevant to their respective fields. For instance, HR professionals may use aspects of a job analysis to generate job descriptions and determine appropriate levels of compensation. Industrial engineers use task analysis to help improve the interface between the workers and the work environment. Quality managers document work pro-cesses, often involving teams of employees as part of the effort, to identify prob-lem situations that occur in the processes, such as non-value-added components, and to implement corrective actions. Safety managers often conduct a job safety analysis to help anticipate and show how to respond to safety hazards in the workplace. And, workforce development specialists may use the information to identify occupational standards for a region or nation. As will be discussed in the next chapter, HRD professionals arguably use information that results from a work analysis in more ways than any other profession. The list of HRD pro-grams that depend on work analysis information is quite extensive.

To clarify, work analysis is not about identifying the learning needs of train-ees to perform certain parts of a job, as might be done from conducting a training-needs analysis. Moreover, work analysis is not the same as analyzing the training objectives to identify the instructional content and to sequence the objectives in a logical order, as would be done with an instructional analysis. Neither is work analysis about identifying performance problems, deducing their probable causes, and determining the most appropriate solutions, as would be the case with a performance analysis. All of these pro-fessional practices differ in their intent from work analysis.

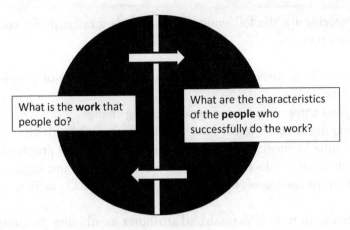

What is the **work** that people do?

What are the characteristics of the **people** who successfully do the work?

Fig. 1.1 Two major components of work analysis

In a broad sense, work analysis focuses on documenting what people do in the workplace, as is suggested by the title of the book. More specifically, work analysis refers to the area of HRD professional practice that seeks to document both the work that people do and the characteristics of the people who successfully do the work. As shown in Fig. 1.1, the definition makes clear that work analysis comprises two major components, or major questions. The first component focuses on analyzing the *work* that is done, regardless of who performs the work. The second component focuses on understanding the characteristics of the *people* who do the work, seeking to find out what makes some individuals more successful in doing the work than others. Because of the fundamental difference between the two components, the figure shows that a conceptual separation exists between them. But the figure also shows arrows that cross over the separation from both directions because, while the components have historically been considered essentially independent from each other, in practice, they often inform and provide context to understanding the other. In this sense, there is an undeniable relationship between them.

Considering both components as the defining aspects of work analysis represents a noteworthy departure from other resources on the topic. Until now, virtually all resources have treated the components as being basically distinct from each other, with little or no mention of one when discussing the other (e.g., Carlisle, 1986; Swanson, 2007; Swanson & Gradous, 1986; Boyatzis, 2008). We now realize that considering both components together responds better to the emerging demands of HRD professional practice in the context of the changing nature of work. For instance, many HRD professionals now have job titles that refer to talent development and management, an emerging area of responsibility that suggests the need for a broader understanding of work and also the people doing the work.

More specifically, the following points provide a rationale for combining the two components:

- Each broadly focuses on understanding the behaviors of people in the workplace.
- Each plays a prominent role when managing change.
- Each requires analysis as the fundamental professional activity.
- Each results in information required for designing HRD programs.
- Each ultimately seeks to facilitate employee learning and improve workforce performance, goals that are consistent with HRD practice.

Admittedly, in spite of these shared attributes, combining the components together in the definition invariably raises some conceptual concerns, as each component has roots in differing traditions of psychology. Consider that the first component—What is the work that people do?—draws mainly from theories of behaviorism, which fundamentally emphasizes a more objective understanding of human behavior.

Behavioral psychology, as described by Edward Thorndike and John B. Watson in the early part of the twentieth century, and then later popularized by B. F. Skinner (1965) in the 1950s, is a perspective of psychology that emphasizes the outward, observable, aspects of human behavior. As a result, most theories of behaviorism generally dismiss, to a varying extent, the importance of internal human processes, such as the constructs related to personality. Human behavior is generally considered best understood from those behaviors that can be objectively demonstrated to exist, and that the behaviors are mostly associated with conditions that occur in the person's environment.

In contrast, the second component—What are the characteristics of the people who successfully perform the work?—draws primarily from theories of personality psychology. In general, personality theory emphasizes understanding how people differ from each other, through an understanding of both their temporary states and enduring traits, and was guided early on to a large extent by the groundbreaking work of Gordon Allport, beginning in the 1930s (Allport, 1968). Theories of personality seek to explain the internal thought processes of individuals, or their cognitive functioning, and to identify those processes as constructs that might be ultimately named and measured.

Even from this brief explanation, the gulf between the two components should be readily apparent. No amount of explanation can really accommodate their differing positions. In brief, one set of psychological theories emphasizes the importance of the environment on human behavior, while the other places more emphasis on the nature of the person as a determiner of behavior. There are theoretical differences between them that simply cannot be bridged.

These differences often appear even greater when groups of researchers get together to discuss their various research and development projects. On more than one occasion, I have witnessed heated professional disagreements occur about which perspective provides better information about a set of work. Comments such as "Oh, you're still doing those old ways of analyzing work" really don't do much to advance practice. Such disagreements have become even more prevalent as behaviorism has been generally perceived as being out of vogue in the social sciences. Why should practitioners discard a set of approaches if they have been shown to be effective in certain situations?

This book takes an informed practical perspective about the differences between the two components. That is, the perspective here is to acknowledge that important differences exist between them, and to suggest that HRD professionals should make wise use of the differences when addressing a broad range of practical problems. For instance, when a manager seeks to find out what people do on their jobs, HRD professionals cannot be first concerned about which theoretical perspective is better. The primary focus should be on matching the appropriate work analysis technique with the question to be addressed, all the while recognizing the theoretical roots of the technique. As stated, considering both components together provides an enhanced opportunity for HRD professionals to address a more comprehensive set of both organizational and societal problems.

For instance, consider that at one point in time the HRD staff of a national retail furniture company had the following HRD projects under way:

- Designing a technical training program for their office employees following the introduction of a new inventory system
- Identifying the sales process used by highly successful sales staff so that this information could be used as part of a sales training program for new hire sales associates
- Creating a long-term leadership development experience that would help individuals with management potential to acquire the characteristics of effective store managers

Both components of work analysis are represented in the HRD projects listed here: the first two projects focus more on the work and the last project focuses more on the characteristics of the people doing the work. HRD professionals should have the ability to recognize the underlying meaning of each situation and respond appropriately.

Work Analysis and the Knowledge Economy

Most readers should be aware that the nature of work continues to undergo much change across all levels of employees. For one thing, in many developed countries, the service sector is now equal in value or greater than the manufacturing sector. Work has invariably trended toward becoming more complex, placing greater demands on the individuals doing the work. Regardless of their level, more and more employees are now expected to engage in higher-order thinking, such as problem solving, decision making, and critical analysis, as part of their jobs, rather than merely performing routine work behaviors.

Peter Drucker (1957) predicted early on that jobs would progressively become more and more complex, coining the term knowledge work. It is interesting to note that Drucker offered these observations long before the introduction of the Internet or the use of advanced information and communications technologies in the workplace. His prescient insights and predictions about the future of work and the effect in organizations continue to resonate among his many followers.

More recently, Jacobs (2017) reviewed what is known about knowledge work and, as a result, introduced the notion of knowledge-based tasks, as a way of seeking a more precise and practical way of understanding knowledge work in the context of HRD practice. How to analyze knowledge-based tasks and develop employees to perform this form of work has become a challenge in many global companies. The fact of the matter is that jobs will likely continue to undergo dynamic change for the foreseeable future.

Understanding the influences of the knowledge economy has become even more important with advancements in using digital technologies in the workplace. Some observers are even now saying that the next economic era has in fact arrived, the Digital Age, which has emerged from the ongoing Information Era. The topic of the Digital Age will be discussed in more depth later in the book. At this point, it is important to briefly consider the implications of knowledge work and digital technology on work analysis.

For instance, consider that almost every job in the health-care field is now being impacted by the introduction of complex technologies, such as imaging devices that rely on algorithms to diagnose and recommend treatments to patients. Beyond health care, consider that jobs in the manufacturing sector no longer rely on simply having workers perform mostly physical work. Instead, most jobs in the manufacturing sector now require an understanding of technology, including the operation of robots when they are linked together, the use of sophisticated lasers to ensure alignment of assembled parts, and even meeting customers' requirements through 3D printing machines. Finally, almost all workers now use, in some way, the Internet, cloud computing, and social media to accomplish their work. There have been dramatic changes in both the intellectual demands placed on workers and the resources used to perform the work.

As new knowledge and advanced technologies are being continually introduced, work analysis has arguably become an even more critical professional skill set, necessary to help identify the changing job requirements and to ensure the efficient and effective integration of the information. How else could organizations and societies alike possibly benefit from the various technological advancements, if no one could actually understand how to use them?

For all of these reasons, the perspective of this book is that previous conceptions of work analysis have necessarily been much too limited. The demands on HRD professional practice now require a more responsive view of work analysis, recognizing the continuing challenges from the knowledge economy.

Historical Roots of Work Analysis

This book seeks to view work analysis from a contemporary perspective. To an extent, many of today's accepted principles about work analysis rest on advances in practice that were developed over a century ago. As a systematic professional activity, work analysis can trace its roots back to the beginning of the Industrial Era in the United States in the 1890s. In this sense, the key advancement made at the time was understanding that work could be understood as being comprised of distinct units of human behavior (Allen, 1922). With careful observation, each unit of the behavior could be written down and made explicit for others to examine as well. This principle—that human behavior can be separated into its component parts—arose from the need to support the manufacturing and production processes used at the time. Even so, this principle continues as a fundamental aspect of work analysis today.

During the Industrial Era, for the first time, large numbers of workers were employed in mass production–related work settings. As a result, consumers could now select from a wide array of products, including readymade clothing, many different household goods, and eventually automobiles. Mass production differed from the previous emphasis on crafts-people making things on a relatively limited scale. Mass production was made possible by a number of technological innovations, the most fundamental of which was the electrification of the industrial work setting. Electricity could now power all the machines required for production and provide a safe way to illuminate the work settings as well.

During this time, companies seeking to achieve high-volume production faced the same basic challenge. That is, how to distribute and organize the work to achieve the most output in the least amount of time, thereby reducing the cost of each product and increasing overall productivity. Perhaps no individual addressed this question with greater success than did Henry Ford, who devised and implemented the belt-driven moving assembly line. Groups of workers were assigned tasks at designated work stations, while the vehicles under assembly passed by them on a moving track at a set speed. Keeping up with the speed of the moving assembly line was a challenge for many of the workers (Lacey, 1986).

Each work station in the assembly line had clearly demarcated sets of responsibilities, however small in their size and limited in responsibility. Each behavior was carefully identified and the entire assembly became a choreography of established sets of actions. Through these advancements in manufacturing technology, from 1908 through 1927, over 16 million Model T Fords were produced. Henry Ford is famously quoted as saying "The man who puts in a bolt does not put on the nut. The man who puts on the nut does not tighten it" (as quoted in Lacey, 1986).

At the same time, Frederick Taylor (1911, 1998) introduced the notion that organizations should adopt a more scientific approach to management. Taylor, who was trained as a mechanical engineer and among the earliest individuals to be considered a management consultant, focused his efforts on devising methods to systematically analyze and then standardize the work. That is, to find the one best way. Using this information, managers could plan which sets of work would be most appropriate for which workers. Of note, the more complex work, which was performed by managers and engineers, was excluded from any analysis.

To achieve higher production volume, each task had to be scrutinized to eliminate any extraneous time-wasting behaviors. To the extent that the work could be made more efficient, the speed of production could be increased and greater production outcomes could be achieved. As a result, Taylor introduced his version of the time-study method, which for the first time sought to find the standard time to perform aspects of a particular task. This could only be accomplished by first analyzing the task according to its discrete behavioral components, and determining how much time was required to perform each component.

In addition to Taylor's groundbreaking work, Frank and Lillian Gilbreth, perhaps better known to some today from the book and film entitled *Cheaper by the Dozen* (Gilbreth & Carey, 1948), devised their own version of the time and motion study approach (Gilbreth & Gilbreth, 1917). Their time and motion study approach has endured even until today, since it uses precise measures to chart the time required to perform each part of the work, based on having a timing device and a list of the component behaviors on hand.

The analyst would observe workers doing the work, identify any wasted motions when doing the behaviors, and then propose alternate ways of performing the behaviors. Today, the time and motion study technique is still conducted by industrial engineers in many organizations, though it has given way to more informative and advanced industrial engineering approaches such as human factors analysis, human error analysis, and lean manufacturing work designs.

The contributions of Frank and particularly of Lillian Gilbreth are worth mentioning further. During the early 1900s, along with a number of collaborators, they produced a number of short silent films showing people performing various types of work, and the analysts using the time and motion study technique to analyze the work. These films were intended as a common reference from which they could devise improvements on how the work was done and also as a means to train the workers on how to do the work. Of particular fascination today is the film showing workers building a brick wall. In their writings, the Gilbreths reported extensively on how they made improvements in the productivity of this job by adjusting the location of the bricks and mortar in the work area (Gilbreth, 1909). Interestingly, the jobs shown in the film, of the bricklayer and the bricklayer's assistant, have not really changed much since that time.

Many of these films have been archived on Youtube.com, and can be easily viewed by using Frank Gilbreth as the search descriptor. The opportunity to view the same work situations that Frank and Lillian Gilbreth observed and later wrote about, over a century ago, is quite enlightening.

Beyond their historical value, the film clips also provide some insight on why individuals and groups, such as organized labor unions, grew to resent most efforts to document what they did on their jobs. In practice, time and motion studies were often perceived as reducing workers' behaviors to mere standardized time sequences—resulting in the sense that workers as individuals were somehow equivalent to machines, often without regard to their safety and physical well-being. Working faster and faster in an effort to increase productivity was the ultimate goal, regardless of the effect on the individuals. Even so, the Gilbreths themselves were sensitive to the psychological effects of constantly finding ways of making work more efficient.

My own experience in the 1980s, when consulting in a General Motors plant, provided insights about some workers' resentments about using time and motion studies. At the time, I sought to analyze certain tasks performed by operators, and to develop training guides to be used with structured on-the-job training programs, which were intended to help future operators learn how to perform the work. Even so, many of them remained suspicious of my intentions, especially since I mistakenly used a clipboard to hold my notes. In general, no one really likes the feeling of being watched and evaluated. What I didn't know at the time was that the clipboard represented one of the hallmark undesirable symbols of conducting a time and motion study, not to mention that the clipboard was being used by a person seeking to appear more important than he really was, and wearing a collared shirt.

From this experience, I learned the importance of first developing an honest and trusting relationship with the individuals being observed and, of course, never using a clipboard from that point forward. A stenographer's note pad is just as useful and often has much less negative symbolism to those people being observed.

It should be noted that, in a historical sense, Frank Gilbreth is often considered the more celebrated partner of this most productive husband-and-wife team. In fact, after Frank's death in 1924, Lillian Gilbreth went on to have an extremely successful career on her own as an innovator, designer, and educator, until her passing in 1972. She was described in a popular publication as being a genius in the art of living. For instance, few people today know that among her many contributions, after doing much research, was that she established the standard height of countertops and appliances—34 inches—which is still in use today. And another little known fact is that she also invented the wastebasket with the pedal-operated lid opener (Gilbreth, 1998).

At first glance, these may seem trivial innovations, but these were simply part of her broader goal of making life easier through solid engineering and an understanding of human behavior. Many people think that Lillian Gilbreth's life achievements, including receiving a Ph.D. in applied psychology in 1915, actually surpassed her husband Frank's. But, because she was a professional woman who excelled during a certain time period, her story has often remained on the sidelines of history.

Today, perceptions about work analysis among some individuals remain decidedly mixed. On the one hand, the techniques devised long ago showed the undeniable value of breaking down human behavior into its constituent parts, which as stated remains a principle that has many uses today. On the other hand, breaking down work behavior has also encouraged the perception that work analysis is best suited for documenting relatively simple, repetitive types of work only, to the exclusion of work that involves both thinking and doing. In addition, as portrayed by Charlie Chaplin in the 1936 silent film

Modern Times, work analysis has also been viewed as a seemingly benign way for management to get the most out of workers, all the while neglecting to respect their basic humanity and well-being along the way.

The use of work analysis techniques developed long ago responded to the needs and prevailing values of organizations at the time. In that context, managers themselves were just learning how to balance the need for productivity and showing sincere sensitivity to their employees.

Today, work analysis has the potential of becoming a strategic partner in guiding change across both organizations and societies, all for the good. But work analysis can do this only if it responds to the challenges of the emerging nature of work. No longer can work analysis focus only on documenting simple, repetitive forms of work. How to analyze all forms of work, including the complex knowledge work that occurs in today's workplace, is an issue of concern and is part of the challenge of this book.

Work Analysis Terms and Techniques

This section defines the basic terms and the major techniques that are associated with work analysis. Additional terms of importance will be defined throughout the book. The definitions presented here establish a beginning understanding of work analysis in the context of HRD. No other resource provides such an integrated set of definitions on the topic of work analysis. The following definitions are grouped to form a logical flow among the basic terms and techniques related to work analysis.

Work

As the underlying focus of the book, work has been selected as the first term to be defined in this chapter. Work can have a somewhat broad meaning, and is defined here as any purposeful activity that involves using an individual's cognitive, physical, and affective abilities that result in outcomes that provide for the livelihood of the individual. Simply put, work is what people do when they are employed and receive compensation for what they do.

Recently, there have been increased efforts to understand the economic and psychological implications of work. Clearly, work influences the well-being of both individuals and societies as a whole, especially since knowledge has become a competitive advantage for nations competing in the global economy. For example, many countries have established national programs to promote the efforts of people to identify the kind of work they find most appealing, and to help them prepare to enter the workforce through organized training, education, and apprenticeship programs.

Nations benefit from such workforce development programs since they help ensure that its citizens have the knowledge and skills to be employed in the types of work that will have value to achieve broader societal goals and that is satisfying and rewarding to the individual as well.

Work also carries with it numerous individual benefits. Being employed relates to many positive social outcomes, such as identity, status, and family stability, among other outcomes (Putnam, 2016). In a more informal sense, work represents a topic of some importance that often arises in conversations among individuals. When strangers meet, the following question is invariably asked: "So, what kind of work do you do?"

The response provides immediate insights about the identity and background of that individual. In sum, work plays a dominant role in the life of most people.

Analysis

In a general sense, analysis is the process of first examining an entity as a whole, and then using a process to systematically take it apart so that its various components can be studied in some depth. Analysis is about deconstructing something—finding the meanings in the individual pieces that are not readily apparent when reviewing the entity as a whole.

Analysis is often a precursor to the act of synthesis, which can be thought of as the opposite of analysis. Synthesis is the process of reassembling the individual components back into a whole entity, often in a form that differs significantly from the original entity. Even the act of simply analyzing something into its constituent parts invariably affects the nature of the whole.

Work Analysis

Work analysis is the primary focus of this book and refers to the various techniques used to both document the work that people do and the characteristics of the people who successfully do the work. As discussed, combining these two major components better reflects the challenges of contemporary HRD practice.

Table 1.1 shows the techniques that are most often associated with the two components of work analysis. Oftentimes, people mistakenly believe that job analysis has the same meaning as work analysis. Job analysis is simply a technique to address certain questions, within the context of the broader understanding of work analysis.

Table 1.1 Techniques related to the components of work analysis

Documenting the work	Understanding the people
• Job analysis—DACUM	• Competency analysis
• Task analysis	• Competency assessment
• Occupational analysis	
• National occupational standards	
• Critical incident technique	
• Work process analysis	

Job

A job represents a formally designated set of responsibilities, as defined by a title and an accompanying description, as a means to define the responsibilities of individuals performing those activities in a particular work context. A job represents what people do in the workplace.

Recently, many organizations have purposely expanded the boundaries of jobs—that is, they have included more responsibilities in them—or have made the boundaries of jobs more permeable and easier to change. Such actions have reduced restrictions on the composition of jobs, enabling greater management flexibility in responding to ongoing challenges that are occurring in many work settings. In this case, many job titles and job descriptions have been written with less specificity, so the meaning of the job often becomes less bounded.

While this trend has benefits for managing change in dynamic work settings, it may also result in some confusion about job expectations and the extent to which workers identify with the content of their jobs. Regardless, the notion of a job remains an important designation and signifies the existence of a specific set of responsibilities within a particular organizational context.

Career

The term career is included in this list to ensure that its meaning is distinguished from job. A career generally refers to the sequence of related jobs that a person may hold over a period of time. A career is an expression of an individual's commitment to the general type of work represented by various jobs, such as a career in law enforcement.

Career denotes the progression of jobs that the individual has done in the past, the individual is currently doing, or the individual plans to do in the future. Regardless of the time referent, career almost always has a relatively long-term meaning attached to it. In this sense, career may refer to the life's work of an individual.

Job Analysis

Perhaps the most well-known work analysis technique, job analysis is the process of documenting information related to a defined role in a specific organizational context. Job analysis can make use of different sources for obtaining information and various methods for gathering the information. A job analysis can generate all or part of the information listed below, depending on the goals and scope of the project:

- The job title and the job description, which provide a high-level overview of the position, the day-to-activities of people in the job, and the workplace environment in which the job is performed
- The broad areas of responsibility or duties within the job
- The individual units of work or tasks within the broad areas of responsibility
- The specific component behaviors within the tasks
- The prerequisite areas of knowledge, skills, and attitudes required to do the work
- The quality information related to the work
- The safety information related to the work
- The various resources related to the work

A scan of this list suggests the potential usefulness of job analysis in organizations. In practice, a job analysis might not document all of this information. The intended goals of the job analysis determine which aspects will be included in the job analysis.

Task Analysis

Often considered as part of job analysis, task analysis can also be considered as a separate technique. Task analysis is the process of documenting the components of individual units of work, commonly known as tasks. As will be discussed, a task is a unit of work that has discernible beginning and end points, discrete from other tasks, and that produces measurable outcomes when the task is completed.

As a self-standing process, task analysis is conducted because there may be interest in knowing more about the behaviors within one or more specific units of work. Or, task analysis can be done as part of a more complete job analysis project, by which some or all the tasks within the job might be analyzed.

Occupation

The term occupation has a broader meaning than that of job. In this sense, an occupation represents a set of similar job titles that occur across different work settings. In this sense, an occupation can also be defined by a title and a description, but this information is necessarily less context-specific than that of a job title and job description. As a result, some referent confusion often occurs when considering the differences between a given job or an occupation.

For example, consider that the title of process engineer can refer to an occupation that appears across different organizations and business sectors. At the same time, process engineer can also refer to a specific job title that occurs within a particular organization. As will be discussed, whether the referent is a job or an occupation has implications for the type of information that will be gathered as part of the work analysis project.

Occupational Analysis

Similar to a job analysis, an occupational analysis is the process of documenting an occupation or a related occupational cluster. Occupational analysis is often perceived to be essentially the same as a job analysis. In practice, an occupational analysis usually provides much more information than a job analysis, with the addition of the following information:

- The business sector in which the occupation occurs
- The occupational cluster or occupations related to a particular occupation
- The current and future availability of position openings related to the occupation, often within a geographic region
- The training and educational requirements for entry into the occupation
- The underlying personality characteristics required of individuals to be successful in the occupation
- The potential for career advancement from this occupation upward to other occupations

As can be seen from the list, occupational analysis also provides a wealth of information useful for planning at the societal, organizational, and individual levels. Later, the book will discuss in depth the use of national occupational standards, which are based on extensive occupational analyses and used to help individuals, primarily youth, prepare to enter the workplace.

Because an occupational analysis represents how the occupation appears across different work settings, many organizations have difficulty making immediate use of occupational analysis information. It is often necessary to identify how the occupation appears within a specific organizational context.

Another focus of an occupational analysis is to document an occupational cluster. An occupational cluster represents a broader perspective than an occupation alone, and often refers to the occupational clusters as they have been identified by the U.S. Department of Labor in their system of Standard Occupational Classification (SOC). For reporting purposes, the federal government has identified 934 separate occupations and has grouped the occupations into 34 occupational clusters. Some of the occupational clusters identified include the following: Information Management and Computing; Managerial, Sales, Marketing, and Human Resources; STEM and Applied Sciences; Transportation, Logistics, and Planning; and, Managerial, Sales, Marketing, and Human Resources. Each of these occupational clusters could have many different occupations categorized within them.

At first glance, one might wonder what is the usefulness of considering occupations and occupational clusters. In fact, this information has much importance for those HRD professionals who work in educational institutions or public-sector agencies. Understanding occupational clusters assists these professionals to plan programs that are responsive to the needs of employers, often within a geographic region. They also provide individuals a means to make more informed career choices for themselves.

Work Process

Since the 1980s, understanding work processes has become an emerging need for HRD professionals. Work processes represent the most prominent aspect of many quality management efforts. The emphasis on work processes makes much sense for improving performance, since this level of organizations represents how the products and services of the organization are actually accomplished.

In terms of a definition, a work process refers to the series of human actions and technology-based events that convert inputs into outputs, involving diverse groups of people, over a period of time, and usually occurring across functional boundaries.

Work Process Analysis

Work process analysis—logically—is the process of documenting the components of a work process. Processes can involve many different components, including direct actions, decisions, inspections, and troubleshooting, among other components. Process analysis typically involves a number of informed individuals, representing the various stakeholder areas in which the work process occurs. Process analysis provides information for many quality improvement efforts including Kaizen and lean manufacturing.

Individual Competency

As stated, the notion of an individual competency draws from a different psychological tradition than the previously defined terms and techniques. An individual competency comes from the personality psychology tradition that is interested in how people differ from each other and how they are similar. The previous techniques focused on the work to be done—occupation, job, and task—and not the individual doing the work.

An individual competency refers to those characteristics, including personality traits, certain abilities, and any other relevant aspects of the individual, such as motivation, that are considered critical for success in a particular job role. Individual competencies are of relevance mostly for individuals at the professional, management, and executive levels of organizations. A job role simply describes the general way in which a person contributes in the organization. For instance, individuals with the job role of middle manager generally oversee and direct the work of others, and this job role can occur across different functional areas. A job role has a broader meaning than a job, and depends on an understanding of the context of the organization.

Of note, an individual competency does not mean the same as an organization's core competency, as defined by Prahalad and Hamel (1990). An organization's core competency describes what an organization does best and how it does it. The selection of which core competencies are of most importance should be reconciled with the organization's mission statement and vision of how it seeks to be viewed by others. As stated, individual competencies focus on the characteristics of individuals, such as their personality traits, not a focus on the organization.

Competency Analysis

As stated, individual competencies refer to the inherent characteristics of individuals, relative to successfully performing the work in the context of a particular job role. Competency analysis is the process of identifying which set of characteristics would be most important for the job role in a particular organizational context. The assumption is that organizational performance can be positively influenced by identifying the characteristics, and then providing that information to individuals for their personal development.

Conducting a competency analysis involves a set of steps that are much different from most other work analysis techniques. For one thing, competency analysis often starts out by asking questions at the highest level of the organization, such as the mission and vision of the organization. These perspectives influence the types of preferred behaviors that individuals should possess to be successful.

Comment

This introductory chapter presents the context of the book—analyzing work has become increasingly complex and based more on knowledge, rather than physical actions alone. Conceptualizing work analysis in response to these changes requires that HRD professionals consider the two major components together. The historical roots of work analysis, founded in the early twentieth century, address the needs of organizations at the time. Now, work analysis should adapt again to meet the needs of contemporary work settings.

Reflection Questions

1. Do you agree with the broader, more comprehensive perspective of work analysis presented in the chapter?
2. Which terms are you most familiar with based on your knowledge and experience in HRD?
3. The term work analysis includes several different techniques, some of which may be new to HRD professionals. Which ones were new to you?
4. By considering the broader term of work analysis, what are the implications for preparing individuals to enter the field of HRD? Does it expand the skill set required of professionals?
5. Competency development differs most when compared to other techniques. Do you agree with this statement? What is the basis for this statement?

References

Allen, C. R. (1922). *The foreman and his job*. Philadelphia: J. B. Lippincott Company.

Allport, G. W. (1968). *The person in psychology*. Boston: Beacon Press.

Boyatzis, R. E. (2008). Guest Editorial: Competencies in the 21st century. *Journal of Management Development, 27*(1), 5–12.

Carlisle, K. E. (1986). *Analyzing jobs and tasks*. Englewood Cliffs, NJ: Educational Technology Publications.

Drucker, P. (1957). *Landmarks of tomorrow*. New York: Harper.

Gilbreth, F. B. (1909). *Bricklaying system*. New York: The M.C. Clark Publishing Co.

Gilbreth, F. B., & Carey, E. G. (1948). *Cheaper by the dozen*. New York: Perennial Classics.

Gilbreth, F. B., & Gilbreth, L. M. (1917). *Applied motion study: A collection of papers on the efficient method to industrial preparedness*. New York: Sturgis & Walton Company.

Gilbreth, L. (1998). *As I remember: An autobiography*. Atlanta, GA: Institute of Industrial and Systems Engineers.

Jacobs, R. L. (2017). Knowledge work and human resource development. *Human Resource Development Review, 16*(2), 176–202.

Lacey, R. (1986). *Ford: The men and the machine*. New York: Little, Brown & Co.

Prahalad, C. K., & Hamel, G. (1990). The core competence of the organization. *Harvard Business Review, 68*(3), 79–91.

Putnam, R. (2016). *Our kids: The American dream in crisis*. New York: Simon and Shuster.

Skinner, B. F. (1965). *Science and human behavior*. New York: Free Press.

Swanson, R. A. (2007). *Analysis for improving performance: Tools for diagnosing organizations and documenting workplace expertise*. San Francisco, CA: Berrett-Koehler Publishers, Inc.

Swanson, R. A., & Gradous, D. (1986). *Performance at work: A systematic program for analyzing work behavior*. New York: John Wiley & Sons, Inc.

Taylor, F. (1911, 1998). *The principles of scientific management*. Unabridged Dover (1998) republication of the work published by Harper & Brothers Publishers, New York, 1911.

2

Human Resource Development and Work Analysis

Human resource development (HRD) professionals typically perform a broad range of activities, often requiring some flexibility on their part, based on the setting in which they practice. For instance, HRD professionals in small and medium-sized companies often have a relatively broad set of responsibilities, compared to their fellow practitioners in large companies. Consider the situation of a 250-employee manufacturing company in Illinois that produces precision, custom-machined products, and which recently decided to seek ISO 9001 certification. A requirement for obtaining the certification is that all tasks and critical work processes should be documented and standardized. The resulting information facilitates efforts to reduce waste, improve quality, and improve on-time deliveries to customers.

The following question might be asked about this situation: Who should be responsible for analyzing the tasks and the work processes necessary to meet the ISO 9001 requirements? Would it be the responsibility of the HRD professional, the HR manager, or the quality manager? It is likely that all of these professionals will be involved in the effort in some way. In fact, the HRD professional may be asked to shoulder more of the responsibility in this regard than the others, simply because training programs would also be planned to ensure that employees are aware of the upcoming certification effort and that everyone can do their jobs properly.

This case study suggests again the broad scope of HRD practice and the range of contributions that many HRD professionals make in their organizations. In this instance, the HRD professional will likely be called upon to design and deliver the awareness training sessions to all employees, develop

© The Author(s) 2019
R. L. Jacobs, *Work Analysis in the Knowledge Economy*,
https://doi.org/10.1007/978-3-319-94448-7_2

a set of performance support guides to be used on the job, and also be involved in analyzing the work processes. Achieving the ISO 9001 certification is a major undertaking for any organization, especially for an organization of this size.

This chapter defines the HRD field in the context of work analysis and the describes four major categories of HRD programs. The categories in effect help define the boundaries of HRD practice. The section also introduces the HRD process, showing how work analysis is part of the first phase of the process, Assess and Analyze.

Human Resource Development

The literature offers numerous definitions of HRD, a fact that often puzzles many newcomers to the field. How can authors define the same field of study and practice in so many different ways? As an applied field of study and practice, HRD has an array of contributing bodies of knowledge, such as adult learning theory, economic theory, organization theory, and system theory. Indeed, depending on their backgrounds, authors can select any one of these theories as the one that best defines the basic nature of the field.

Beginning from the mid-1980s through even today, authors continue to offer their considered perspectives, based on well-established scholarship, about how best to view the HRD field (For example, Jacobs, 1990). At first glance, considering the different perspectives may appear to have uncertain practical usefulness. In fact, the differing perspectives suggest the relative diversity of thought among HRD scholars, which inevitably influences matters of practice at some point. All of this suggests that the HRD field comprises an engaged, vibrant group of global scholars, in spite of the fact that the HRD field may not be as large as some others, such as human resources (HR) management.

Swanson and Holton (2009) provide a relatively comprehensive discussion about HRD as an applied discipline and a listing of the various published definitions at that point in time. A review of the definitions suggest that authors have viewed the field from at least three somewhat distinct perspectives, each having their own respective theoretical underpinnings. The three perspectives will be briefly introduced here, with comments on how each perspective relates to work analysis.

Humanistic

The humanistic perspective generally focuses on fostering employees' need to fulfill their own individual desires and capabilities in the workplace. People are naturally driven toward exploring new areas to learn, and through this learning they can achieve greater quality of work life, job satisfaction, and self-actualization. All of these constructs should be considered of importance in organizations (Merriam, Caffarella, & Baumgartner, 2007).

From this perspective, it is axiomatic to say that when individuals have the opportunity to realize their potential to the fullest extent, they can make more valuable contributions to their organizations. But they can only do this if there is an array of learning possibilities available to them. From the humanistic perspective, HRD practice generally seeks to find ways to help individuals identify meaningful learning opportunities consistent with their own personal goals and of relevance to the workplace.

Not unexpectedly, the humanistic perspective of HRD does not directly focus on work analysis to any extent, since it places greater focus on the needs and interests of individuals than on the work per se. Indirectly, the humanistic perspective seemingly reduces the otherwise important role of expert employees.

From the humanistic perspective, it is generally considered that all employees should have the opportunity to acquire and reflect on information on their own accord, without necessarily having someone else show them the one best way. In this sense, experts are sometimes viewed as using their expert power to impose their knowledge on others, as opposed to encouraging individuals to generate the knowledge for themselves. From a long-term perspective, the learning process may be considered as important as the outcomes of the learning.

From the humanistic perspective, greater value would be given to the use of discovery-based versus didactic training methods, so that employees might generate their own meanings about the work. As will be discussed, the role of experts, or at least experienced employees, plays an important contributing role when conducting almost any work analysis technique. How to reconcile the role that expert employees should play with principles from the humanistic perspective appears problematic.

Learning

The learning perspective generally focuses on the importance of facilitating change through individual and group learning (Watkins & Marsick, 1993). The learning perspective suggests that enduring change can occur only when individuals engage in learning in all its various forms in the workplace. In this sense, employees might learn through a number of different situations: formal, informal, or incidental.

Each of these situations has its own unique characteristics: formal learning occurs as a planned event in a location designated for learning; informal learning occurs as a natural result of individuals sharing their ideas and thoughts about the work, in the actual context of the work setting; and incidental learning occurs in unexpected, almost serendipitous, instances in which insights are gained from doing something else, and the individual realizes some information might be useful in another situation. Not unsurprisingly, the underlying principles of the learning perspective derive mostly from adult learning theory.

The learning perspective appears to recognize the importance of work analysis, but this area of practice does not necessarily play an especially prominent role among its authors who have written about this perspective. When work analysis might be considered, it would be primarily used in formal learning situations, and only in those formal learning situations that have a direct relationship with work expectations. So the use of work analysis is often bounded by a narrow set of circumstances when it is considered appropriate.

From the learning perspective, HRD practice should generally focus on enabling employees to engage in learning in all its various forms. While there is common agreement about the need to promote learning, the overemphasis on informal learning, especially, often overlooks the need to document what is to be learned on a systematic basis in the first place.

Many scholars from the humanistic and the learning perspective dismiss work analysis as being simply obsolete today, based on the view that work analysis is best suited to document the mostly physical and repetitive sets of work, similar to jobs of the early and middle part of the twentieth century. As discussed in the previous chapter, no one can deny the historical roots of work analysis, but the need exists today, perhaps more than ever before, to have the ability to analyze all types of work, particularly the emerging forms of complex knowledge work, and this fact should be acknowledged as well.

Performance

The performance perspective generally focuses on the behaviors of individuals and the outcomes of the behaviors (Gilbert, 2007). That is, how HRD programs are used as a means to influence behaviors that, in turn, will lead to changes in the outcomes of the behaviors, at the individual, work process, group, and organization levels. Performance outcomes can refer to a relatively wide range of measures, through the categories of quality (accuracy, classification, or novelty), quantity (frequency, rate, schedule), or some combination of these when considered in the form of productivity.

The performance perspective generally views employee learning as being important, but learning may not always be necessary for planned change of some kind to occur. For instance, when appropriate, sometimes simply making explicit the performance expectations or implementing some sort of a feedback system about one's performance may be sufficient alone to accomplish the desired change.

Fundamental to the performance perspective is the principle that HRD professionals should identify the desired outcomes of a situation first, before undertaking how to achieve them, since understanding what is desired provides a sense of the goal and what might be the most appropriate HRD program to achieve the goal. That is, starting out by stating the desired results, and then identifying the means to achieve the results afterwards (Jacobs, 2014). Indeed, this basic principle—starting out at the end first—will be referred to throughout the book, as it seems to have relevance across many different situations.

Differentiating between the means, or the nature of the HRD program, and the ends, or the outcomes of implementing the program, constitutes a core aspect of the performance perspective. As a result, this fundamental principle links the performance perspective to system theory as its underlying body of knowledge. System design—logically, the process for the design of a wide range of systems—forms the most identifiable aspect of system theory. As will be discussed later in the chapter, the HRD process is an application of system design.

It is not necessary to determine which one of the three perspectives described here might be best in a relative sense. That discussion is best reserved for venues of a scholarly nature that encourage the exploration of new ideas about the HRD field. Many readers may already have selected their own preferred perspective from previous experience and upon reading the brief summaries in this chapter. In fact, any of one of the three perspectives might be considered the most informative for practice, depending on the nature of the practice and assumptions made about the context in which HRD is being considered.

Of importance here is considering which perspective of HRD provides the most productive way of viewing work analysis. As organizations and nations realize the need to prepare a skilled workforce and respond to changes in the nature of work, there is an increased need for knowledge and skills in work analysis. It is critical for professionals to have the appropriate resources to help make this happen in practice. In this sense, most professionals, knowingly or not, rely upon information drawn from the performance perspective when engaged in their practice, including work analysis. With its reliance on system theory as a basis, the performance perspective provides the most logical viewpoint for understanding work analysis, though the other perspectives contribute as well.

Consistent with this understanding, Jacobs (2014) defines HRD as the process of improving workplace performance and facilitating the learning that supports the performance through the accomplishments that result from employee development, organization development, career development, and performance support programs.

As presented in the definition, four major categories of HRD programs are said to comprise the field:

- Employee development
- Organization development
- Career development
- Performance support

Some references identify three major components of HRD, as was done in the HR Wheel presented in the *ASTD Models for Excellence* study (McLagan & Bedrick, 1983). Though published almost 40 years ago, the study continues to help distinguish the boundaries of the HRD field. In contrast, Swanson and Holton (2009) basically identified only two major categories of the field: training and development and organization development. The four categories of HRD programs as presented are responsive to the ways that work analysis information is used to support the design of HRD programs.

As shown in Table 2.1, employee development programs focus on the different ways that individuals learn through various training, education, and experiential opportunities that help the individuals meet current and future work expectations, as adapted from Jacobs (2014). Employee development programs might be understood through the type of program, the type of program content, the locations where the program would be delivered, and the approaches, methods, and media used to deliver the program.

Organization development programs focus on the human and structural processes to facilitate change among individuals, groups, and organizations. Organization development programs can be grouped according to whether the programs emphasize human relations and self-awareness, individual and group change, or structural change.

Table 2.1 Categories of HRD programs

Employee development	Organization development	Career development	Performance support

Types of learning
• Awareness
• Managerial
• Technical
Learning locations
• On the job
• Off the job
Learning approaches
• Self-study
• One on one
• Small group
• Group
Learning methods
• Discovery
• Presentation—
  Discussion
• Role play
• Drill and practice
• Games and
  simulations
Learning media
• Live trainer
• Recorded
• Computer-based
• Printed materials
	Human relations/
	self-awareness
	• Team building
	• Diversity training
	• Stress
	  management
	• Rope climbing
	• Group
	  experiences
	• MBTI
	Individual/group
	processes
	• Goal setting
	• Performance
	  management
	• Leadership
	  development
	• Coaching
	• Mentoring
	• Commitment
	• Engagement
	• Problem-solving
	  groups
	Structural redesign
	• Task redesign
	• Work process
	  improvement
	• Information
	  technology
		Career planning
		• Talent
		  development
		• Job search
		  programs
		• Career
		  counseling
		• Tuition
		  assistance
		• Job rotation
		Career
		management
		• HR
		  forecasting
		• Talent
		  management
		• MBOs
		• Job rotation
		• Tuition
		  assistance
			Location
			• External
			• Mobile
			• Embedded
			Type
			• Step by step
			• Parts and
			  purposes
			• Reference
			• Artificial
			  intelligence
			Message
			• Text
			• Table
			• Figure
			• Diagram
			• Picture/Icon
			Audience
			• Previous
			  experience
			• Literacy level
			• Relevance
			• Conditions of
			  performance

Adapted from Jacobs (2014)

Career development programs focus on the educational and experiential opportunities to address the future needs of organizations or the interests of individuals. In this sense, career management derives from the needs and priorities of the organization. Career planning comes from the interests of individuals, on what they wish to pursue.

Finally, performance support programs focus on guiding the use of certain behaviors at the time of expected performance, in situations where learning is not necessarily a priority or a desirable outcome. Performance support programs can be used at different locations, using different types of formats and message formats, consistent with considerations about the intended audience.

HRD Design Process

Figure 2.1 presents the general process for designing HRD programs, as adapted from Jacobs (2014). The process is considered general because it includes virtually all aspects of HRD practice. As shown in Fig. 2.2, a more targeted design process might also be considered, such as the ISO 10015 guide for designing training programs, as proposed by Jacobs and Wang (2007) or even the well-known Analyze, Design, Develop, Implement, and Evaluate (ADDIE) training design process. All of these are derived from the

Assess and Analyze the Context and the Work	Design and Implement the HRD Programs	Evaluate and Improve the HRD Programs
• Strategic Planning	• Employee Development	• Performance outcomes
• Needs Assessment	• Organization Development	• Changes in behavior
• Performance Analysis	• Career Development	• Attitudes and perceptions
• Work Analysis	• Performance Support	

Fig. 2.1 General process for designing HRD programs. Adapted from Jacobs (2014)

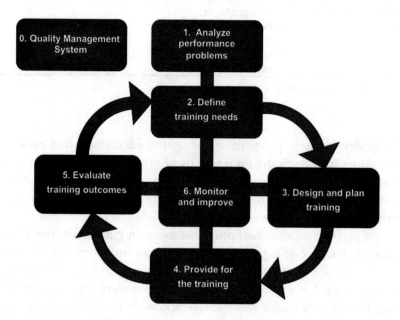

Fig. 2.2 ISO 10015 guideline for designing training programs (Jacobs & Wang, 2007)

general design process. Similarly, Chap. 3 will introduce a work analysis process that is also derived from the HRD process.

All design processes have distinct major phases and, in turn, each phase has a specific set of activities. As shown in the HRD design process, work analysis is a component within the first phase, Assess and Analyze. Each component of the Assess and Analyze phase addresses a broad question of importance.

Briefly, strategic planning addresses questions related to what should be the mid- and long-term focus and direction of the organization? Needs assessment addresses questions related to identifying the priorities that should be addressed for change in the organization. Performance analysis addresses questions related to the nature of the performance problems, their likely causes, and the HRD programs that might be used to address the problems. As shown in Fig. 2.1, work analysis is part of the Assess and Analyze phase, and addresses questions related to the nature of the work and the characteristics of the people doing the work.

The various components of the Assess and Analyze phase suggest that they are logically interdependent on each other. That is, one component might be expected to follow the next one in a logical, orderly sequence. In practice, each component is often considered independent and conducted as a stand-alone professional activity, depending on the needs of the organization. In this sense, work analysis is mostly conducted based on having a specific purpose in mind beyond the work analysis itself. As presented in the following section, work analysis provides information critical for guiding subsequent phases of the HRD process.

Uses of Work Analysis

Information generated from most work analysis projects is literally useless by itself. This statement may appear startling at first glance. But work analysis, regardless of the technique involved, is always used for a purpose, and so the practice of work analysis seldom stands alone. For instance, when a job analysis is conducted, the duties and tasks identified have little meaning unless the information is used later on to develop, say, a training program or establish job standards. The job analysis information should be viewed as inputs to the training design process.

Table 2.2 presents a list of the potential uses of work analysis information, listed across the four major categories of HRD practice. Specifically, the table describes the various ways that work analysis information is used to support the design of programs related to employee development, organization development, career development, and performance support.

Table 2.2 Uses of work analysis information

Categories of HRD practice	Potential uses of work analysis information
Employee development	• Identify the objectives of training programs • Identify content of training and education programs • Design classroom-based training programs • Design structured on-the-job training (S-OJT) programs • Construct performance-rating scales • Construct cognitive test items • Identify potential safety hazards • Identify quality criteria for performing the work • Identify job expectations
Organization development	• Develop job descriptions • Develop job standards • Develop job performance evaluations • Document "what is" and "what should be" of work processes • Provide the basis of performance improvement activities • Meet quality management requirements • Conduct audits of the HR function
Career development	• Construct selection and promotion tests • Match people with the right jobs during selection • Identify the prerequisite knowledge, skills, and attitudes of jobs • Match special skill requirements and disability • Develop national occupational standards • Design technical training and educational programs matched with occupational standards
Performance support	• Prepare company manuals, work instruction sheets, and standard operating procedures • Develop virtual performance guides • Develop physical performance guides

The extensiveness of the list supports the assertion made in Chap. 1 that HRD makes use of work analysis information to a greater extent than any other applied field, and makes work analysis an essential part of HRD professional practice.

Reflection Questions

1. To what extent is the definition of HRD presented here consistent or inconsistent with your own ideas of the field?
2. Can you identify instances of practice that represent each of the categories of HRD practice?

3. Which components of the HRD design process have you had the most experience with, or know the most about?
4. Were you aware that information from a work analysis contributed to such a lengthy list of practices?
5. Of all the practices that depend on work analysis information, which ones have been used currently in your own situation? Which ones might you consider to use in the future?

References

Gilbert, T. (2007). *Human competence: Engineering worthy performance*. San Francisco, CA: Pfeiffer.

Jacobs, R. L. (1990). Human resource development as an interdisciplinary body of knowledge. *Human Resource Development Quarterly, 1*(1), 65–71.

Jacobs, R. L. (2014). System theory and human resource development. In N. Chalofsky, L. Morris, & T. Rocco (Eds.), *Handbook of human resource development*. San Francisco, CA: Jossey-Bass.

Jacobs, R. L., & Wang, B. (2007). A proposed interpretation of the ISO 10015 guidelines for training: Implications for HRD theory and practice. In F. Nafuko (Ed.), *Proceedings of the annual conference of the Academy of Human Resource Development*. Bowling Green, OH: AHRD.

McLagan, P., & Bedrick, D. (1983, June). Models for excellence: The results of the ASTD training and development competency study. *Training and Development, 37*(6), 10–12, 14, 16–20.

Merriam, S. B., Caffarella, R. S., & Baumgartner, L. M. (2007). *Learning in adulthood: A comprehensive guide*. San Francisco, CA: Jossey-Bass.

Swanson, R. A., & Holton, E. F. (2009). *Foundations of human resource development*. San Francisco, CA: Berrett-Koehler Publishers, Inc.

Watkins, K. E., & Marsick, V. J. (1993). *Sculpting the learning organization: Lessons in the art and science systemic change*. San Francisco, CA: Jossey-Bass.

3

Work Analysis Roles and Process

Many human resource development (HRD) professionals may be uncertain about what is their role when involved in a work analysis project, and what process steps they should use to actually conduct the work analysis. Consider the following situation where the director of HRD at a regional furniture chain called together her staff to plan how to develop future store managers. The organization was soon facing the likely retirement of a large number of their current store managers.

Early on, she posed the following question to her staff: What are the characteristics of our best store managers? In response, the various staff members offered their respective opinions in response to the question. They all soon realized that their opinions differed to some extent, and that a more systematic approach to addressing the question should be considered. The HRD director suggested that a competency analysis should be conducted to address the question.

In this situation, the HRD director decided that she would serve as the primary analyst with assistance from some staff members and, in that role, she planned to conduct a number of in-depth interviews with individuals across the organization who were knowledgeable about the store manager position. These included senior executives, regional managers, and respected store managers. All of these individuals would be considered as subject-matter experts (SMEs) of the competency analysis. The HRD director had never served as a store manager herself so, in this situation, she would be considered a content-free analyst.

From the interviews, the HRD director was able to synthesize the information and generate a list of individual competency statements that described the characteristics of effective store managers. The competency statements provided important insights into how to develop the next generation of store managers.

© The Author(s) 2019
R. L. Jacobs, *Work Analysis in the Knowledge Economy*,
https://doi.org/10.1007/978-3-319-94448-7_3

Work Analysis Roles

The preceding brief case study illustrates the importance of understanding the two major roles of those individuals involved in work analysis projects. The HRD director realized that to identify the competencies of store managers, she would be required to obtain information from a relatively wide range of knowledgeable individuals from the organization, because she had never served as a store manager herself. Most work analysis projects involve a group of individuals who serve in one of two basic project roles: (1) analyst and (2) SME. In general, these two roles can be identified, with some expected variation in their arrangements, across most work analysis projects, regardless of the settings in which they occur. The following section discusses the two major roles in more depth.

Analyst

Logically, the analyst is usually the person who is responsible for most aspects of a work analysis project. The next section of this chapter introduces the work analysis process, which the analyst would use to guide how to actually conduct the work analysis. The analyst role is the major focus of this book.

Individuals in the analyst role might be an internal staff member, usually from the HRD function, or the analyst might be an external consultant. Regardless, the issue for both types of individuals is the amount of knowledge they have about the work to be analyzed. One perspective suggests that the analyst should be relatively *content-bound* in relationship to the work. That is, analysts themselves should be, or should be close to being, highly knowledgeable about the work. Thus, the person serving in the analyst role would have dual roles in the project: analyst and SME.

As a rationale for this perspective, the following question is often posed: Who else would be better suited to serve as the analyst other than those individuals who have at least some knowledge and experience about the work? In practice, when knowledgeable employees are asked to analyze their own work behaviors, the decision may be based on expediency—it seems the easiest or quickest way to get the information—or a lack of understanding about what is required to conduct a work analysis.

Another perspective suggests that the analyst should instead be relatively *content-free* in relationship to the work. That is, the analyst would have limited if any knowledge of the work to be analyzed—never having performed it before. In this case, content-free analysts would be expected to collaborate with other individuals who have been identified as SMEs.

In general, the preferred perspective here is for the analyst role to be relatively content-free, recognizing the following two assumptions. First, the analyst has in-depth knowledge and skills in the work analysis process, along with at least some general understanding of the work being analyzed. In practice, the analyst cannot be completely unfamiliar with the work being analyzed. Consider that in the preceding case study, as stated, the HRD director never served as a store manager, but she likely had some understanding about the position based on her many visits to the stores. In an increasing number of instances, the content may be highly complex, such as designing telecommunications networks, requiring that the analyst seek assistance from more knowledgeable employees who also have some experience as an analyst.

Second, it is assumed that other individuals who have the most knowledge about the work will be available to meet with the analyst as needed, recognizing that everyone involved has their own busy work schedules. Again, from the case study, the HRD director had to schedule the interviews with the senior managers well in advance. Today's flatter and leaner organizational structures often make securing access to SMEs all the more difficult.

Many HRD professionals may express concerns about being a content-free analyst. After all, this may be a new role for them and the prospect of trying to make sense of highly complex work content can be intimidating. As a result, some HRD professionals themselves may mistakenly believe that the analysis should best be done by others, such as an SME (Lin & Jacobs, 2008).

In response, the HRD professional should keep in mind the added value of being content-free for achieving the goals of the project. In being content-free, the analyst can be in a better position to ask more probing questions and delve into certain areas of the work content that might be overlooked by a person who is content-bound. In this sense, the content-bound analyst is more likely to simply document what that particular person knows and does in regard to the work. Instead, the content-free analyst is more likely to document what the ultimate user of the information should know and do, such as a future trainee. Knowing how the information will be used later on is a critical aspect of being an effective analyst.

For instance, without meaning any disrespect, whenever engineers in an organization are called upon to serve as analysts, they oftentimes document the work as they see it from their highly knowledgeable perspective, and do not gather the information from the perspective of those who will be using the information, who may be just learning the information. This observation is based on reviewing many technical documents and standard operating procedures over the years that were presumably intended for others to use.

The reader should reflect on the two mindsets that have been presented here, and realize that there are subtle but important differences between them. The role of the content-free analyst can be said to be a fundamental attribute of HRD professionals. How else could HRD professionals effectively focus on different forms of work across different organizations in their careers?

The following list presents some required attributes of individuals in a content-free analyst role:

- Is knowledgeable of the work analysis process
- Has some knowledge or awareness of the work content
- Has respect for the people doing the work
- Has a fundamental curiosity about the work of others
- Understands the interconnectedness of events and things
- Is persistent in seeking to understand complex information
- Can focus both on details and broader views at the same time
- Can express complex ideas clearly in written form

Perhaps the last attribute on the list—the ability to express ideas clearly in written form—is the greatest developmental challenge for many individuals serving in the analyst role. A critical approach to writing is essential, keeping in mind who will be the readers of the information later on.

Finally, in my own experience, there is a fundamental need for the analyst to have a sense of curiosity about the work. I have often playfully used the term "informed knucklehead" to describe the role of the analyst. Admittedly, this is not a very attractive label to place on anyone. But in a somewhat crude way, the term seems to capture the basic approach of the analyst. That is, informed about the work analysis process, perhaps not well informed about the content of the work, but curious and eager to learn about the information nevertheless.

Subject-Matter Experts

As will be discussed in this section, the work analysis process depends on selecting the most appropriate sources of information, the most prominent of which are the individuals who serve in the role of SMEs. As discussed, if the analyst is content-free, conducting the analysis calls for the close collaboration of that person with SMEs, often over an extended period of time.

In many organizations today, the notion of being an SME is a relative term. In fact, most SMEs are seldom considered experts per se. Being considered a true expert results from a long journey of learning and experience for most individuals. While the term SME is most frequently used, perhaps a more appropriate understanding of the role is to identify the employees who possess the most knowledge and experience in a relative sense.

In practice, being identified as an SME simply recognizes that this individual is the most knowledgeable person available relative to the set of work being analyzed. As a result, the SME might even be an employee who has been on the job for as short a time as six months. Or, it could be an employee who is on a short-term contract with the organization. Or it could be a contract employee, who actually works for another organization. Or, in the most distressing situation encountered, it could be an employee who is soon to be laid off, and his or her knowledge was critical to document before leaving the organization. In today's organizations, one should not be surprised by the many different types of individuals who are asked to become SMEs.

The job level of the SME depends on the nature of the work analysis project. Oftentimes, an SME is thought of as a frontline employee, who can operate a certain piece of equipment or is involved in a work process. In practice, almost all levels of employees might be asked to serve as an SME. In the case study at the beginning of this chapter, the SMEs were, in fact, senior managers since they were the most knowledgeable about the store manager position.

Similarly, in projects seeking to document occupations for a national standard, the SMEs were individuals who could be nominated from a variety of sources, including trade associations, industry councils, vendors of the equipment used in the occupation, and community colleges.

Among the general criteria used for selecting SMEs, either formally or informally, are the following considerations:

- Knowledge and skills related to the work
- Length of time involved in the work
- Recognition as being a high-performing individual
- Previous training or educational experiences related to the work
- Formal credentials in topics related to the work
- Willingness to share what they know and can do
- Availability of time they can devote to the project

At first glance, one might believe that being asked to serve as an SME would be welcomed by most individuals, based on the recognition and status it often bestows. In fact, for some individuals, being asked to serve as an SME represents an unwanted disruption in their work schedules, and they may even try to turn down the request. Since the HRD professional works closely with SMEs, they should know what issues and dynamics might hinder the working relationship between them. Regardless of the selection process, being an SME is often a new experience for most individuals. Some individuals might even question why they were selected in the first place.

The following summarizes the common concerns of individuals who are asked to serve as SMEs:

- They have never been involved in a work analysis project before, and are uncertain how the process works and what is expected.
- They are extremely busy with their own work, and cannot see how they can possibly spend the required time collaborating with the analyst.
- They may lack confidence in their knowledge of the work, as they may be comfortable with some of the work content, but not all.
- They dislike being called an SME because it denotes a certain level of competence they are uncertain they possess.
- They may have performed the work for a period of time, but have never really reflected on it before this time.
- They don't want to feel responsible for being the sole source of information about the work.
- They may have other issues with the organization, which are unrelated to this project, that inhibit their motivation to serve in this role.

Many of the reasons stand out as being derived from a lack of understanding of the work analysis process, most prominent of which, especially with work that is highly technical or that has a high consequence if an error is made, is the feeling of not wanting to be responsible for the content as the sole source of information. SMEs should be informed that they are not expected to know everything, that they are just one of several sources of information that will be used as part of the project, and that others will review the information later on for its consistency and accuracy. Regardless, a formal orientation session that clarifies the project goals, the process being used, and the expectations of the respective roles is almost always necessary when working with SMEs.

Analysts Working with SMEs

As stated, in many instances, work analysis involves the close collaboration between analysts and SMEs. How the analyst manages the relationships with the SMEs determines, to a large extent, the success of the project. One of the underlying principles throughout this book is the need to be respectful of all individuals doing work, regardless of their level in the organization.

This book seeks to expand work analysis into addressing knowledge work, which usually involves individuals who have professional education and training of some kind. But by necessity, the book also recognizes that work analysis is used with frontline jobs as well. These jobs may not require extensive prerequisites, so the SMEs may not have the same level of training and educational experience. Regardless, the analyst must always show respect for what the SME brings to the project.

Perhaps one of the most important abilities of the analyst in working with SMEs is helping guide the SME toward providing the necessary information. In a sense, the analyst's role is similar to that of a journalist, who is conducting a purposeful interview for a story, just seeking to get facts about a situation. The analyst is seeking to gather information about a set of work. In both roles, listening skills are critical.

Analysts should especially practice on how to listen at more than one level. In too many instances, the analyst has a list of questions for the SME, and the analyst simply goes through the list, asking the questions and writing down what the SME says. In this way, the analyst does not seem to process the information being received to any extent.

Listening at more than one level means that the analyst both listens to the response given by the SME and allows the SME to finish the thought. At the same time, the analyst listens at another level that would begin to filter the information in context. Internally, the analyst should keep asking: "Am I getting what I need?"

Perhaps the SME has unknowingly strayed from the topic on hand. Perhaps the SME is providing information that is clearly out of sequence. Perhaps the SME is either providing too much detail or insufficient detail about the topic. Perhaps the SME does not really know the information. The analyst should be both respectful in responding to the SME and purposeful in obtaining the information that is required. In effect, the analyst is beginning to impose a structure or framework on the information being received. Figure 3.1 presents a logic flow when the analyst poses questions to an SME, and the process of probing the SME for additional information.

Some resources suggest using a recording device when interviewing or observing an SME (Patton, 2015). In my own experience, using a recording device—whether audio or video—with permission can be helpful because the analyst can then review what was said afterward, when the analyst might be alone and synthesizing the information gathered. At the same time, a recording device should not be used to replace the primary set of interactions between the analyst and the SME, as the use of a recording device might encourage some passivity on the part of the analyst and intrude on the SME.

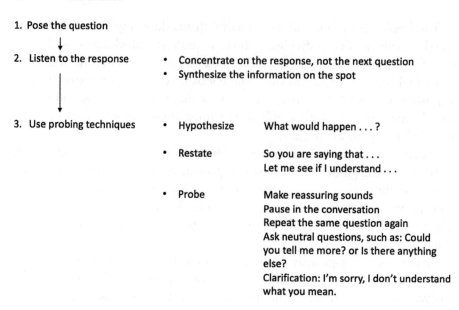

1. Pose the question

2. Listen to the response
   - Concentrate on the response, not the next question
   - Synthesize the information on the spot

3. Use probing techniques
   - Hypothesize — What would happen . . . ?
   - Restate — So you are saying that . . .
     Let me see if I understand . . .
   - Probe — Make reassuring sounds
     Pause in the conversation
     Repeat the same question again
     Ask neutral questions, such as: Could
     you tell me more? or Is there anything
     else?
     Clarification: I'm sorry, I don't understand
     what you mean.

Fig. 3.1 Posing questions and follow-up probing

Working with SMEs can sometimes be frustrating for the analyst, simply because of the nature of the work being analyzed. Early on, analysts often confront what is known as the principle of the extruded middle. From a work analysis perspective, the principle of the extruded middle means that when referring to whether a set of work behavior is actually performed, one SME may say yes and another SME may say no, and they both may fully believe they are giving accurate information. Similarly, from a work analysis perspective, the principle of contradiction also might be confronted, when two versions of the same information cannot both be true at the same time.

The role of the analyst, similar again to the journalist's, is to identify the truth of the matter, but truth in this instance almost always is based on conditions and situations. After all, the SMEs are reporting from their own respective knowledge base and experiences, which may differ from person to person. It is for this reason that using more than one source of information is always recommended in conducting a work analysis.

Work Analysis Process

As stated, work analysis represents the collective of techniques that can be used to address two major questions: What is the work that people do? and What are the characteristics of people who successfully perform the work?

I. Plan the Analysis
   a. Specify the purpose of the analysis
   b. Decide which work analysis techniques will be used
   c. Develop a proof of concept prototype

II. Select the sources and the methods
   a. Select the sources of information
   b. Select the methods of gathering the information

III. Conduct the work analysis
   a. Review the technique-specific process
   b. Use the technique-specific process

IV. Prepare the work analysis report
   a. Prepare the draft version of the report
   b. Review the report
   c. Prepare the final version of the report

Fig. 3.2   Work analysis process

Information from a work analysis can be used to support the design of a wide range of HRD programs. To achieve this goal, a planned process should be used, ensuring that all aspects are considered, making use of resources in the most effective and efficient ways possible. The process supports the accomplishment of a project—which seems the best way of describing the effort required to conduct a work analysis.

Figure 3.2 presents the four phases of the work analysis process and the components of each phase of the process. The purpose of the process is to serve as a general guide for action, regardless of the intent of the project or the techniques used. The process helps practitioners get a work analysis project started and guides their actions along the way. As will be discussed, the sub-processes for carrying out specific techniques, such as conducting a job analysis, will be identified in Part II of the book. The work analysis process can be used to guide the use of the various techniques discussed in the book.

As with all system-theory based planning processes, the work analysis process is seldom followed in a lockstep fashion, without any flexibility. Instead, certain aspects of the process can be repeated or revised based on updated information as required. Whenever the process is used, one can usually expect some back and forth movement during the project, toward achieving the goal. That is simply the nature of using a system approach.

The following discussion introduces each phase of the process and then comments on the components that comprise each phase.

I. Plan the analysis

Logically, the first phase of the work analysis process is to plan the analysis. Within the first phase, there are three related components to consider:

a. *Specify the purpose of the analysis.* In general, the purpose statement addresses two basic questions: (1) what information is sought to be gathered and (2) how will the information be used? Including both questions in the purpose statement maintains the focus on the ultimate reason for conducting the work analysis. By itself, the work analysis information has limited usefulness. The following are examples of purpose statements, showing how both questions are addressed:

- Document the characteristics of successful store managers for the purpose of designing a talent development initiative.
- Identify the process steps used by customer service representatives when troubleshooting a customer's problem, that will be used as part of a new-hire training program.
- Analyze the duties, tasks, and task components of petroleum engineers for the purpose of designing a long-term development program for new-hire engineers.
- Analyze the components of an entire occupation for use as an occupational standard by an industry group.
- Analyze an area of competence within an occupation as part of a curriculum development project in a community college.
- Document the customer fulfillment process that links staff actions from the Contracting, Pricing, and Sales functions for the purpose of cross-training individuals from these various areas.

b. *Decide which work analysis techniques will be used.* Based on the purpose of the analysis, the various work analysis techniques should be considered and the appropriate ones identified. Table 3.1 presents a decision table listing several categories of purpose statements and suggested work analysis techniques to be used with each. The underlying point is that deciding which work analysis technique to use should be guided foremost by the purpose of the work analysis. The separation of means (the various work analysis techniques) and the ends (the purpose statements) is an example of system thinking.

c. *Develop a proof of concept prototype.* In too many instances, a work analysis has been conducted only to realize that the information gathered is not exactly what is required for later use. This can occur in both relatively small projects, such as when a task analysis is conducted to design a performance support document, and a large-scale project, such as when an occupational

Table 3.1 Matching purpose statements and work analysis techniques

If the purpose of the work analysis project is to document the following:	Then the following work analysis technique should be used:
A. Major responsibilities, units of work within the responsibilities, and other descriptive information about a specific job in an organization	Job analysis
B. Behavioral components of units of work in a specific work setting	Task analysis
C. The series of actions over time that lead to an outcome	Work process analysis
D. Underlying characteristics of individuals who are successful in their job roles	Competency analysis
E. Thoughts and actions of individuals when they perform complex knowledge-based tasks	Critical incident technique
F. Major responsibilities, performance criteria, and other descriptive information of related jobs across work settings	Occupational analysis

analysis is conducted to guide the development of a national occupational standard, which will guide curriculum development. In fact, many national occupational standards have low adoption rates, partly because of the difficulty of adapting the information later on.

A proof of concept prototype provides an example upfront on how the work analysis information will be used. It is a way of demonstrating how the end product will appear, for all stakeholders to review. For instance, for the occupational analysis, a proof of concept prototype would show the format of the information to be gathered, and how the information would be adapted for instructional use, with actual examples of course objectives and plans.

II. Select the sources and methods

The next phase of the work analysis process is to select the sources of the information, the methods of gathering the information, and the individuals who will serve as SMEs.

a. *Select the sources of information.* Table 3.2 presents a relatively comprehensive list of the possible sources of information. Sources of information address the question of where will the information come from?

b. *Select the methods of gathering the information.* Table 3.3 presents a list of the most common methods of gathering the information. The methods of gathering information address the question of how the information will be gathered.

Table 3.2 Work analysis sources of information

Job incumbents—Individuals who currently perform a job or a job role, and have knowledge and skills about the work being analyzed.

Managers and supervisors—Individuals who oversee the job incumbents and likely have some knowledge and perspective about the work being analyzed, as they may also have been a job incumbent themselves at one time.

External experts—Individuals who are outside of the work setting and, through their unique backgrounds or experiences, have knowledge and skills related to the work being analyzed.

Instructors and trainers—Individuals who may not actually perform the work, but have some knowledge and skills about the work, based on their experiences in delivering training or educational programs.

Senior managers and executives—Individuals who have an understanding of the mission, vision, and other high-level sets of information, which provide a context for the work being analyzed.

Job postings and descriptions—Documents that provide useful background information about the work being analyzed, but the information is typically broad in nature.

Standard operating procedures and other internal documents—Documents that are used as resources for guiding current practice and, since they were generated in the past, the documents should be reviewed carefully for their accuracy.

Training and educational program materials—Instructional materials that accompany training and educational programs in the immediate work setting, a postsecondary vocational school, or a technical-training institution.

Organizational mission, vision, and value statements—Documents that provide an understanding of the strategic direction of the organization.

Professional organizations—Many professional organizations, such as in the health-care, engineering, and teaching professions have conducted studies to establish performance standards for their respective occupations.

Technical information from vendors—Reference documents provided by those supplier organizations that have provided the tools, equipment, and other resources used as part of the work, and could be in the form of user materials, technical manuals, reference guidelines, and online libraries, among others.

Employment and wage reports—Government agencies and nonprofit organizations that publish employment reports focusing on certain occupations and business sectors.

*O*NET*—Website https://www.onetonline.org is the primary resource about occupational information in the United States. O*NET is a free resource managed by the U.S. Department of Labor, Employment and Training Administration. The database contains information about approximately 1000 occupations, allowing individuals, organizations, and educational institutions the ability to obtain comprehensive information about the occupations. It was originally developed in 1933 as the *Dictionary of Occupational Titles* to assist individuals with their job search. Copies of these encyclopedia-sized volumes, updated every five years, could be found in every public library in the United States. In 2000, the Dictionary of Occupational Titles became a web-based resource, known as O*Net

Research articles—Publications in scholarly journals and the non-scholarly popular literature that report the results of occupational analyses.

Consulting firms—Private-sector firms that have developed extensive databases of individual competencies, which can be accessed for free as a public service or for a fee as part of a contractual agreement with a client.

Table 3.3 Work analysis methods of gathering information

Observe work behaviors—The most commonly used work analysis method is simply to observe people doing the work. The logic is simple—if you want to know what is done, then watch someone doing it, and document what you see. Observation is a good method to use with behaviors that are mostly observable and have a relatively fixed sequence of behaviors.

Observe work samples—A form of observation, this method can be used when continuous observation is not possible and when the work occurs at irregular intervals. Various parts of the work day/week cycle may be selected for sampling. The observer keeps a running log about what is observed. This method is time-consuming and may have internal organization considerations. This method is often used to document work behaviors of managers and professionals.

Conduct individual interviews—Asking questions about the work content can be directed to individual job incumbents or others that know about the work. Interviews are almost always structured in nature and often used in combination with observations. Interviews can also be used to identify information for a questionnaire.

Conduct small group interviews—Mostly structured in nature, but the interviewer raises questions and records the range of responses. Could be done in different ways, such as a focus group setting. Focus groups consist of 8–12 experts with a leader who initiates the discussion on a specific topic. Focus groups are useful in providing a sense of the issues and comparing attitudes, approaches, and knowledge and skills of stakeholders. Experience as a group facilitator is essential to use this method.

Gather critical incidents—A variation of the interview method, the analyst seeks to identify specific incidents from an individual's experience that describe when the job incumbent was effective or ineffective in performing a set of work. The critical incidents are descriptions of the actual job behaviors. An analysis of the incidents helps identify the underlying factors or task clusters that are critical for job performance. The method has been used to analyze work that involves complex decision-making and has multiple means for achieving the outcomes. The critical incident was originally devised in the 1950s to understand how test pilots responded to emergencies in experimental jet aircraft.

Facilitate panel discussions—This method involves facilitating a group of approximately 8–15 stakeholders who have knowledge of the work. The most prominent example of this method is Developing a Curriculum (DACUM). This specific method has proven to be an efficient way of gathering job information as the panel is convened over a two- to three-day period of time. The method requires a skilled person to facilitate the panel. The DACUM method generates much useful information about the job duties, tasks, prerequisite information, among other aspects of a job. The panel sessions occur away from the work setting, which may detract from the accuracy of the information.

Review documents—This entails applying techniques to analyze text information, such as organization websites, internal reports, HR documents, previous job analysis studies, benchmarking studies, and research articles, among others. The output of the review might be in the form of a synthesis table, summary notes, outlines, and so on.

Administer surveys—This method is used to reach many people at a relatively low cost. The major issues with surveys are the uncertain accuracy of the results and the low return rates of the respondents. Survey results may be misinterpreted because of the uncertain backgrounds of all respondents. Surveys may be used in combination with other methods, such as observations and a panel session, as a means to verify that the results are accurate.

Many analysts assume they know which source and method will be used for a work analysis project upfront, without giving much additional consideration to the decision. It makes sense to review the various sources and methods to be used for each project, in case some helpful insights might occur.

For instance, when asked how a job analysis would be conducted, most analysts would simply say they will be interviewing a panel of SMEs. In fact, before conducting the interviews, the analyst also reviewed information about the job on O*NET and some internal documents from the company as well. So while the most apparent source and method was interviewing SMEs, the analyst in fact used other sources and methods as well.

A review of the sources and methods suggests that conducting a work analysis requires some advanced skills in using qualitative research methodologies (analyzing documents, interviewing, and observing) and quantitative research methodologies (survey instrument design, data analysis). Analysts should have knowledge and skills in both of these data-gathering traditions. Information about these skills will be embedded in the following chapters, but readers are encouraged to seek out more in-depth resources, as presented at the end of this chapter, as required.

III. Conduct the work analysis

As stated, the work analysis process serves to guide the actions of practitioners in conducting a work analysis project. Projects differ in their goals, techniques used, and nature of the information that result from the project. In this sense, each project situation likely calls for a technique-specific process that is embedded within the broader work analysis process. For instance, in Chap. 4, the job analysis technique of DACUM will be introduced, which has its own set of steps to follow. In this regard, here are the components of this phase of the work analysis process:

a. *Review the technique-specific process.* Each work analysis technique that is described in this book has a process of its own on how it should be used. The analyst should review the steps of the process and make any modifications based on the goals and any unique aspects of the project.

   For instance, if the DACUM technique was selected, and if all panel members cannot attend the event in person, then the DACUM process needs to be modified to accommodate this change. In practice, if more than one technique is used, then the analyst should be aware of all the technique-specific processes that need to be reviewed.

b. *Use the technique-specific process.* Obviously, this component calls for the analyst to actually conduct the analysis. This is the occasion for using the knowledge and skills that will be introduced in Part II of this book.

IV. Prepare the work analysis report

The analyst should prepare a report that presents the information in a form that satisfies the project goals.

a. *Prepare the draft report.* At the conclusion of the data gathering, a draft report needs to be prepared. The report presents the findings to the clients and stakeholders, and is the core reference document moving forward. To many observers, work analysis reports often appear to be written for a limited audience. The following are some inspection points to keep in mind when preparing the draft report. Make sure of the following:

- The format of the report is clear and obvious to anyone reviewing it.
- The headings are logical and defined without overuse of jargon.
- The use of terms is consistent throughout the report.
- The use of underlines, boldface, and other grammatical conventions are consistent.

b. *Review the report.* The completed draft report should be distributed to the various stakeholders for review and feedback. The analyst should establish some criteria for the review, based on the following questions:

- Is the information presented clearly and easy to understand?
- Does the information accurately represent the work that was analyzed?
- Is the information presented in a way that will be useful later on?

c. *Prepare the final report.* Upon completion of the review, the final version of the report can be prepared. It is important to ensure that the final report becomes a stand-alone document. That is, the report includes all the information that has been generated as part of the project, including the proof of concept prototypes.

Comment

This chapter introduced the two major roles when conducing a work analysis: the analyst and the SME. To be most effective, the analyst should be relatively content-free. That is, it is not necessary for the analyst to have knowledge of the work. In this situation, SMEs play a critical role as a source of information, often the primary source of information. As an analyst, working with SMEs can be either a pleasure, in that each looks forward to the interactions as the project progresses, or it can be difficult. Certainly the analyst has some control in this regard, in terms of how they approach the relationship. Most SMEs respond better when they perceive that the analyst is taking a keen interest in the content, and making a concerted effort to represent the information as best as possible.

The chapter also introduced the work analysis process, which should generally guide all work analysis projects, regardless of the goals of the project and the techniques being used. Each of the chapters in Part II presents a specific process which should be used as part of the general work analysis process. This will occur during Step 3 of the work analysis process. The work analysis process provides an overall sense of how to get started on the project and the issues that should be addressed along the way.

Reflection Questions

1. Have you ever considered the challenges of being a content-free analyst? Is this a role you have ever been involved in before?
2. What are your perceptions of being either a content-bound or a content-free analyst? Do you think being a content-free analyst would be especially difficult?
3. Have you ever been in the role of an SME? What challenges do you think come with this role?
4. Have you ever been involved in a relatively large project, and felt that there was not enough direction on what was happening at each stage of the project?
5. Does the work analysis process make sense to guide work analysis projects? Can you foresee using the process as the basis for your current or future project planning?

References

Lin, Y., & Jacobs, R. (2008). The perceptions of human resource development professionals in Taiwan regarding their working relationships with subject matter experts (SMEs) during the training design process. *Human Resource Development International, 11*(3), 237–252.

Patton, M. Q. (2015). *Qualitative research & evaluation methods: Integrating theory and practice* (4th ed.). San Francisco, CA: Sage.

4

Structures of Work

Regardless of the goals of a work analysis project or the techniques that are used, it is important for the analyst to first recognize that all forms of work have an underlying conceptual structure. As will be discussed in this chapter, most analysts may not fully realize that such structures in fact exist, because they are not always easily observable. But they exist nevertheless, and knowing about them greatly assists when conducting a work analysis. Knowing this information is part of the tool kit of most reflective analysts.

In this sense, the structures themselves represent informal theories that seek to make sense of the behaviors of people when they work. Interestingly, it can be said that each time a work analysis project is conducted, the validity of the theory, as represented by the structure, is tested. The major question would be: Did the structure provide the most useful way of representing the work behaviors in this instance? Throughout my own experience, the structures have always, without exception, proven to be of high value in supporting the analysis of work. The structures presented here are not especially esoteric or complex in nature, as the structures are presented for practical reasons. Understanding the various structures has at least three related implications for work analysis.

First, having a structure provides the analyst with a way of organizing the information across instances according to some established rules. Otherwise, each time a work analysis is conducted, the analyst would in effect be starting over in thinking about how to make sense of the information. Similar to all instances of human behavior, work behavior is often messy and confusing at first glance, and relying upon a structure of some kind begins to provide a means to untangle the situation on hand.

© The Author(s) 2019
R. L. Jacobs, *Work Analysis in the Knowledge Economy*,
https://doi.org/10.1007/978-3-319-94448-7_4

For instance, consider that each time a job analysis is conducted, the analyst can rely upon the structure to help organize the information, even though the job being analyzed at this time might differ to a great extent from the last one. Having an organizing structure imposes a reliable framework for the analyst to use.

Second, having a structure provides a systematic way to communicate the results of the work analysis, providing greater consistency in how the information is formatted and the way the various terms are used. Similar to other professional activities, work analysis has its own technical vocabulary that gives specific meaning to the information presented. This vocabulary becomes important for HRD professionals to adopt as part of their practice and to share with their colleagues as well.

This is not to say that all individuals involved in work analysis necessarily use the exact same rules and guidelines. In practice, there is often much variation in how similar sets of work analysis information are presented. For instance, this is clearly evident when reviewing the various formats and terms used in national occupational standards. Each country seems to have its own way of presenting the information. And variation is even evident when reviewing documents from the same company, such as the different ways that work processes might be analyzed. But, in general, the similarities among these documents are often greater than the differences, and the use of an organizing structure helps make this consistency occur to the extent possible.

Finally, having a structure provides guidance on how one might make best use of the work analysis information later on. As stated, by itself, information from a work analysis has limited meaning by itself, unless a purpose has been identified for it. For instance, as will be discussed in Part III, task statements are in fact the basis for preparing performance-oriented training objectives, which is the beginning phase of designing a training program. And the documents that result from analyses of work processes easily become useful for individuals involved in performance improvement activities. Without the conceptual structures, information from a work analysis would be far less useful.

Structure of Jobs

Figure 4.1 presents the underlying structure of all jobs. This structure is used to help organize the data gathering at the initial stages of a job analysis, arrange the different sets of information gathered during the job analysis, and provide a logical means to present the job analysis information in the final report. This

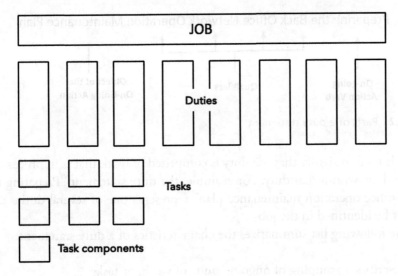

Fig. 4.1 Structure of all jobs

is true regardless of the nature of the job; whether the job happens to be, for instance, a frontline job, a skilled technician job, a professional job, or a senior management job, the structure provides a template that has many practical uses for HRD professionals.

The structure shows that jobs typically have four levels, organized somewhat like a hierarchy based on the amount of information covered at each level. In addition, the structure shows that jobs have various supporting sets of information as inputs that further describe what is required to perform the job.

The highest level of the structure identifies the formal title of the job that makes it distinctive from other jobs. It is at the highest level because it has the broadest perspective of the job. How to prepare a job description will be discussed in Chap. 5.

On the second level, the structure shows that jobs are comprised of entities called a duty. A duty represents an inclusive set of behaviors related to the job. A duty is similar, in a sense, to a family name, since it is composed of a set of related units of work or tasks, which is the next level. Experience suggests that the number of duties within any given job may range from 7 to 12. But the actual number will depend on the results of the job analysis, reflecting the relative complexity and amount of responsibility associated with the job.

As shown in Fig. 4.2, a duty is represented by a duty statement, which, by some convention, is presented in the present participle verb form—that is, ending in "ing"—and the statement starts with the action verb followed by the object of the verb, along with modifiers of the object. The present participle

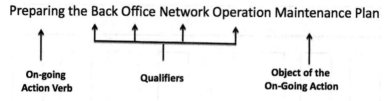

Preparing the Back Office Network Operation Maintenance Plan

On-going
Action Verb
Qualifiers
Object of the
On-Going Action

Fig. 4.2 Parts of a duty statement

form is used to signify that the duty is comprised of work that is in process, or being done within that duty. For example, the duty statement "Preparing the back-office operation maintenance plan" represents one of several duties that might be identified in the job

The following list summarizes the characteristics of a duty statement:

- Describes a grouping of ongoing units of work, or tasks
- Has an in-process orientation
- Action verb that usually ends in "ing" form
- Usually at least 7–12 duties per job, but this depends on the job analysis
- Represents the largest set of outcomes from the job analysis

The third level of the structure comprises the units of work, or tasks, that exist within each duty, and represents the core aspect of understanding any job. Figure 4.3 shows that a task is represented by a task statement which again starts with an action verb followed by the object of the verb, along with modifiers of the object. For example, the statement "Troubleshoot IP network fault problems" represents one of several tasks that might be identified within the duty stated earlier. There may be any number of tasks associated with a duty, but usually the number ranges from 5 to 15 or so. Again, this depends on the results from the job analysis.

As distinct units of work, tasks have some defining features:

- They have definite beginning and end points when performing the task.
- They are performed over a defined period of time, which can be relatively short or long in duration.
- They represent a set of behaviors that are separate from other tasks, though tasks may be related to each other.
- They have a result that is measurable, which could represent a product produced, a service provided, or some other type of result.
- They represent behaviors that can be either observable or non-observable in nature.

Fig. 4.3 Parts of a task statement

Table 4.1 Example list of duties and related tasks

Job title: Network Engineer
A. *Analyzing the IP network*
A.1. Analyze the IP network capabilities
A.2. Gather network performance information
A.3. Analyze the network service history architecture
B. *Identifying IP network preventive measures*
B.1. Develop an evaluation plan for monitoring IP problems
B.2. Formulate daily report on IP problems
B.3. Present preventive solutions to senior management
C. *Managing IP network tier 2 trouble tickets*
C.1. Analyze trouble ticket–related information
C.2. Troubleshoot IP network fault problems
C.3. Develop IP network solution plan

Table 4.1 provides an example list of three duties and the associated tasks within each duty for the job of Network Engineer. For the purposes of the example, only three tasks are shown for each of the three duties. More examples of the relationship between a duty and associated tasks will be shown in Chap. 5, in the discussion about the Developing a Curriculum (DACUM) job analysis technique.

The final part of the structure of jobs includes the individual behaviors that comprise each of the tasks. More information about the nature of tasks will be introduced in Chap. 6, including an explanation about the meanings of the verbs used for duty and task statements. As stated, the task level represents the core aspect of understanding many jobs. An understanding of the components of tasks is called task analysis.

Structure of Occupations

As defined in Chap. 1, an occupation represents how related jobs titles might be viewed across different work settings. Because of their somewhat similar nature, a job and an occupation are often mistakenly viewed as having the same meaning, which is obviously not true. This difference is important for understanding the structure of occupations.

Back-Office Engineer   Technical Support Engineer   Telecom Engineer
Company A   Company B   Company C

Fig. 4.4 Structure of the occupation: telecommunications engineer

Figure 4.4 presents the framework for understanding an occupation. For instance, the occupation of telecommunications engineer typically occurs across several different work situations, and can have different job titles in each organizational context. Again, this structure is used to help organize the data gathering at the initial stages of an occupational analysis, arrange the different sets of information during the occupational analysis, and provide a logical means to present the occupational analysis information in the final report.

This is true regardless of the nature of the occupation. Whether the occupation happens to be, for instance, a technical occupation, a professional occupational, or a senior management occupation, the structure provides a template that has many practical uses for HRD professionals.

Occupations have a title which is the most inclusive and broadest level of the structure. The occupational title may or may not differ from the related job titles. For instance, consider that the job title of Network Administrator can occur in the context of one company. The job likely has unique requirements relevant to the context of that company. But Network Administrator might also be considered as an occupational title when it is understood as occurring across companies or even across business sectors. After all, the job of network administrator can be commonly found in the telecommunications, financial services, and manufacturing business sectors, among several others as well.

In this sense, the occupational title might represent how this occupation occurs within a specific business sector. Following from the preceding example, the title of the occupation might be presented as Telecommunications Network Administrator. The selection of the occupational title depends on the intent of the analysis.

Similar to the structure of a job, the structure of an occupation has a similar set of hierarchical components. In addition, there are inputs to the occupation that are typically more extensive than what is shown for the structure of a job. As will be discussed in Chap. 7, this is necessary because an occupation typically has a broader set of intended uses.

Beyond the title of the occupation, the structure of occupations also includes identifying broad clusters of work, which may be called a duty or a similar term. From the duty statement comes the more specific units of work, most frequently called tasks. As will be discussed, the terminology used for understanding the structure of occupations may not parallel exactly the terminology used for understanding jobs. The structure of occupations does not necessarily include the further analysis of the tasks, simply because of the inherent difficulty in conducting a task analysis at that broad level. As stated, occupations represent related jobs across different workplace contexts. From this understanding, it would not be possible to analyze tasks as part of an occupational analysis, because of the differences in each context. The task level assumes that the behavioral components of the tasks—identified through a task analysis—would need to be identified within each work context.

Structure of Work Processes

As defined in Chap. 1, a work process is the series of human actions and technology-based events that occur over time, often taking place across functional boundaries and involving diverse groups of people, that convert inputs into outputs. Previous perspectives of work analysis have focused on the behaviors of individuals. Instead, a work process emphasizes the series of events that connect the individuals, which fundamentally represents a much different focus.

Figure 4.5 presents the framework of work processes, showing that a work process is essentially composed of a series of pass offs between entities that together function as both suppliers and customers. The figure identifies three entities by the letters A, B, and C. In reality, these entities might have the names of a function, a department, a group of people, or even one individual. By definition,

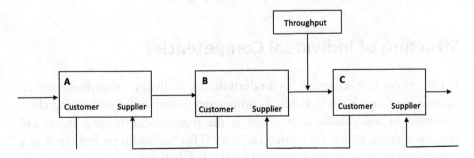

Fig. 4.5 Structure of work processes

suppliers are entities that use their resources to produce something to give to another entity. A customer is an entity that receives what is given by the supplier. As stated, work processes appear as strings of these relationships to achieve the intended goals.

All work processes have inputs, which is where the work process starts, and may be in the form of a connecting work process. The performance outcomes that occur during the work process can be thought of as throughputs. Throughputs are especially critical parts of work processes since they contribute directly along the way to the outcomes. The performance outcomes that occur at the end of the process can be thought of as outputs. Moving from the beginning until the end of the work process can be understood as cycle time. As systems, work processes themselves have inputs, likely another work process, and customers who receive the completed product or service.

This structure is used to help organize the data gathering at the initial stages of a work process analysis, arrange the different sets of information gathered during the work analysis, and provide a logical means to present the work process analysis information in the final report. The structure provides a template that has many practical uses for those seeking to understand the components of the work process and how to improve it.

Work processes can be identified by a title of the work process, which operationally defines the boundaries and what is accomplished. For instance, the work process "Develop IP network maintenance plan" suggests that the output of the work process will be a formal document that presents the components of a plan. Developing the plan likely requires the involvement of several individuals who are knowledgeable of the work process. In this instance, one individual is usually expected to be responsible for ensuring that the events are accomplished and the outcome is produced as a result. The example presents a management type of work process. Chapter 9 will discuss in greater depth the notion of work processes, their different types, how to analyze them, and the various ways they might be represented at the end.

Structure of Individual Competencies

Finally, there is a structure for understanding individual competencies. As defined in Chap. 1, an individual competency refers to the underlying characteristics of individuals, most often at the professional, management, and executive levels, which are considered critical for successful performance in a particular job role—not necessarily in a single job alone.

For instance, a competency, such as Sensitivity to Others, might be considered critical for success regardless of the management level or functional area.

Individual competencies based on:

- Personality dimensions
- Motives
- Knowledge and skills
- Experience

Fig. 4.6 Structure of individual competencies

A competency is a characteristic that exists within certain individuals, with the understanding that others might acquire the competency through a developmental experience.

Figure 4.6 presents the structure for understanding individual competencies. Since the competency is said to exist within the person, the structure portrays an individual and the sources of their competencies, which may include personality dimensions, individual motivations, knowledge and skills, and sometimes experience.

Comment

Some readers may at first be skeptical about the practical value of understanding the structures of work as presented in this chapter. After all, some of the information may simply appear as common-sense information. In practice, the structures have much value for analysts, subject matter experts, and other project stakeholders as well. The structures help clarify for all what the focus of the project is and the necessity of the information being gathered. Having structures is helpful both for the analyst to keep in mind and to communicate the information to others.

Reflection Questions

1. Have you ever considered that all types of work have an underlying structure? Does this make sense as a way of understanding all types of jobs?
2. Now that you know about structures, does this information seem helpful for conceptualizing a set of work you are familiar with?

3. Jobs and occupations differ from each other—can you identify an occupation title that represents a job you have now or have held in the past?
4. Can you visualize what is meant by a work process at this point? What work processes have you been involved with in your work experiences?
5. What is your perception of an individual competency at this point? Does the structure help make the idea more clear? What individual competencies might be important for a position you hold now or have held in the past?

Part II

Work Analysis Techniques

The chapters in Part II begin the transition from discussing the conceptual aspects of work analysis to actually presenting how to use the various work analysis techniques. The techniques presented in the following chapters are the ones viewed as being most relevant for human resource development practice. Additional techniques exist, as well as other ways of using the work analysis techniques included in the discussion. Whatever differences occur, the focus should be on how the resulting information will be used, not necessarily on preferences in gathering the information. How the information will be used seems the most crucial criterion for using the techniques.

Part II

Work Analysis Techniques

5

Job Analysis and the DACUM Process

Of all work analysis techniques, human resource development (HRD) professionals are likely most familiar with job analysis. The term job analysis is commonly used in organizations, though its precise meaning may differ across individuals. For some, the term job analysis somehow encompasses all work analysis activities. On more than one occasion, I've heard a manager say something like "We should do a job analysis so that people will know how to operate the new equipment". In actuality, conducting a job analysis would result in much more information than what is required to achieve this particular goal. And job analysis may not provide all the details to help the operators perform the new work. Task analysis would be the technique that would more accurately address this request.

For others, the term job analysis represents a way of determining what information is required to help recruit and select new employees. In fact, the use of job analysis in this way is more closely associated with the responsibilities of a human resource professional, not an HRD professional. When HRD professionals hear the term job analysis referred to in so many ways, they are often uncertain of what it means in terms of their own areas of practice. This chapter seeks to provide a clear understanding of job analysis, with a focus on the well-known job analysis technique called Developing a Curriculum (DACUM). DACUM has been used on a global basis across many different situations.

© The Author(s) 2019
R. L. Jacobs, *Work Analysis in the Knowledge Economy*,
https://doi.org/10.1007/978-3-319-94448-7_5

Job Analysis

As defined in Chap. 1, job analysis is one of the major techniques that are part of work analysis. In general, job analysis is the technique to use when there is a need to provide information about a defined job as it exists in a specific workplace context. A job analysis can result in all or part of the information listed below, depending on the goals and scope of the project:

- Job title and job description, which provides a high-level overview of the position, the day-to-activities of people in the job, and the workplace environment in which the job is performed
- Broad areas of responsibility or duties within the job
- Units of work or tasks within each of the duties
- Prerequisite areas of knowledge, skills, and attitudes required to do the work
- General quality requirements related to the work
- General safety requirements related to the work
- Various resources that are used as part of the job
- Additional information that would enable an individual to be successful in the job

A scan of this list suggests the potential usefulness of job analysis. In practice, some job analysis projects might not document all of this information. The intended use of the information will determine which aspects will be included in the job analysis.

For instance, a regional bank in the Midwest shifted its strategic focus so that it can begin to offer extended customer services within each branch office, through the job called personal banker. As a result, the bank undertook a comprehensive job analysis of the major responsibilities and specific units of work within this newly identified constituted job. The job analysis also included information about the educational prerequisites of the job. The results of the job analysis were used in a number of different ways, including the design of a training program, a coaching program to be delivered by branch office managers, and the content of the performance review document to be used by the managers at each branch.

It should be noted that the job analysis was conducted on a job that essentially did not formally exist in the bank, though managers were already performing some aspects of it. The job was now being established on a formal basis for the first time. As a result, the job analysis focused on what management envisioned the job should entail in the future, not what it currently looked like. Most job analysis projects more often focus on documenting the components of existing jobs, but that does not need to be the case in all instances. Obviously, the context of the project will determine the nature of the data gathering.

In addition, the results of the job analysis helped identify that there was a need for developing a proprietary customer service process, that the personal bankers would follow when they meet with customers. This was considered a critical part of the job. The following job duty was pinpointed: Identifying the financial needs of customers. And with that duty came the realization that the personal bankers should have a formal process to follow when they actually work with a customer.

Conducting a Job Analysis—DACUM

The literature discusses several different approaches on conducting a job analysis. The focus of this chapter will be on the job analysis technique called Developing a Curriculum (DACUM). DACUM was first developed in the late 1960s to analyze the content of occupations as the basis for designing technical courses in community college settings. Since that time, DACUM has been used across a wide range of jobs, both professional and nonprofessional, and work settings, including community colleges and technical schools, national policy centers, nonprofit nongovernmental organizations, and business and industries.

Today, a relatively large number of universities, community colleges, and private-sector consultants provide services related to DACUM, including programs that train individuals on how to use the technique and certify individuals on how to become facilitators in using the technique in practice. Most prominent among these various training providers is the DACUM services provided through the Center on Education and Training for Employment (CETE), at The Ohio State University, as promoted for many years by Robert Norton (Norton & Moser, 2008).

As will be discussed in Chap. 7, DACUM has also become one of most frequently used techniques to conduct an occupational analysis and to establish national occupational standards as well. No other single technique used to conduct a job analysis or an occupational analysis has attracted more adherents than DACUM.

DACUM is essentially a group process, in which a panel of several subject-matter experts (SMEs) of varying numbers of people, depending on the situation, are brought together for one to two days, and are guided through the process by a trained facilitator, who is likely content-free. DACUM makes three assumptions about the work being analyzed. For one thing, DACUM assumes that SMEs, or the most knowledgeable individuals about the job, will be available to participate in the process and because of their designation as SMEs, will be able to describe what they do better than anyone else. The reliance on SMEs is a fundamental part of the DACUM process.

Second, DACUM also assumes that the technique can be used to analyze any job, given that the job can be separated into its component parts. Admittedly, while this is a core assumption about work analysis in general, it also has some limitations at least from a job-level perspective. The responsibilities of some contemporary jobs, such as entrepreneurs in start-up companies, are often more fluid in nature, given their inherent unpredictability and the need for flexibility. In addition, the assumption may be difficult to accept for emerging jobs that involve new technologies that tend to change rapidly over short periods of time or that have ill-defined and emerging sets of responsibilities, simply because no one has ever performed them before.

Finally, DACUM assumes that, in the end, individuals who possess the prerequisites that have been identified during the process will be able to learn how to perform the job from the information generated from the technique. This assumption is based on the perspective of mastery-learning, as used in technical education and training. Mastery learning, a notion that is also referred to as competency-based or criterion-referenced instruction, proposes the alignment of the learning objectives, the instructional content, and the means for measuring learning outcomes, such that learners will know in advance what they should learn and be able to perform as expected at the end.

Table 5.1 presents the steps of the process for conducting a job analysis using the DACUM technique. The process can be separated into three major phases: (1) Prepare to conduct the DACUM, (2) Conduct the DACUM, and (3) Verify the results of the DACUM. The DACUM process is presented from the perspective of the facilitator. That is, what the facilitator should do to effectively use the DACUM technique.

The first phase involves the facilitator getting ready before bringing together the panel of SMEs, as a means to become more familiar with the job. This could involve the use of different sources of information—oftentimes the use of O*NET occurs here—and methods of gathering the information. Indeed, the facilitator might even conduct some one-on-one interviews to find out more about the job. The facilitator should not conduct the DACUM without becoming fully aware of the job.

Clearly, the second phase is the most critical phase for the facilitator as it represents the actual meeting with the panel of SMEs. The most important resource at this point for the facilitator, believe it or not, is the sticky posts and

Table 5.1 DACUM process

I. *Prepare to conduct the DACUM*
   a. Identify the job title.
   b. Become familiar with the job using a range of sources and methods.
   c. Prepare a summary of the job information for reference during the DACUM.

II. *Conduct the DACUM*
   a. Bring together the subject-matter experts (SMEs).
   b. Provide an orientation to the SMEs: Purpose, Process, Definitions, Outputs, Rules.
   c. Present the first prompt question: What are the major activities (duties) of this job?
   d. Post responses for group discussion and consensus.
   e. Present the second prompt question: What are the tasks within each duty?
   f. Post responses for discussion and consensus.
   g. Present draft DACUM chart for panel review.
   h. Manage group process of panel.
   i. Present the third prompt question: What are the prerequisite competencies, prerequisite knowledge and skills, resources, key terms?

III. *Verify the results of the DACUM*
   a. Prepare final DACUM chart and additional information for review.
   b. Conduct final review of DACUM chart from panel.
   c. Obtain final management and expert approvals.

---

flipchart sheets. Anyone who has had experience with DACUM, or has conducted a search on the Internet on the topic, will almost immediately be able to find photographs of a DACUM panel and facilitator, with the walls of the meeting space filled with ideas about the duties and tasks for each duty. Using sticky posts and flipchart sheets have almost become synonymous with the DACUM technique.

Figure 5.1 presents the pages of an abbreviated example of a completed DACUM chart, and presents the names of the SMEs, the analysts, the duties of the job, the associated tasks for each duty, the perquisites necessary for performing the job, the resources used when performing the job, and some of the future trends. The example provides an overall view of how a job analysis report would appear at the end of the process. Some job analysis charts present the required characteristics of the individuals performing the job, but this information can be considered as individual competencies, and represents a separate process. The information on a typical DACUM chart includes the following:

- Names of the subject-matter experts
- Names of the analysts
- Display of the duties
- Tasks for each duty

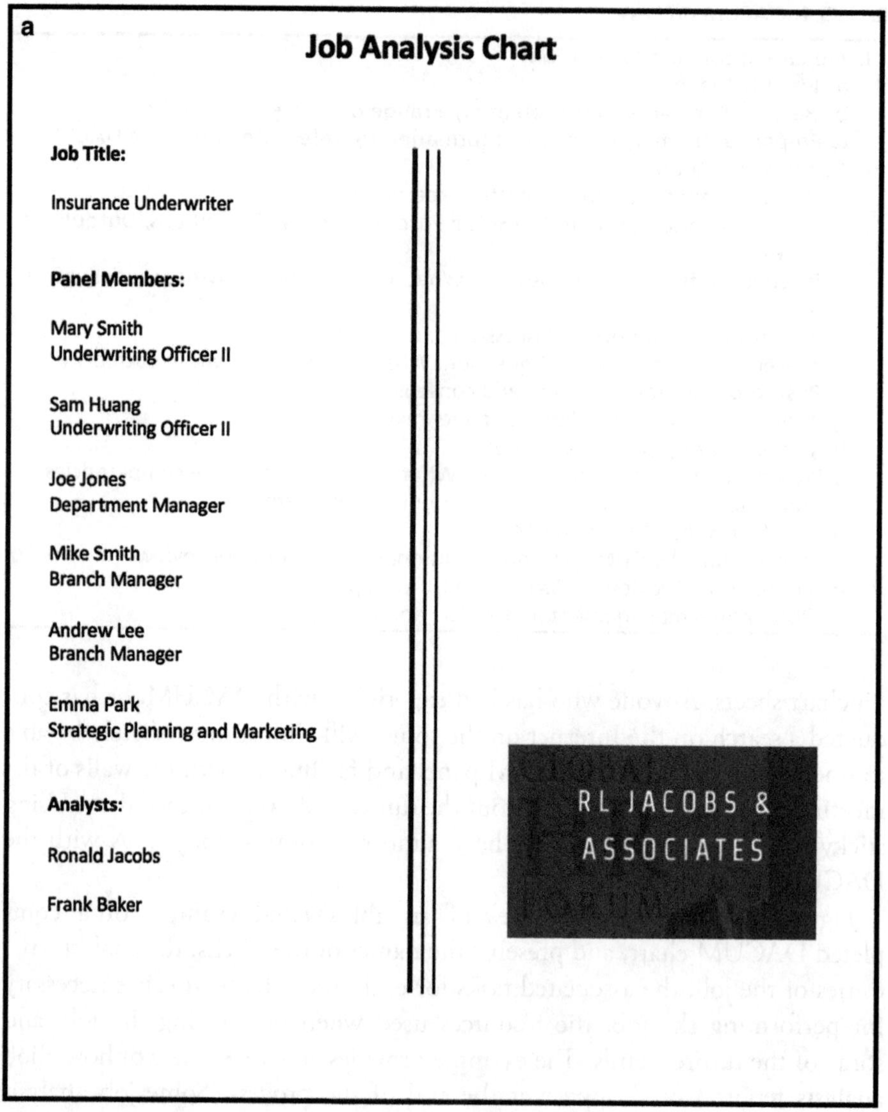

a

Job Analysis Chart

Job Title:

Insurance Underwriter

Panel Members:

Mary Smith
Underwriting Officer II

Sam Huang
Underwriting Officer II

Joe Jones
Department Manager

Mike Smith
Branch Manager

Andrew Lee
Branch Manager

Emma Park
Strategic Planning and Marketing

Analysts:

Ronald Jacobs

Frank Baker

RL JACOBS &
ASSOCIATES

Fig. 5.1 (a–c) Example job analysis chart

b

Job Title: Insurance Underwriter

Duties	Tasks				
A. Preparing production reports	A001. Prepare re-insurance analysis report	A002. Prepare compulsory third-party report	A003. Prepare customer quality report	A004. Troubleshoot government yellow-card reports	A005. Inspect report formats to ensure conformity with standard
B. Calculating insurance premiums	B001. Determine level of commercial customer risk	B002. Determine the customer's risk category	B003. Calculate the basic premium rate	B004. Manage premium rate structures	B005. Schedule premium requests for commercial customers
C. Assessing insurable risks	C001. Conduct pre-risk survey with commercial customers	C002. Identify insurable risk criteria for commercial customers	C003. Ensure insurable risk criteria are appropriate for commercial customers	C004. Prepare report for commercial customers to explain risk criteria	C005. Manage insurable risks to meet unit goals
D. Managing communications with customers	D001. Generate internal reports for branch offices	D002. Conduct presentations with customer groups	D003. Troubleshoot customer policy problems	D004. Manage data-base of customer service inquiries	D005. Manage data-base of customer contact information
E. Developing technical and administrative staff	E001. Prepare internal training programs on reviewing customer applications	E002. Conduct training sessions with new-hire underwriters	E.003. Conduct coaching sessions with new-hire underwriters	E004. Conduct coaching on firm software sessions with administrative staff	E005. Manage the development progress of staff underwriters

(Continued)

Fig. 5.1 (continued)

c

Prerequisites

Topics of Knowledge
- Insurance underwriting
- Risk analysis
- Premium rate setting
- Service quality

Areas of Skill
- Calculating insurance premiums
- Determining risk levels
- Training delivery
- Coaching
- Technical writing

Firm Policies
- Basic premium structures
- Acceptable levels of risk
- Customer Service

Education Degrees and Training
- Minimum of bachelor's degree
- Company programs on underwriting
- Company programs on risk analysis

Individual Characteristics
- Analytical skills
- Team player
- Customer orientation
- Honesty
- Detail oriented

Resources

Software
- Company data base
- Company underwriting software
- Company risk analysis calculator
- Company premium calculator

Documents
- Company mission statement
- Statement of Service Quality
- Underwriter Reference Manual
- Risk Analysis Reference Manual
- Training program materials
- S-OJT modules

Equipment
- Desk top computer
- Printer
- Photocopier
- Internet

Future Trends
- Increased automation of tasks
- Emergence of new risk levels
- E-insurance market
- Reduced need for underwriters

Fig. 5.1 (continued)

- Prerequisite knowledge, skills, experiences
- Resources: tools, equipment, software, documents
- Future trends and issues
- Additional information about the job

Often, the DACUM chart is presented in landscape orientation to show this information more clearly. The format of the chart is often the most recognizable aspect of using the DACUM technique.

The final phase requires that the information from the DACUM be verified by other stakeholders in the job analysis. That is, individuals who have an interest in ensuring the accuracy and comprehensiveness of the information. The verification might be done by different stakeholders, including other SMEs who were not part of the DACUM, such as job incumbents, quality and safety staff, and senior managers. In many instances, the verification is done simply by having the facilitator send the completed DACUM chart to them and asking them to make comments. Or the facilitator can present the results to various stakeholder individuals and small groups.

As shown in the abbreviated example in Fig. 5.2, the verification may also use a survey instrument, which calls for gathering information about the tasks of the job. Such an instrument is used when there may be a sizeable number of stakeholders who are involved in the verification process, and the instrument calls for collecting some additional information as well. Today, most of these instruments are delivered through a web-based platform. DACUM verification instruments typically list each of the tasks, and respondents are asked to rate the task in terms of three categories: the importance of the task within the job, the relative difficulty in performing the task, and the relative frequency of performing the task.

The results of the survey can provide some additional insights into the composition of the job. The results can show the perceptions of respective sets of stakeholders about each task and across the categories, the discrepancies among the three categories for each task, and perhaps most interestingly how, through a cross tabulation, different groups of respondents, such as managers, supervisors, and other job incumbents, may differ in their responses. In the end, the additional information from the survey can be used for setting priorities for instructional planning.

To a large extent, the success of using DACUM depends on the ability of the facilitator to obtain the required information from the various SMEs participating in the process. Most participants in a DACUM have never had this experience before, and certainly do not know what the result of the process should look like. The following list provides further information about the requirements of an effective DACUM facilitator:

a

Instruction: Please read carefully!

On the pages that follow, you will find a list of 76 task statements, clustered into seven major duties that relate to the job of Insurance Underwriter. These tasks were identified through meetings with several subject-matter experts from several offices of the company.

We now require your reactions to these tasks, based on three questions for each task statement:

   a. How important is the performance of each task to this job?

   b. How difficult is it to perform this task, relate to other tasks in the job?

   c. How frequent is this task performed in the job?

Respond to these questions by completing the following steps:

   1. For each task, indicate how **important** is the performance of the task, relative to the job. Select which one of the following most accurately reflects your beliefs about the task:

       5 = Extremely Important
       4 = Highly Important
       3 = Important
       2 = Somewhat Important
       1 = Less Important
       0 = Not important

b

   2. For each task, indicate how **difficult** is the performance of the task, relative to other tasks in the job. Select which one of the following most accurately reflects your beliefs about the task:

       5 = Extremely Difficult to Perform
       4 = Quite Difficult to Perform
       3 = Difficult to Perform
       2 = Somewhat Easy to Perform
       1 = Quite Easy to Perform
       0 = Extremely Easy to Perform

   3. For each task, indicate how **frequent** is the task performed, relative to other tasks in the job. Select which one of the following most accurately reflects your beliefs about the task:

       5 = Once Daily or More
       4 = Once Per Week
       3 = Once Per Month
       2 = Five to Ten Times Per Year
       1 = One to Five Times Per Year
       0 = Almost Never

Fig. 5.2 (a–d) Example job analysis verification instrument

c

Task Verification: Insurance Underwriter

Task Statements	Task Importance						Task Difficulty						Task Frequency					
	How important is this task relative to other tasks?						How difficult is this task to perform?						How frequent is this task performed?					
	Extremely Important				Not Important		Extremely Difficult				Extremely Easy		Daily or More					Almost Never
Duty A: Preparing production reports																		
A001. Prepare re-insurance analysis report	5	4	3	2	1	0	5	4	3	2	1	0	5	4	3	2	1	0
A002. Prepare compulsory third-party report	5	4	3	2	1	0	5	4	3	2	1	0	5	4	3	2	1	0
A003. Prepare customer feedback quality report	5	4	3	2	1	0	5	4	3	2	1	0	5	4	3	2	1	0
Duty B: Calculating insurance premiums																		
B001. Determine level of commercial customer risk	5	4	3	2	1	0	5	4	3	2	1	0	5	4	3	2	1	0
B002. Determine the customer's risk category	5	4	3	2	1	0	5	4	3	2	1	0	5	4	3	2	1	0
B003. Calculate the basic premium rate	5	4	3	2	1	0	5	4	3	2	1	0	5	4	3	2	1	0

(Continued)

d

General Information

Name of Organization: _____

Name of Branch Office: _____

Your Current Job Title: _____

Highest Level of Formal Education:

_____ a. High School   _____ d. Master's Degree
_____ b. Two-Year Degree   _____ e. Ph.D. or other Terminal Degree
_____ c. Bachelor's Degree   _____ f. Military Qualifications

Which of the following best describes your current job relative to the Insurance Underwriter:

_____ a. Area Supervisor   _____ c. Trainer
_____ b. Department Manager   _____ d. Human Resources

How many years have you served in this role? _____

Fig. 5.2 (continued)

- Should be content-free in terms of the job
- Should be an expert in the DACUM technique
- Should be able to listen actively to all contributions
- Should encourage contributions from all SMEs
- Should control participants who try to dominate
- Should probe responses with questions—open ended
- Should manage conflicts—allow some disagreements if appropriate
- Should maintain an open climate
- Should understand the meaning of verbs

A review of this list suggests that most of the requirements for being an effective DACUM facilitator are similar to those of being a group facilitator in general. The one exception is the last point on the list, an understanding of the meaning of the verbs used for the duty and task statements. The selection of the verbs may seem relatively unimportant within the context of the entire process. But, in fact, the selection of the verbs is a critical part of the facilitator's contribution to the DACUM process. While the facilitator is usually content-free, the facilitator should have a clear sense of the meaning of the verbs that will be used for the duty and task statements.

In this sense, Table 5.2 presents a list of commonly used verbs and their definitions. As stated, the facilitator should help guide the SMEs in identifying the verbs that best match the intent of the duty and task statements. The importance of doing this often reveals itself during the process when the facilitator is seeking to help the panel reconcile the duty statement with the various tasks, and perhaps more importantly when the task statements are being used for a specific purpose later on. For instance,

From experience, I have found visualization skills can be extremely helpful for ensuring the accuracy between the observed work behavior and the language used to describe the work behavior. The ability to match an observation with the language used to describe the observation is a crucial ability for DACUM facilitators, and for all analysts for that matter. In practice, the SMEs would seek guidance from the facilitator to use the best language possible. As for facilitators, they should be an expert in this ability.

The final aspect of conducting the job analysis is constructing a job description. In practice, there are several different approaches for writing job descriptions, as evidenced by the wide differences that one might find in organizations. HRD professionals seldom make use of job descriptions per se, since this information is more likely used for purposes of recruitment, selection, and compensation, which are usually not part of HRD practice.

Table 5.2 Work analysis verbs and their definitions

Adjust—to change something for the purpose of improving the product or process of interest. The outcome often appears as a set of physical actions or verbal behaviors.

Analyze—to study a situation or a problem, to separate take something apart and look at the relationships. The outcome often appears as a report or a presentation.

Assemble—to collect or gather things in a predetermined order, to put something together. The outcome often appears as a tangible object.

Assign—to give specific responsibilities to someone else to perform. The outcome often appears as a memo or a set of verbal instructions.

Attach—to bind, fasten, or connect things together. The outcome often appears as an object or thing.

Attend—to participate in some event. The outcome often appears as verbal comments such as during a meeting. Merely being present at a meeting is not sufficient.

Audit—to examine or review a situation, condition, or set of practices. The outcome often appears as a report or a presentation.

Build—to put something together, often of a large or complex nature. See Assemble. The outcome often appears as a physical object (product) or the actions to perform the task (process).

Calculate—to use mathematical formulas to derive a result from a set of numbers. The outcome often appears as a report or representation.

Check—to examine or inspect a product or a process. The outcome often appears as an inspection report that includes the inspection points, steps, criteria for each inspection point, and the overall rating.

Collect—to gather facts or data. The outcome often appears as information presented in a document.

Compose—to make up something that seems original or novel. The outcome often appears as a plan or some other entity that required some original thought.

Conduct—to carry out something, to lead others in doing something. The outcome often appears as an observable set of actions or documents.

Consult—to seek the advice of others. The outcome often appears as a meeting with a document as a result.

Control—to exert power over something, to guide something toward a set of behaviors. The outcome usually appears as a set of actions or documents.

Coordinate—to bring two or more actions or conditions into alignment, to take into consideration a set of conditions and bring them to a conclusion. The outcome often appears as a set of behaviors or documents.

Decide—to decide among options, based on a set of decision conditions, each of which varies in some way. The outcome often appears as a set of verbal statements or documents.

Delegate—to assign a set of responsibilities to someone else to achieve an objective. The outcome often appears as a set of verbal behaviors or a document.

Design—to consider a set of specifications and constraints, in combination with a set of ideas for the purpose of achieving a goal. The outcome often appears as a plan, presentation, or report.

Determine—to make a decision, see Decide.

Develop—to facilitate the progress of some activity or event that changes over a period of time, similar to Design but with a changed emphasis. The outcome often appears as a plan, presentation, or report.

(continued)

Table 5.2 (continued)

Disassemble—to take something apart. The outcome often appears as an object or thing in its separate parts.

Discuss—to exchange ideas that lead to a conclusion or result of some kind. Discuss would not be appropriate without the result. The outcome often appears as a decision made or some set of information.

Ensure—to make certain that something is in place, or an occurrence of some kind takes place. See Check, Inspect. The outcome often appears as a physical action or set of observable behaviors judged against a standard.

Enter—to place information or data from one location to another location. The outcome often appears as a set of physical actions.

Evaluate—to examine something carefully based on a referent or set of standards. The outcome often appears as a report, memo, or presentation.

Identify—to find a set of possible choices that meet a set of criteria. The outcome often appears as a set of verbal behaviors, a plan, or a report.

Implement—to put a plan, project, or design into action following phases of a process. The outcome often appears as a document or set of verbal behaviors.

Inspect—See Check.

Install—to put something into place, to put a component onto a larger object. The outcome often appears as a completed physical action and possible verbal behaviors.

Manage—to exert control over a set of events or the efforts of others to achieve a result. The outcome often appears as a set of verbal behaviors or a document.

Negotiate—to use a process involving others to reach agreement on an issue or area of concern, based on an understanding of the advantages and disadvantages of the positions. The outcome often appears as the use of verbal behaviors in using a specific process.

Perform—to carry out something, to act, to accomplish something. The outcome often appears as a set of physical or verbal behaviors.

Plan—to undertake a process or set of events that will lead to an outcome of some kind. The outcome often appears as a document or presentation.

Prepare—to put together elements as a means to get ready to do something else. The outcome often appears as a set of physical actions, verbal behaviors, or a document.

Provide—to give something to another person or group, for the purpose of them acting on what is given. The outcome often appears as a document, verbal behaviors, or physical actions.

Recognize—to single out a person or group for performance that is beyond the average or commonplace. The outcome often appears as a set of observable behaviors.

Review—to examine something, usually with the intent to approve or dissent, to analyze the components of something. The outcome often appears as a document or presentation.

Revise—See Adjust.

Schedule—to consider more than one variable from which a time line or set of arrangements can be made. The outcome often appears as written document, a plan, or a report.

(continued)

Table 5.2 (continued)

Shut down—to make a piece of equipment stop operating. The outcome often appears as a set of physical behaviors.

Select—to pick out which option or possibility among the identified ones best meets the established criteria. The outcome often appears as a physical action, verbal behavior, or written document.

Solve—to address a problem and derive a solution, see Troubleshoot. The outcome often appears as a set of cognitive behaviors followed by observable actions.

Start up—to make a piece of equipment begin to operate. The outcome often appears as a set of physical behaviors.

Supervise—to oversee an activity done by others, to lead others in doing something, all of which focuses on achieving a result. The outcome often appears as verbal behaviors or physical actions.

Train—to deliver a set of training materials using a planned process. The outcome often appears as a set of observable behaviors.

Troubleshoot—to identify the problem situations, the likely causes, and the actions to take to address the problem situations. The outcome often appears as a set of physical actions, verbal behaviors, or documents.

Verify—to prove something to be accurate, to test something, to check the accuracy of something. The outcome often appears as a set of physical actions, verbal behaviors, or documents.

The following example shows the relationship between a description and the duties of a job.

Job Title: Senior Software Project Manager

Job Description The Senior Software Project Manager oversees a diverse team of professionals to achieve software development project goals. The Manager ensures timely execution of project plans, essential for maintaining high levels of productivity and the competitiveness of our organization in the marketplace. The Manager must perform the job in accordance with internal and industry-wide software development standards.

Job Duties

A. Planning the development of software projects
B. Coordinating assignments across software development team members
C. Coordinating all development steps with regional software managers
D. Ensuring that all applicable processes contribute to improvements
E. Coordinating the resolution of technical issues across platforms
F. Ensuring compliance of the development process within regulations
G. Allocating resources to achieve financials goals
H. Managing new software development project budgets

As shown in the example, job descriptions should not simply summarize the duties, as many job descriptions seem to do. In their most basic form, job descriptions might have the following three-sentence format. The first sentence often provides a general statement of responsibility of what individuals holding the job actually do, sometimes on a daily basis. The second sentence states the importance of the job in regard to achieving the organizational or departmental mission. The third sentence states the expectations of the job in terms of meeting safety, quality, and customer service requirements, consistent with the mission of the organization. In this three-sentence format, the job description should be no longer than about 75 words in length.

In many instances, job descriptions are mistakenly written upfront, before engaging in the job analysis process. In practice, this approach seems difficult, unless there are previous documents that can be reliably referred to that provide information about the job. More logically, job descriptions should be prepared after the job analysis is conducted, once there is a more comprehensive understanding of the job. The duties often provide critical information for formulating the job description.

Comment

This chapter introduced how to conduct a job analysis, with a specific focus on using the DACUM technique. The DACUM technique has been used in a wide range of situations to document the components of a job in a particular workplace context. At least one issue should be emphasized about job analysis. That is, while most job analyses provide much important information, it should be noted what in fact they don't provide. Most importantly, job analysis, especially when DACUM is used as the method, does not in itself provide information about the behavioral components of tasks, which represent an important set of information in many organizations. That is, the specific work behaviors that comprise the task statements.

Identifying the component behaviors of tasks requires the use of another work analysis technique, called task analysis, which will be addressed in Chap. 6. The realization that most job analyses do not provide this additional information often comes as a surprise to many HRD practitioners and managers. They mistakenly believe that job analysis provides all the information required to design a training program or some other HRD program. As will be noted in the following chapter, task analysis requires a unique set of analyst skills different than those of job analysis.

Refection Questions

1. In what capacity might you undertake a job analysis project? Could you envision yourself being a facilitator of the process?
2. Have you ever performed in the role of a facilitator, in which there would likely be six to ten SMEs involved?
3. Does the DACUM chart make sense, as a means to communicate the various duties and tasks of a job?
4. From a review of the list of verbs, can you visualize what the meaning of each word is, and help explain them to others?
5. The DACUM process assumes that the facilitator will provide feedback to the group about the appropriateness of the statements. Do you feel comfortable in providing feedback about the duty and task statements generated by the SMEs?

Reference

Norton, R. E., & Moser, J. (2008). *DACUM handbook* (3rd ed.). Columbus, OH: Center on Education and Training for Employment, The Ohio State University.

6

Task Analysis

A task represents a specific unit of work, which often becomes the most useful set of information taken from a job analysis. For human resource development (HRD), understanding the component behaviors of a task, or conducting the technique called task analysis, provides information that has a wide range of uses relevant for designing human resource development programs. Perhaps no other work analysis technique provides as much useful information as does a task analysis. For instance, when designing a training program, the training objectives are derived from the task statements and its components, the training content comes directly from the behavioral components of tasks, and the performance rating scale used to measure trainee learning are all derived from the task analysis.

Consider the following case study example. A leading global consumer electronics manufacturer sought to train new hire test engineers, using structured on-the-job training, on how to inspect and troubleshoot completed circuit boards. The tasks actually represent two unique and relatively complex units of work. In general, in the first task, the test engineers are required to examine, or to inspect, the component parts, and make a judgment about their acceptability, according to industry standards. In the second task, they are required to figure out why certain products don't operate as required, or to troubleshoot, and communicate this information back to other personnel across other functions of the organization, such as manufacturing, design, and sales. How to understand the component behaviors in each of the two separate sets of actions calls for use of the technique called task analysis.

© The Author(s) 2019
R. L. Jacobs, *Work Analysis in the Knowledge Economy*,
https://doi.org/10.1007/978-3-319-94448-7_6

Task Analysis

As defined in Chap. 1, task analysis is the technique to use when there is a need to analyze the components of individual units of work, commonly known as tasks. A task is a defined unit of work that has discernible beginning and end points, is discrete from other tasks, is carried out over a defined period of time, and produces measurable outcomes when the task is completed. In terms of measuring the quantity of the outcomes, the following requirements are often considered:

- *Volume*—the number completed
- *Rate*—the number completed over a period of time
- *Schedule*—the timeliness in meeting a deadline
- *Productivity ratios*—the outputs divided into the inputs

In terms of measuring the quality of the outcomes, the following requirements are often considered:

- *Accuracy*—the match between a model and a sample
- *Class*—the perceived features of a product or service
- *Novelty*—the perceived extraordinary nature of a product or service

For some, the term task itself raises issues of concern. For instance, the term task perhaps harkens back to much earlier times, when the word task was primarily used to identify extremely small, specific units of work behavior, that were mostly physical and repetitive in nature, such as those found in traditional manufacturing and production work settings.

The image of people doing menial repetitive work, and the task analysis techniques that were developed to guide people to perform this work, has left a lasting impression on many people today. And the impression is not always positive. For good reasons, documenting tasks as part of work efficiency efforts is perceived as being oppressive and exploitative of the workers. After all, the basic point is how to get more and more productivity from the person, without thinking that there might be implications on the people doing the work. The people ceased to be human beings, and merely became extensions of the things around them.

As discussed in Chap. 1, readers are urged to reflect about these early industrial times and the way that task analysis information was gathered and used at that time. To be sure, things are not the same as they were at the turn of the century, at the time of Henry Ford and other early industrialists. In fact, without the use of task analysis, Henry Ford could not have successfully implemented the moving assembly line, which reduced the actions of employees at each station of the assembly line to their most basic elements: positioning the part to be assembled, attaching a bolt, and tightening the bolt.

In today's environment, task analysis plays a more positive and helpful role in understanding the work that people do in their jobs. The information is not necessarily meant to be imposed on employees. Rather, task analysis has now become a much more collaborative, flexible, process, taking into account not only the physical aspects of work, but the cognitive aspects as well. In this regard, a more recent issue related to task analysis has arisen from the emergence of knowledge work, and the uncertainty of how to define work that is often free-flowing, creative, and lacking in any obvious ways of it being measured. In fact, the difficulty of measuring the outcomes when performing knowledge-based tasks has been discussed at length in the management literature (Arthur, Defillippi, & Lindsay, 2008; Jacobs, 2017).

In this sense, I recently undertook an analysis of a large number of DACUM charts, all of which focused on various engineer-level jobs that occur across three petroleum refinery settings (Jacobs & Bu-Rahmah, 2012). The opportunity was unique in that, while all the DACUM charts focused basically on one occupation—petroleum engineer—the jobs were in fact quite different from each other, and the job analyses had been conducted by the same set of analysts. It was presumed that the tasks performed in these various petroleum engineer jobs would essentially be considered knowledge-based tasks.

The analysis was conducted for the purpose of identifying what are the common behavioral patterns might exist across the tasks—over 300 of them. The results as reported in Jacobs (2017) showed the emergence of five categories of behavioral patterns of knowledge-based tasks:

1. Troubleshooting problem situations, finding their causes, and proposing a solution
2. Making decisions based on established standards and best practices
3. Conducting a critical analysis, or an inspection, of an ongoing operation or object
4. Designing a plan that they would execute or that someone else would produce later on
5. Facilitating a work process across functional boundaries that involves others at certain points in time

The meaning of these patterns of behavior will be discussed further in the following section of the chapter. The five patterns of behavior serve to operationally define what is meant by a knowledge-based task.

Some HRD professionals might find the term task problematic. Depending on the context, alternate terms that serve the same purpose as the term task might be assignment, project, or plan. Regardless of the term preferred, the meaning should remain the same. These terms basically refer to a specific unit of work behavior. As stated, task analysis can be used as part of a job analysis—usually done after the duties and tasks have been identified—or it can be done as a self-standing activity. As part of a job analysis, it often represents the missing set of information whenever a job analysis is conducted. That is, people will say that it is nice to know the duties and tasks of a job, as provided by a DACUM. But, for the job analysis to be really useful, we now need to know what the components of the tasks are. In general, task analysis is conducted when there is interest in knowing more about what are the individual behaviors required to carry out the task. Task analysis represents the opportunity to analyze the smallest forms of work behavior.

In a sense, task analysis is often another way to verify the accuracy of the DACUM technique. That is, certain task statements may have been generated during the DACUM which at the time seemed clear and logical. Yet, when seeking to analyze the task statements, one often realizes that one or another task statement may not adequately describe the behavior in mind, or that the task statement might even be separated into two tasks. Thus, the actual analysis of the task often reveals more information about the accuracy and comprehensiveness of the original job analysis. One can never say that a job analysis is necessarily altogether finished, as additional information might come along to reveal new insights into the work, which should be integrated into the documentation.

Or, task analysis can be done as a self-standing activity, when there is a need to simply document certain units of work, irrespective of the other aspects of the work around them. For instance, when a new set of software is adopted in a customer service call center, there would be some critical tasks that should be documented, aside from the general reference documents that the developers of the software typically provide. In this case, the task analysis would focus on how to use the software to accomplish sets of work that are relevant to this particular call center context.

Patterns of Task Behaviors

As stated, task analysis identifies the behavioral components of tasks. Those work behaviors might comprise both observable and non-observable behaviors. Even unseen work behaviors, such as when individuals need to think about a problem or reflect on a situation, can be documented. In practice, analysts begin to realize that the behavioral components of tasks have certain patterns that reoccur with some consistency. That is, the patterns occur irrespective of the business sector and level of the job, because they represent basic sets of actions done by all humans.

For instance, many tasks can be identified that have the basic pattern of performing a series of steps, such as installing the new software. And many tasks can be identified that have the basic pattern of solving a problem, such as troubleshooting why a specific function in the software does not work as expected. Even though the two basic patterns of behavior mentioned in the example focus on the software program in the call center, each is independent from the other, and should be considered as distinct units of work. Each places different requirements on the people doing the work.

From experience, it has been observed that the behavioral components of tasks tend to differ in relatively consistent ways. That is, regardless of the job, most jobs are composed of work that requires problems to be solved, work that requires decisions to be made, work that requires inspections to be done, work that requires a set of sequential steps to be performed, and so on.

Table 6.1 describes six characteristic patterns of work behavior commonly found when analyzing tasks. In a sense, aside from the procedure analysis, which is more or less straightforward in nature, the remaining patterns can be considered as part of cognitive task analysis (Crandall, Klein, & Hoffman, 2006). Cognitive task analysis is the general term used to describe those units of work that require more than simply following a set of steps. Instead, the tasks require some thinking to occur, before taking an action. The premise of this book is that more and more tasks are now moving in this direction, and are called knowledge-based tasks, which describe the nature of the behaviors involved, not the task analysis technique.

In practice, some tasks can contain more than one behavioral pattern, as when performing a procedure requires a decision to be made within it, or a problem to be solved within an inspection. It should be noted that work processes are included as a behavioral pattern, even though, as will be discussed in Chap. 10, work processes are typically performed by more than one individual. Yet, increasingly, there are occasions when individuals have a task as part of their job which requires them to facilitate a work process, which is common among managers and professionals.

The behavioral patterns associated with particular units of work are usually related to the levels of the job. For instance, management and supervisory jobs are likely to have units of work involving the behaviors of planning and organizing resources that affect others, while skilled technical jobs are likely to have units of work involving behaviors that make use of tools or equipment. Today's work expectations have created many exceptions to this rule. That is, many skilled technical employees can also be expected to be involved in the planning and organizing of work.

Table 6.1 Summary of patterns of task behaviors

Task behavior	Description	Information to document
Procedure	Performing a series of steps in a specific order	• Steps • Quality requirements • Safety information • Embedded decisions and problem components
Troubleshooting	Matching problem situations or symptoms with probable causes, and the actions required to resolve the problem situations	• Problem situations • Probable causes • Actions to take
Inspection	Determining the match between a given instance of a product or service and an established model	• Decision conditions that vary • Decisions related to each set of decision conditions
Decision making	Determining the action to take based on considering the varying conditions	• Inspection points • Steps to inspect • Criteria for each point • Overall criteria
Adjustment and revision	Changing a product or process to make it better or to match a referent	• Adjustment or revision points • Effects of making each adjustment or revision • Steps required to adjust or revise
Manage a work process	Facilitating the progress of a work process	• Process step • Additional comments or information • People involved in performing the step

Nevertheless, the ability to see and anticipate discrete patterns of work behaviors, regardless of the job involved, is an important aspect of understanding the patterns of task work involving the behaviors of planning and organizing resources that affect others, while skilled technical jobs are likely to have units of work involving behaviors that make use of tools or equipment.

Conducting a Task Analysis

Again, the process of conducting a task analysis should be considered as part of the broader work analysis process, specifically as the primary component of Phase 3 which calls for Conducting the Work Analysis. The process for conducting a task analysis includes the following steps.

1. *Review the tasks to be analyzed*

The first step of the task analysis process is to review again the tasks to be analyzed. More specifically, this step requires a review of the task statements, to ensure that the task statement is representative of the actual task to be analyzed. In particular, the verb component of the task statement is a key indicator for the analyst, and requires that the analyst ascertain the appropriateness of this component.

Some analysts may believe that doing this review is not really important or they believe that they should vary the verbs used, just so they don't repeat the same ones over and over. In fact, the most important criteria is whether the verb of the task statement truly represents the behavioral pattern of the task. For instance, if the pattern of the behavior components is a procedure, then one would expect the following verbs to be used in the task statement: assemble, disassemble, install, prepare, and so on.

2. *Prepare the templates to guide the task analysis*

In preparation for gathering the task analysis information, the analyst should prepare the templates that will be used, based on the behavioral patterns of the tasks. Tables 6.2 through 6.7 present relatively straightforward examples of a task analysis representing each of the patterns, showing the task statements and recommended analysis templates to be used for each. The various examples show that each of the templates basically follows a landscape page orientation, and each has three columns of information to be gathered.

For instance, for the procedure analysis, the analyst should focus on the steps, the safety and quality information related to each step, and any additional information of importance that should be documented related to each step. Conducting a procedure analysis is much like preparing a list of steps for a recipe or showing how to find a particular location. So many people have some experience in doing a procedure analysis, even though it may not be from a work perspective. The procedure analysis is perhaps the most commonly occurring behavioral pattern, and often the easiest to analyze.

When discussing how to perform a procedure analysis, some resources present examples that include the listing of the steps and also include what might be considered associated sub-steps as well. That is, relatively smaller steps that may be associated with some of the steps. For instance, the following is a brief example of having steps and associated sub-steps:

Table 6.2 Example procedure analysis

Task name: Conduct a laboratory test		
Job title: Laboratory Technician	Job code: AP133	Work area: product testing
Step	Quality	Health/safety
1. Obtain distilled water, ethanol solution, and buffer solutions		The following safety guidelines must be observed: A. Protective eye glasses B. Protective gloves C. Safety Guideline L-106 D. Safety Guideline L-108 E. Safety Guideline L-110
2. Wash probe electrode assembly with distilled water	• Probe must be fully immersed in the distilled water • Probe must be completely clean	
3. Wash probe electrode assembly with ethanol solution	• Probe must be fully immersed in the ethanol solution • Probe must be completely soaked in the ethanol solution	Caution: Ethanol solution should not be spilled on any surface
4. Inspect the probe assembly	Probe assembly inspection points are the following: • Deep scratches on the electric tip • Signs of wear on the contacts • Flecks or cracks on the plastic handle Contact the supervisor if any of these conditions are observed	
5. Place the probe on clean, absorbent paper	All parts of the probe should be resting on the absorbent paper	

1. Remove the protective cap from the vial.

   a. Clean the vial stopper with an alcohol wipe, let dry.
   b. Attach a transfer needle to the syringe tip.

2. Transfer the fluid from the vial to the syringe.

   a. Pull out the plunger on the syringe to fill it with air.
   b. Insert the needle into the center of the rubber stopper.
   c. Push the plunger on the syringe down.

In practice, this approach has not been advised in this book, based on the following questions as criteria:

- Does the sub-step constitute a distinct behavior when performing the task?
- Does the sub-step have its own safety, quality, and other considerations attached to it?
- Does the sub-step actually represent a part of or provide additional explanation on how to perform the associated step?
- When the procedure analysis is used later on, does the sub-step help clarify when to perform the associated step?

In most instances, the use of sub-steps has not been found to provide any further value for how the information would be used later on. For instance, if the planned use of the procedure analysis information was to develop a performance guide of some kind. As a result, sub-steps are not included in the example shown in Table 6.2. In some instances, the use of sub-steps may be warranted.

Most of us have done a procedure analysis at one time or another, likely aside from a professional situation. When a person gives travel directions to a location in a step-by-step format, that is a procedure analysis. When a person documents a favorite recipe, that is a procedure analysis. Similarly, in a professional setting, the analyst seeks to document the steps that occur in the same sequence in which they are performed.

For the troubleshooting analysis, the analyst should focus on the various problem situations or set of symptoms, the probable single cause or the possible multiple causes of each problem situation, and the actions to take to address each of the problem situations. In a troubleshooting analysis, the task statement represents a grouping of related problems: Troubleshoot telecommunications network transmission problems. In practice, two words stand out in importance: the verb used, signifying what action the employee will be doing—that is, to troubleshoot—and the word problems at the end of the statement, signifying that the task comprises a group of related problem situations.

As shown in Table 6.3, conducting a troubleshooting analysis is often more difficult than a procedure analysis, because the analyst must be careful to differentiate between problem situations and their probable causes. Consider how even in general conversation people sometimes fail to differentiate between a problem situation and the cause of the problem, such as when an automobile engine won't start. People often mistakenly say that the problem is that there is a dead battery, when in fact the problem situation is actually that the engine does not turn over when the ignition key is turned, and the probable cause is that the battery lacks sufficient charge to engage the starter, which starts the engine. In practice, the analyst should be careful to differentiate

Table 6.3 Example troubleshooting analysis

Task name: Troubleshoot laboratory test result problems		
Job title: Laboratory Technician	Job code: AP133	Work area: product testing
Problem situations	Probable causes	Corrective actions
A. Test results vary more than +/− 0.04 across test batches	• Probe not fully immersed in test solution	Make certain that probe touches the bottom of the test container
	• Probe not completely clean	Inspect probe for film, reclean if necessary
	• Sample batch numbers differ	Contact Production Supervisor to ensure that batch numbers match
B. Test result consistently exceeds upper limits	• Test instrument counter not reset to zero default	Reset instrument counter to default position
C. Test result within specification, but sample does not meet visual inspection	• Contaminated test container	Follow decontamination steps:
	• Sample temperature not within specified range	1. Identify correct disposal container
	• Unannounced batch change	2. Dispose of current sample
		3. Identify contamination source
		4. Refill test container
		5. Reset test instrument counter
		Heat or cool the sample to meet requirements
		Contact production supervisor to confirm batch number

these aspects, especially when the analyst is content-free and works with the subject-matter expert (SME) to identify this information.

As shown in Table 6.4, for the inspection analysis, the analyst should focus on the various inspection points, whether they be a physical location or an ongoing process to be inspected, the procedural steps required to inspect each of the points, and the criteria to judge the adequacy of the inspection points. As a task behavior, an inspection is relatively easy to document as the analyst should simply ask the SME to explain how to know when quality is achieved.

Inspection represents one of the tasks most frequently engaged in, and it can be expressed in many different ways. Inspection can be done on a product or physical object or an ongoing process. Consider that when a person reviews a billing document to ensure its accuracy, that is the inspection of a product.

Table 6.4 Example inspection analysis

Task name: Inspect the fuel filler door assembly		
Inspection point	Inspection steps	Criteria
A. Part/net surface flush	1. Place the flush block on net surface with pin in bushing hole 2. Place the lower edge of flush template on part and net edge on net surface 3. Slide flush template around part A. NOTE: At the finger, lift net edge on flush block 4. Slide flush template around part B. NOTE: At the finger, lift net edge on flush block	• Low edge of flush template must touch part all around • High edge of flush template should not touch the part
B. Part edge/net block clearance	1. Place feeler gauge between part edge and net block, then slide around outer edge 2. Slide feeler gauge completely around outer edge	• Go portion of the feeler gauge should fit between net block and part • No Go portion of feeler gauge should not fit between the net block and part
C. Part edge finish	1. Place part face down on inspection surface 2. Visually inspect all around the part edge 3. Use finger to feel around the part edge	• All edge surfaces must appear smooth • All edge surfaces must be free of burrs or metal flakes

When a person reviews a final report or design, that is also an inspection of a product. When a person reviews the adequacy of a manufactured part to see if it meets customer requirements, that is inspection as well. When a supervisor listens in on a customer service representative using a customer service process, that is also inspection, but of the ongoing process.

As shown in Table 6.5, for the decision analysis, the analyst should focus on identifying the decision conditions, and how each of them might vary, and then matching them with the action that corresponds with the combination of decision conditions. As a task behavior, making a decision is perhaps the most difficult pattern to analyze. For one thing, in practice, documenting a decision is oftentimes confused with solving a problem—that is, troubleshooting, and this makes it difficult for some SMEs to differentiate between them.

One way to differentiate between making a decision versus solving a problem is when each of the tasks occurs. Solving a problem typically occurs after some other tasks might be done. For instance, problems arise when something

Table 6.5 Example decision analysis

Task name: Select paint additives for painting truck frames		
If you require this amount of paint ...	And if ...	Then use this amount of paint additive
A. 2.25 gallon of solid paint	• No other colors will be used on the frame	• 99 oz 1586 activator and 4 oz 398 accelerator
	• Other colors will be used on the frame	• 80 oz 1586 activator and 4 oz 398 accelerator
B. 2.35 gallon of metallic paint	• No other colors will be used on the frame	• 99 oz 1386 activator and 8 oz 398 accelerator
	• Other colors will be used on the frame	• 80 oz 1386 activator and 8 oz 398 accelerator
C. 2.50 gallon of solid paint	• No other colors will be used on the frame	• 110 oz 1586 activator and 6 oz 398 accelerator
	• Other colors will be used on the frame	• 100 oz 1586 activator and 6 oz 398 accelerator
D. 2.50 gallon of metallic paint	• No other colors will be used on the frame	• 110 oz 1386 activator and 6 oz 398 accelerator
	• Other colors will be used on the frame	• 100 oz 1386 activator and 6 oz 398 accelerator

can't be done as planned, such as the simple example of when a person seeks to turn on their mobile phone, and it doesn't respond. At that point, a person should engage in the behavior to figure out why the mobile phone doesn't work. In this sense, troubleshooting can be understood as back-end analysis—as it occurs after actions have been taken.

In contrast, making a decision often occurs at the beginning, as a way to guide future actions. For instance, a decision must be made about which mobile phone to purchase in the first place, based on a set of decision conditions, such as amount of memory required, size of screen, and budget. At this point, a person should engage in behavior to determine which actions to take, based on the decision conditions and options. In this sense, decision analysis can be understood as front-end analysis—as it occurs before actions are taken.

As shown in Table 6.6, for a revision and adjustment analysis, the analyst should focus on the areas of an object or an ongoing activity that requires change, the steps to make the change, and the outcome of making each adjustment or revision. Analyzing this task pattern tends to be relatively straightforward, as the analyst should inquire how changes are made from the SME.

The term adjustment most often seems appropriate to use when referring to changes that can be made on equipment and similar physical objects. Often these adjustments already exist on the piece of equipment, and the analyst should seek to understand what each one of them actually does. So the analyst should seek to identify the adjustment points and the information related to each one. The analyst should realize that the purpose of the analysis is not to

Table 6.6 Example adjustment-revision analysis

Task name: Perform adjustments on bolt-maker machine		
Adjustment	Purpose	How
A. Stock Gage	• Adjusts the length of the cut-off	• Turn clockwise—increases the stock length • Turn counterclockwise—reduces the stock length
B. Feed Knob	• Adjusts feed roller travel	• Turn clockwise—reduces the amount of travel • Turn counterclockwise—increases the amount of travel
C. Back-Up	• Adjusts how deep slug enters the die	• Turn clockwise—moves rod closer toward the die • Turn counterclockwise—moves rod further away from die
D. Rocker Arm Travel	• Adjusts travel by height of cam shoe retainer cap	• Lower the arm—longer length of arm travel • Raise the arm—shorter length of arm travel

replicate expert behavior. Rather, the purpose is to document the possible changes that can be made. For instance, the task statement might be as follows: Adjust the filament alignment on the 3D printer to meet the specifications for the product to be produced.

The term revision more often seems appropriate when dealing with certain objects, such as plans, designs, and reports, and also to ongoing activities such as a presentation. In a revision, the analyst may be required to identify the revision points. These could also be considered as revision categories, such as when a weekly quality report is revised based on feedback received from other team members. The revision categories might be accuracy of the numbers, clarity of the presentation, usefulness of the recommendations. The analysis should include operational descriptions to ensure an understanding of each category.

Regardless of whether the term used is to adjust or to revise, the intent remains the same. That is, to make act upon something to show how to improve it or change the conditions around something in some way.

As shown in Table 6.7, to document how to manage a work process, the analyst should focus on the steps of the process, any additional comments about performing the process step, and the other people who are involved in performing the step. Some explanation of this pattern of task behavior is required at this point. As stated, this pattern of task behavior focuses on when individuals have, as part of their jobs, the requirement of taking the lead to ensure that a work process is accomplished. That is, it is part of a person's job to make the process occur.

Table 6.7 Example of how to manage a work process analysis

Task name: Manage archive of maintenance reports		
Step	Comments	Staff involved
1. Verify electrical activities carried out	Collect reports, drawings, and documents for the following completed activities: • Routine maintenance • Preventive maintenance (PM) • In-house projects • Contractor projects • Modifications jobs • Problem rectifications	• Area Supervisor • Maintenance Supervisor • Maintenance Planning Division
2. Review reports with drawings and documents	Verify the following (PM) activities: • Activities carried per maintenance manual • Any used spares recorded • Activities carried out as per PM schedule • Activities carried out as per work order • Job completion report submitted to maintenance planning division • For both in-house and contractor projects, ensure the following: • Job completed as per project documents • Drawings are updated	• Supervisor—Maintenance Planning Division • Area Supervisor • Lead Engineer • Team Leader
3. Verify accuracy of the drawings	Review all As Built drawings that are available. Ensure the following: • As Built drawings match the executed jobs • All comments are incorporated into the drawings • Activities were executed as per standards • Spare parts are available	• Contractor Engineer • Team Leader • Supervisor—Maintenance Planning Division

Consider the instance when the production supervisor's job at an automobile assembly plant includes the following task: *Prepare the weekly missing parts inventory report*. Clearly, the manager cannot perform this task alone, and will need the involvement of a number of different functions other than his own to provide the required information, including assembly, inventory, and the warehouse. While many individuals may be involved, the completion of this task is led by the production supervisor.

Many other situations call for managing a process, when it is considered as a task. For instance, when a job requires the preparation of a design for a customer, or the preparation of a maintenance plan, or the preparation of an extensive report, all of these instances involve a series of steps over time, involving others as required, and with the responsibility of completing the process tied to one job.

Later, Chap. 10 will discuss how to analyze work processes, or the series of steps that occur in all organizations that often cross over functional lines that convert the inputs into outcomes. As will be discussed, work processes are documented to show all the jobs that contribute to a work process. In this instance, the analysis shows the responsibilities of one job, that is, the person who is most responsible for the success of a particular work process.

Finally, as shown in Table 6.8, a unique use of task analysis is called a safety task analysis. In this type of analysis, the most typical behavior pattern is that

Table 6.8 Example safety task analysis

Part A: Replace worn bucket elevator belt		
Step	Potential hazards	Precaution

1. Prepare safe working area:
  a. Barricade area with signs, cones, or barrier tape
  b. Lock out/tag out elevator
  c. Verify that electrical supply has been shut down
  d. Inspect for loose objects
	• Electric shock and burns
	• Arc flash/blast
	• Struck by loose belt or belt parts
		a. Follow approved sign, cone, and barrier tape approach distances
		b. Follow lock out/tag out policy
		c. Verifying electrical supply is an added confirmation that power is off
		d. Loose objects may fall from belt

2. Loosen bucket elevator take-ups	• Pinch points in bucket belt • Slippery surface leading to falls	• Use the correct tool to loosen bolts • Maintain balanced footing
3. Open side access door of elevator	• Belt parts • Salt lumps	Always stand beside elevator when removing cover. *Never* place head or other body parts into elevator shaft

4. Determine if belt is broken:
  a. If broken, carefully remove loose pieces and other debris, then remove belt
  b. If not broken, remove belt from elevator
	• Pinch points
	• Back strain from lifting
	• Struck by belt
	• Struck by salt lumps
		• Always stand to side or a safe distance from elevator door
		• Use extension tool to grasp belt
		• Use knife to cut worn belt into manageable pieces
		• Use safe knife-cutting techniques
		• Wear cut-resistant gloves
		• Place belt pieces on cart for disposal

of a procedure, in which the steps are documented, then the potential hazards of doing the step, and finally the precautions that should be considered based on the potential hazards.

Another unique use of task analysis is to conduct a disability analysis. In practice, a disability analysis is used to document the behavioral components of a task, the cognitive and physical requirements of the task components, and to use that information to identify what reasonable accommodations would be necessary for individuals with a certain disability to perform each component. Title I of the Americans with Disability Act of 1990 prohibits private employers with over 15 employees, state and local governments, and labor unions from discriminating against qualified individuals with disabilities in all aspects of employment. Reasonable accommodations are defined as any modification of the task or the work environment that will enable individuals with a disability to perform the task, as well as any other individual. Such a disability analysis is often conducted in cooperation with public agencies seeking to ensure employment access and opportunities for all qualified job seekers.

3. Gather the task analysis information

Because of the nature of conducting a task analysis, gathering the information almost always involves direct contact between the analyst and the SME. In many instances, this requires that the analyst observe the SME in the work setting or having an in-depth interview with the SME. As stated, task analysis requires the most fine-grained level of detail among the various techniques discussed in the book. But how much detail is appropriate? Is there a way of determining what is best in all instances?

Figure 6.1 presents a graphical representation, with the horizontal axis showing the seven steps of a hypothetical procedural task and the vertical axis showing the relative level of description used to describe each step, or the depth of description. The resulting profile, which some call a depth of criterion profile, shows that for some steps, the depth of the description is relatively low, requiring fewer words, and for some other steps the depth is high, requiring more words. The profile is a conceptual way of making the following statement: The level of detail required when documenting each component of a task analysis differs, depending on who will be using the information later on and the context of the work setting.

Here's an example of this principle. A large truck manufacturer asked whether the set of task analyses conducted at the Ohio plant could also be used in the Seattle plant. The task statement for both locations was the same. In practice, the result was that the documents from the Ohio plant

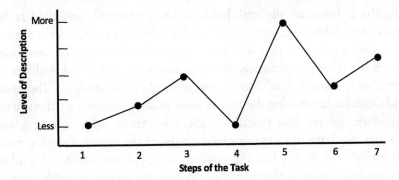

Fig. 6.1 Depth of criterion profile of a procedure task

represented the employees and the context there, differing much from the situation in Seattle. In the end, separate task analyses were required to be conducted at each location, simply because this was the most effective approach to be used overall.

Obtain Approvals from Stakeholders

It is recommended that a routing should be established to ensure that all stakeholders have an opportunity to review and eventually approve the task analysis document. The stakeholders may include the following: job incumbents, supervisors, managers, quality staff, and safety staff, among others. To obtain the approvals, the analyst must first synthesize all the rough notes into a formal document, using the task analysis templates as a guide. Then the documents are presented to each of the stakeholders for their review. The analyst should explain that there are four questions to be satisfactorily addressed in order for the task analysis to be approved:

1. Is the task analysis accurate, without any misinformation or errors?
2. Is the task analysis complete in all respects, without any missing or inadequate information?
3. Is the task analysis presented clearly, following established formatting rules, without any misleading or inconsistent uses of grammatical or editorial conventions?
4. Overall, does the task analysis appear useful for its intended purpose?

Only after all the questions have been addressed in the affirmative can the task analysis be approved for use. In practice, the analyst may find that the task analysis document may require two to three iterations of revisions, representing the feedback from all the stakeholders. Only after all stakeholders have reviewed the updated versions can the task analysis be approved for use.

The analyst may find that obtaining approvals of task analysis documents can be a frustrating experience. In some instances, some stakeholders may disagree with some others about aspects of the task analysis. The analyst should facilitate identifying the precise areas of disagreement, to identify what might be considered best practice in this context. In other instances, some SMEs may not have the time to spend on doing the review, delaying getting the approval completed. Getting commitment upfront often helps address this issue. Finally, some SMEs may prefer that the analyst sit with them and lead them through the document.

Whatever the situation, the analyst is responsible for ensuring that the task analysis receives all the appropriate approvals. The analyst should realize two points about getting the approvals. First, the analyst can help reduce any unnecessary questions or concerns from the stakeholders by ensuring that the task analysis documents are well designed and logically presented. Having the documents presented in a pleasing manner helps eliminate any potential misunderstandings.

Second, the analyst should recognize that whenever SMEs disagree about something, there is a high probability that the disagreements are in fact over some relatively small, but important, points. In practice, stakeholders have been observed to express dismay about the overall low quality of the information in the task analysis. But, upon further follow-up, the reality was that only one or two points represented areas of disagreement, not the entire document. The lesson was that SMEs should be probed on the areas of disagreement during the review, with the expectation that the probing will illuminate the exact points to be considered for revision.

Comment

Being able to conduct a task analysis is a critical skill for many HRD professionals. Many HRD programs depend on the information from a task analysis, to the extent that HRD programs depend more on a task analysis than almost any other work analysis technique. Task analysis requires that the analyst develop a way of recognizing the various patterns of task behavior. Otherwise, the analyst will believe that task analysis is simply about listing the steps of a procedure, without realizing that tasks vary in their patterns. Six different patterns were identified and examples of templates have been provided to show how they can be analyzed. Most templates follow a landscape format, and have a three-column format.

Reflection Questions
1. Why is task analysis viewed as a critical area of practice for HRD professionals?
2. Have you ever considered that there may be recurring, consistent patterns of task behavior?
3. Troubleshooting and decision making are often confused as being the same, though they differ in important ways. What are the ways the these patterns of task behavior differ from each other?
4. Can you imagine what might be the challenges of conducting a task analysis with an SME?
5. Task analysis depends on the analyst being able to visualize the requirements of the task behavior. Have you tried to visualize the behaviors for each of the task patterns as a way of practicing this ability?

References

Arthur, M. B., Defillippi, R. J., & Lindsay, V. J. (2008). On being a knowledge worker. *Organizational Dynamics, 37*(4), 365–377.
Crandall, B., Klein, G., & Hoffman, R. (2006). *Working minds: A practitioner's guide to cognitive task analysis.* Boston: MIT Press.
Jacobs, R. L. (2017). Knowledge work and human resource development. *Human Resource Development Review, 16*(2), 176–202.
Jacobs, R. L., & Bu-Rahmah, M. (2012). Developing employee expertise through structured on-the-job training (S-OJT): An introduction to this training approach and the KNPC experience. *Industrial and Commercial Training, 44*(2), 75–84.

7

Occupational Analysis

Consider the following situation in which a global telecommunications equipment manufacturer recommended to its customers—that is, companies that provide mobile services to its consumers—that they should adopt the job title of Back-Office Engineer as part of their operations. To support this recommendation, the human resource development (HRD) staff from the equipment manufacturer conducted an occupational analysis to analyze the components of how this job occurs across several customer settings. Subject-matter experts (SMEs) for the occupational analysis were selected from the various customer companies.

At the end of the project, the HRD staff prepared a report describing the duties, the tasks, the prerequisite areas of knowledge and skills, the educational requirements and required certifications, and a listing of the resources, including technical documents, equipment, and software. In addition, the report also included an analysis of the major work processes in which a Back-Office Engineer was likely to be involved in.

The report provided a basis for understanding how this job appears across different organizational settings. Although the report was relatively comprehensive, the customer companies were also informed that further analysis, such as a follow-up job analysis and a task analysis, would be required in their own situations beyond the occupational analysis, to ensure relevance in their own situations. The case study illustrates that anytime the analysis focuses on more than one work setting, occupational analysis is the appropriate technique to use.

Occupational analysis is often considered as being essentially the same technique as a job analysis. Consider that both of them often make use of Developing a Curriculum (DACUM), or a similar technique, from which to

© The Author(s) 2019
R. L. Jacobs, *Work Analysis in the Knowledge Economy*,
https://doi.org/10.1007/978-3-319-94448-7_7

gather the information, and both rely upon SMEs as the primary source of information. In those respects, occupational analysis and job analysis may appear to be the same. But occupational analysis differs from job analysis in at least three related ways.

First, the frame of reference of occupational analysis is, logically, based on an occupation, not on a job. An occupation has a broader scope than a job, since an occupation refers to a group of related jobs across different work settings. A job is a defined role that occurs in a specific work setting only. As a result, the SMEs selected for an occupational analysis often come from more diverse settings and perspectives, representing all aspects of the occupation.

Second, an occupational analysis typically requires that more information be gathered than a job analysis, such as forecasts of future hiring outlooks, the career pathways from this occupation to other occupations, and the educational and credentialing requirements of the occupation, among other information. In this sense, an occupational analysis typically offers a more complete picture of the work involved than does a job analysis.

Finally, as a result of its broader focus, occupational analysis can be used for a wider range of purposes than a job analysis. Indeed, this chapter and the following one both focus on occupations. It takes two chapters to cover all the information related to this work analysis technique. Occupational analysis can be used in the following ways:

- Developing the curricula and courses that focus on an occupation as offered by secondary and postsecondary vocational and technical schools
- Establishing occupational standards that guide the development of certification and licensure processes, as prepared by trade associations and professional societies
- Developing apprenticeship programs that focus on specific high-skilled technical occupations as offered by skilled-trade unions
- Designing a variety of employee development and career developing programs in organizations
- Developing a framework for national standards that establish a consistent set of information about certain occupations

Regardless of how information from an occupational analysis is used, the basic purpose remains the same. That is, using occupational analysis to help support the development of skills and increase the opportunities for employment, all of which leading presumably to employment opportunities. These outcomes seek to benefit a wide range of stakeholders, including individual job seekers, businesses and industries, and communities as well.

In this sense, occupational analysis often has a decidedly broader societal focus to it. Readers should note that this chapter is followed by a related chapter that specifically focuses on national occupational standards (NOSs), a topic of increasing importance globally. No discussion of occupational analysis would be complete without also including a discussion of this topic.

In practice, identifying the precise boundaries of an occupation has become more and more difficult, simply because of the shifting nature of jobs that may comprise a given occupation. Consider the following three illustrative examples of the changing relationship between an occupation and its related jobs.

First, consider the occupation of Physician Assistant, which was established with the intent to allow properly prepared individuals to perform certain duties once performed only by physicians. As time has passed, the Physician Assistant occupation has become more and more specialized, increasing the number of job titles that focus on providing advanced medical care services, but not necessarily requiring a physician. Areas of specialty for a Physician Assistant now include psychiatry, dermatology, and urgent care, among others.

The second example focuses on the occupation of Petroleum Engineer, which often occurs in a refinery setting. This occupation has also seen an increased number of specialized job titles associated with it, including Control Room Engineer, Process Engineer, and Safety Engineer, among others. These and other related job titles have emerged as the number of petroleum-based products has increased, quality and safety standards have been emphasized, and advanced production technologies have been introduced. In all, the occupation of Petroleum Engineer has become at once more complex and demanding, involving more specialized knowledge and skills.

The final example is the occupation of Network Engineer, which has seen a proliferation of new job titles related to Internet security, such as Cybersecurity Analyst. Reports suggest that Internet security jobs are subject to the highest job growth, relative to other jobs within this occupation. Indeed, the growth and diversity of these jobs may in fact call for a new occupational title, which better describes the emerging group of related jobs. There can be no doubt that understanding occupations has a distinct role within organizations and external agencies, such as technical-education schools.

Types of Occupational Analysis

Many examples of occupational analysis reports, across a range of occupations, can easily be found in the literature. Many of these are posted by professional organizations that have used an occupational analysis to help define the components of their respective professions (e.g., Balasa, 2015; MacKenzie & O'Toole, 2011). A review of these various sources of information suggests that occupational analysis has been used in three basic ways, as a means to analyze the following:

1. An entire occupation
2. An area of competence that occurs across certain occupations
3. A set of prerequisite knowledge and skills that are required when performing in any of the jobs related to the occupation.

Entire Occupation

Analyzing the components of an entire occupation appears to be the most frequent use of occupational analysis. That is, using occupational analysis to document the commonalities of a group of related jobs as they occur across different work settings. Of note, the phrase "a group of related jobs" is a critical aspect for understanding the meaning of an occupation in this instance.

The phrase suggests that the jobs are related because they share some or all of the following characteristics in a relative sense: the same underlying bodies of knowledge that support practice, the same sets of prerequisites, the same certifications or licensure requirements, the same general settings in which practice is carried out, and some of the same actual duties and tasks. In a sense, an occupation is a way of understanding a certain group of jobs at a higher level of abstraction.

A relatively complete example of an occupational analysis of registered nurses, in a particular geographic region, as conducted by the Great Lakes Bay College in Michigan, can be found at the following web address: https://www.delta.edu/workforce-training/_documents/glbr-rn-report.pdf. In addition, the following list presents some examples of the many occupations that are available for review in the literature:

- Supply Chain Manager
  http://www.supplychaincanada.org/assets/u/CSCSCOSFinalSupply ChainManager.pdf
- Information Systems Manager
  http://www.supplychaincanada.org/assets/u/CSCSCOSFinalInformation SystemsAnalyst.pdf
- Digital Security Manager
  https://itactalent.ca/wp-content/uploads/2015/04/BTM-NOS_final_ 2016.pdf

- Enterprise Data Analyst
  https://itactalent.ca/wp-content/uploads/2015/04/BTM-NOS_
  final_2016.pdf
- Information System Technician Submarines
  http://www.public.navy.mil/bupersnpc/reference/nec/NEOCSVol1/
  Documents/ITS_o CH63_Jul15.pdf

Upon review of these examples of occupational analyses, it should be apparent that there seems to be no standard format for presenting a report on the occupational analysis information. Each situation calls for a somewhat different form, based on its intended use. In general, occupational analysis reports typically have some or all of the following sets of information:

- Name of the document usually in the form of the title of the occupation
- Reference number that identifies this report within a series of reports
- Level of the analysis, such as whether the analysis is targeted to an entrant to the occupation, an experienced employee, or an expert employee
- General description of the occupation
- Relevant jobs that comprise the occupational title
- Forecasts of future job openings
- Pathways from other occupations to this occupation
- Qualification structure that describes the sequence of the training programs, based on the analysis
- Credentialing information as to whether the qualification structure leads to a certificate or a license of some kind
- Prerequisite areas of knowledge and skill required for learning the occupation
- Underlying characteristics of effective employees in the occupation, including interpersonal skills and other assumptions about the individuals
- Cross-reference information on the training for this occupation to other occupations
- Knowledge-based learning outcomes and performance criteria for each of the learning outcomes
- Areas of competence related to the occupation, often stated in the form of duties and tasks
- Salary ranges as the occupation occurs in different settings

Readers are encouraged to conduct their own search to find examples of occupational analyses and the information provided in each document. As can be easily surmised, this list of information offers a relatively comprehensive perspective of an occupation which can be of use for a variety of professionals.

Areas of Competence

Another use of occupational analysis has been to document specific areas of competence, considered to have some importance, that occur across occupation, or a cluster of occupations. That is, analyzing a certain aspect that occurs across more than one occupation, and not necessarily analyzing the entire occupation. This use of occupational analysis in this way is more focused than using the technique to analyze an entire occupation. Identifying which areas of competence to focus on likely requires an understanding of each of the relevant occupations, nevertheless.

Focusing on specific areas of competence across occupations often provides a more strategic perspective of the occupations. In this sense, there seem to be some advantages for using this more limited approach to analyze occupations. For one thing, it signals which areas of competence should be emphasized for future training and education programs. It provides greater program efficiency, since there is a reduced need to offer the same information more than once across training programs. It provides trainees with greater flexibility in their occupational choices, since they can realize the extent to which occupations are interconnected and then target more than one occupation, and by extension more than one apprenticeship program, for their consideration. Finally, focusing on areas of competence forms the basis of establishing standards from which an occupational framework can be devised.

As will be discussed in the next chapter, many countries, such as the United Kingdom, have implemented a national system of standards for a relatively large number of technical occupations, and the standards are based on various areas of competence derived from related occupations. Occupational frameworks are based on standards, and provide a roadmap, in a sense, to guide individuals on how to acquire the various areas of competence, leading to being qualified for an occupation.

The following list provides some examples of occupational analyses that focus on areas of competence within their related occupations, as taken from the National Occupational System from the United Kingdom:

- Implement DevOps Digital Delivery Infrastructure Processes
  https://www.ukstandards.org.uk/PublishedNos/TECIT50731.pdf#search=digital%20analyst
- Organize Local Telecoms Engineering Activities
  https://www.ukstandards.org.uk/PublishedNos/SEMRET324.pdf#search=telecom
- Conduct Specified Testing of Telecoms Systems

https://www.ukstandards.org.uk/PublishedNos/SEMRET320.pdf# search=telecom
- IT/Technology Solution Testing Level 3 Role https://www.ukstandards.org.uk/PublishedNos/ESKITP5033.pdf# search=telecom

As stated, there are advantages in demonstrating how the areas of competence relates to many different occupations. At the same time, there are some obvious disadvantages as well, the most prominent of which is that when seeking to analyze the areas of competence for several relevant occupations, the level of specificity of the information as it pertains to any one occupation may necessarily be reduced. That is, the more inclusive the number of occupations, the greater is the risk for reducing the context of the area of competence. It is incumbent on educators and HRD professionals to address this issue in the design of training programs based on the areas of competence.

In general, these occupational analysis reports typically have some or all of the following sets of information:

- Name of the area of competence, usually in the form of a duty or task statement
- Reference number that identifies this report within a series of reports
- Overview of the area of competence, which provides a context for the work involved
- Prerequisite knowledge and skills, including other areas of competence
- Knowledge-level learning outcomes
- Relevant occupations that comprise the area of competence
- Occupational clusters or business sectors that the various occupations belong to
- Framework showing how this area of competence relates to other areas of competence, and the pathways to acquire this area of competence
- Credentialing information as to whether the qualification structure leads to a certificate or a license of some kind
- Career guidance on selecting this occupation for future study
- Glossary of technical terms and abbreviations

Prerequisite Knowledge and Skills

The final type of occupation analysis that has emerged is to document specific areas of prerequisite knowledge and skills that support individuals when performing in one or more occupations. These reports are often the most general in nature, leading some informed readers to question whether, in fact, the document actually represents an occupational analysis? Or do the reports simply report on some information of some interest. To be clear, such reports should clarify what role the information in the report plays in understanding an occupation. Because of its general nature, the information in this type of occupational analysis might relate to more than one occupation.

There seems to be no standard template for presenting occupational reports that focus on prerequisite areas of knowledge and skills. Most of the reports include the same sets of information as presented in reports from the previous types of occupational analyses. Some examples of this type of occupational analysis are the following:

- Working with Computers
  https://www.ukstandards.org.uk/PublishedNos/PPLRPTO11.
  pdf#search=computer%20systems
- Using Data with Computers
  https://www.ukstandards.org.uk/PublishedNos/SFJZH2.
  pdf#search=computer%20systems
- Capturing Biometric Intelligence
  https://www.ukstandards.org.uk/PublishedNos/SFSHIB11.
  pdf#search=computer%20systems
- Using Computer Software Packages to Assist with Engineering Activities
  https://www.ukstandards.org.uk/PublishedNos/SEMPEO263.
  pdf#search=computer%20systems

Conducting an Occupational Analysis

Table 7.1 presents the general process for conducting an occupational analysis. As discussed in Chap. 3, the occupational analysis process is based on the broader work analysis process. The following discussion introduces each phase of the process and then comments on the components that comprise each phase.

I. Plan the analysis

Logically, the first phase of the work analysis process is to plan the occupational analysis. Within the first phase, there are three related components to consider:

Table 7.1 Process for conducting an occupational analysis

I. *Plan the occupational analysis*
   a. Specify the purpose of the analysis
   b. Decide which techniques will be used
   c. Develop a proof of concept prototype
II. *Select the sources and the methods*
   a. Select the sources of information
   b. Select the methods of gathering the information
III. *Conduct the occupational analysis*
   a. Review the technique-specific process
   b. Use the technique-specific process
IV. *Prepare the final report*
   a. Prepare the draft version of the report
   b. Review the report
   c. Prepare the final version of the report

---

a. *Specify the purpose of the analysis.* In the context of occupational analysis, the purpose statement focuses on whether the focus will be on an entire occupation or on an area of competence within a set of related occupations. It makes sense from the start of the project to ensure that there is clarity about the focus of the analysis. The following are examples of purpose statements, showing how both questions are addressed:

- Analyze the components of the Back-Office Engineer occupation across various customer telecom locations, from which to develop a set of occupational standards and a training program on this occupation.
- Analyze the components of the area of competence: Managing Network Changes across various customer telecom occupations, from which to develop a common training program for the occupations involved.

It should be noted that these examples of purpose statements were intended to be related to each other, to show how the occupational analysis technique might be used, in fact, within an organization setting. In this instance, the first purpose statement focuses on an entire job as it appears across work settings and the second purpose statement focuses on a specific area of competence that exists across related jobs, across work settings.

b. *Decide which work analysis techniques will be used.* Based on the purpose of the analysis, the various work analysis techniques should be considered and the appropriate ones identified. For instance, beyond using the occupational analysis technique, there may be instances in which the critical incident technique may be appropriate to achieve the purpose as well.

This technique may be especially useful when analyzing an area of competence, not an entire occupation, and no systematic analyses has been conducted of the occupations related to the area of competence. As will be discussed in Chap. 10, the critical incident technique is uniquely suited to analyze knowledge-based tasks.

c. *Develop a proof of concept prototype.* Given that information from an occupational analysis has many uses in practice, a proof of concept would seem to have particular relevance in this case. Developing the proof of concept would help maintain the focus of the analysis, as it is being conducted. For instance, the proof of concept could show the format that will be used to present the information later on.

Stakeholders could then provide comments on the perceived usefulness of the format in terms of achieving the intended purpose of the occupational analysis. Further, the proof of concept would show how to use the information to develop certain academic courses or training programs. It's a way of demonstrating how the end product will appear, for all stakeholders to review.

II. Select the sources and methods

The next phase of the occupational analysis process is to select the sources of the information, especially who will serve as the SMEs, and the methods of gathering the information.

As stated, the primary source of information for many occupational analyses are SMEs coming from a diverse range of settings. Because of the scope of many occupational analyses, the sources might likely include reports of employment forecasts, previous occupational analyses, such as from O*NET, and leaders from the pertinent business sectors.

As stated, DACUM has been used to a large extent as the primary method when seeking to address purposes of conducting an occupational analysis. When used in practice, DACUM is sufficiently flexible to accommodate different prompt questions. That is, what question is used to begin the session with the SMEs. For instance, the prompt question posed to SMEs at the start of using DACUM for a job analysis might be the following: We are here to document the components of a certain job. Logically, the prompt question when using DACUM for an occupation analysis would be the following: We are here to document the components of the occupation.

III. Conduct the analysis

As stated, an occupational analysis often entails gathering a broader set of information than a job analysis does. As such, the analyst should carefully plan out the sequence of the techniques used. In general, it is advisable for the analyst to gather information from various printed sources first, as a means to be oriented first to the occupation or area of competence. The DACUM should be among the last methods used to gather information.

IV. Prepare the final report

The scope of most occupational analyses requires that several different stakeholders should review the draft versions of the report. It is important that the analyst manage the process of identifying the reviewers, providing a feedback form for the reviewers, and responding to the feedback from the reviewers. In essence, the report should be presented in a way that facilitates use of the information as intended.

Of note, such reports may also include information about the proof of concept, showing how the information in the report will actually be used in practice. This aspect is often overlooked, giving the impression that the information is the most important outcome to be considered. Because of the various stakeholders involved, occupational analysis reports are often professionally produced and printed.

Comment

Occupational analysis is a work analysis technique of emerging importance, since it is often used by organizations and governmental agencies. Understanding occupational analysis depends on distinguishing between what is meant by a job and an occupation. As stated, an occupation title is a way of naming a collection of related jobs that occur across work settings.

Occupational analysis tends to be a longer, more involved, process than a job analysis, simply because of the additional information that is included in the report. An occupational analysis usually necessitates having a project team involved in the occupational analysis process.

Reflection Questions

1. Can you distinguish between a job and an occupation? Do you have a personal experience that might help you distinguish between the two?

2. Does identifying the types of occupational analyses help better understand the myriad of documents that can be found that purport to be occupational analyses?
3. In what role would you prefer to serve in conducting an occupational analysis? Analyst? Labor market forecaster? Program implementation?
4. What do you think is the impact of an occupational analysis on the career choices of individuals? Do you think the information would be helpful to individuals? To career guidance counselors?
5. What do you see as the major issues in conducting an occupational analysis, given that jobs are undergoing constant changes?

References

Balasa, D. A. (2015, July–August). Occupational analyses: Why such studies are important for examination and curriculum development. *CMA Today*, pp. 5–7.
MacKenzie, L., & O'Toole, G. (Eds.). (2011). *Occupational analysis in practice*. San Francisco, CA: John Wiley.

8

National Occupational Standards

Readers likely have noted that the topic of national occupational standards (NOSs) was mentioned several times in the previous chapter, which introduced the process for conducting an occupational analysis. NOSs specify what an individual is required to perform in an occupation, as the occupation appears across various workplace settings, at a regional or a national level. NOSs also specify the background knowledge and skills individuals should possess to meet that standard. Each NOS defines one occupation or an area of competence across occupations. NOSs are used for the following reasons:

- To forecast employment priorities and trends by government agencies and educational institutions
- To provide a benchmark for companies so they can compare their job expectations with the occupational standard
- To provide the basis for designing training and education programs
- To construct job descriptions by human resources (HR) staff members for use with recruitment and selection
- To identify occupational options and their respective educational requirements by individual job seekers

Because of their overall importance globally, NOSs are discussed in depth separately in this chapter. Numerous examples of NOSs can be easily found both in the research literature and on various government websites. For instance, information about the occupational standards that relate to health and safety occupations in the United Kingdom can be found at

© The Author(s) 2019
R. L. Jacobs, *Work Analysis in the Knowledge Economy*,
https://doi.org/10.1007/978-3-319-94448-7_8

https://www.britsafe.org/training-and-learning/find-the-right-course-for-you/nvqshealth. Logically, regional and national governments make such information easily accessible, because of the desire to have individuals use the information to make decisions about career choices. To a large extent, NOSs are in the public domain, intended for as much use as possible.

Most HRD professionals in the United States have a relatively limited understanding of such documents and the notion of national occupational standards. NOSs are not as prevalent in this country compared to many other countries. Indeed, some HRD professionals may have never even heard of them at all. Table 8.1 compares and contrasts job standards and occupational standards across a number of different categories of importance to HRD professionals. Many HRD professionals are typically more familiar with job standards as their primary frame of reference. The focus of this chapter is on the broader understanding of occupational standards as they are presented in NOSs.

HRD professionals in many countries have necessarily become well aware of their national own occupational standard systems, and the information has become a critically important part of their professional practice. For instance, HRD professionals in the Republic of South Korea, employed in both smaller and larger companies, must consider their nation's National Competency Standards (NCS) whenever they design training programs for many of the employees in

Table 8.1 Comparing occupational standards and job standards

	Job standard	Occupational standard
Definition	Through a job analysis, job standards provide an understanding of a specific job in a certain work context	Through an occupational analysis, occupational standards provide an understanding of a set of related jobs across settings
Components	• Job description • Duties • Tasks • Task components • Additional information	• Prerequisites • Values • Attitudes • Duties • Tasks • Additional information
How it is used	• Design HRD programs • Guide curriculum development	• Guide curriculum development • Inform business sectors • Inform employers • Inform job seekers • Labor market balance
Determination of validity	Does the standard accurately represent what is done in the specific job in this context?	Does the standard represent a consensus among the stakeholders about this occupation?
Measures of success	• Performance rating scales	• Cognitive tests • Performance rating scales

their companies. As will be discussed later in the chapter, the NCS is a national database that provides standards of over 500 occupations developed from a series of occupational analysis studies.

HRD professionals in many other Asian countries, including Malaysia, Singapore, and Thailand, most European countries, and Australia and New Zealand as well have the same experience. Each of these countries has a well-developed workforce development system, including the use of NOSs, which to an extent influence HRD practice. So an understanding of NOSs is an important part of understanding this broader use of occupational analysis.

Historical Context

NOSs are a relatively recent phenomenon, formally established in most countries during the 1970s and 1980s, in response to the need to better match the skills of job seekers and the needs of employers. Today, NOSs have become a global phenomenon and are a common component of most national workforce development systems.

Table 8.2 presents a partial list of countries and their respective workforce development efforts which include the use of NOSs. Information about NOSs and their use has become readily available from a variety of sources: consulting firms, government agencies, nongovernmental organizations, and the scholarly literature. Some historical context is appropriate as part of this discussion.

For many centuries and until the recent past, individuals were essentially left on their own to acquire the skills necessary to enter the workforce. The primary way for individuals to receive skilled training was through an apprenticeship. For instance, the early apprenticeship system in Europe, starting in the Middle Ages, required that young persons would, on their own, approach

Table 8.2 Partial list of countries that have National Occupational Standards (NOSs)

- United Kingdom—Regulated Qualifications Framework (RQF)
- Germany—National Occupational Standards (NOSs)
- South Africa—National Qualifications Framework (SANQF)
- Scotland—Scottish Credit and Qualifications Framework (SCQF)
- Australia—Australian Qualifications Framework (AQF)
- New Zealand—Qualifications Framework (NZQF)
- Republic of Korea—National Competency Standards (NCS)
- Singapore—Workforce Skills Qualifications (WSQ)
- ASEAN—Competency Standards for Tourism
- The Netherlands—National ICT Competency

a recognized expert in an occupation, such as a furniture maker, blacksmith, painter, or watchmaker, and request to be taken on for a period of time.

The master could refuse the request or could accept the request, and require payment for his service to the apprentice. In China, following the writings of Confucius, apprenticeships had been a major part of the training of handcraft workers, for over a thousand years. Today, traditional apprenticeships remain in the arts and traditional medicine. In the United States, in the early days of our national history, apprenticeships sought to follow the European model, which many individuals were already familiar with.

In fact, it is interesting to note that Paul Revere, one of the heroes of the American Revolution, was in fact an accomplished silversmith, who had begun as an apprentice to learn that trade when he was 13 years old. Presumably, he produced with his own hands and talents the lanterns which were used to signal the arrival of the British troops in Boston.

In general, efforts to implement national educational systems for developing workplace skills began during the era of industrialization at the turn of the twentieth century. In the United States, vocational education as a national concern came about in 1917 with the Smith–Hughes Act, which provided federal funding to establish separate educational entities in each state to oversee the training of youth in various technical occupations. Today, almost all vocational high schools derive their existence from this important piece of legislation. Even so, until the 1950s, the United States and most other countries did not have any coordinated national policies related to skills development beyond the funding of vocational and technical schools.

In the 1950s, the emerging global economic situation prompted many countries to begin to reconsider how best to achieve and maintain a skilled workforce. No longer could individuals be left on their own to make decisions about their future employment. And the vocational schools alone were not providing sufficient numbers of individuals with advanced skills. Among the related issues at the time were the following:

- There was still a global need for reconstruction and industrialization following the devastation of World War II, calling for more individuals with specialized skills in many countries.
- The nature of work began to shift from being mostly physical and repetitive to the emergence of knowledge work, as was first observed by Peter Drucker in 1957.
- There was a growing sense that unemployment, especially among youth, was an important social issue of concern, and that the public and private sectors should work together in search of solutions for the common good.

Economists introduced the term human capital in the 1960s, which suggested the relationship between wages and education. That is, the higher the level of educational achievement, the greater the earning power of individuals, for the benefit of individuals and society as a whole. The theory of human capital development continues to support the use of NOSs today. Finally, in response to societal needs and advances in technology, many new applied occupations began to appear, especially in the health-care, management, engineering, and computer science business sectors. In fact, many specialized occupations today, such as HRD, can trace their origins to addressing needs that arose during the post–World War II era, each of them requiring a unique set of specialized knowledge and skills.

Within this context, many policy makers, business leaders, and educators began to realize that a more articulated, nationally based system of workforce development was required to meet the challenges of the future. This seemed especially true when considering what is referred to as the middle occupations. That is, occupations that are not managerial in nature, but focus mostly on technically based occupations that require an extensive set of prerequisite knowledge and skills to perform. Along with the emergence of national workforce development systems was the recognition that a system of occupational standards would also be required. As a result, occupational standards were established as a core element of the national workforce development systems. It is from this context that NOSs emerged, as we know them today.

Two major national workforce development systems have emerged which remain influential globally today:

- The German dual work-learning system
- The British National Vocational Qualification (NVQ) system

German Dual System

The German dual work-learning system was first implemented through the National Training Act in 1969. Before that time, workplace learning was mostly governed by individual guilds, which oversaw and managed each occupation. Indeed, the German-speaking countries—Germany, Austria, Switzerland—have had a well-established apprenticeship system, dating back over 500 years. The role and recognition of the master craftsman has been well documented in German-speaking countries. In fact, consider that the wide-scale adoption of the moveable-type printing process in Europe from around 1490 could not have occurred without the apprenticeship system in place. Apprentices went out on their own after spending time with the master printer, and began to use the emerging technology.

Legislation that established the dual system in Germany basically formalized the ongoing learning to work system. In addition, the legislation formalized on a national scale the social agreement among the guilds, the local chambers of commerce, and employers, to work together to serve the needs of individuals entering the workforce. As a national initiative, other aspects linked to the German dual work-learning system included reforming the K-12 educational system, managing the number of entrants into occupations, and, for the first time, systematically documenting the components of the occupations.

British National Vocational Qualifications

The British (United Kingdom, Wales, Northern Ireland, and Scotland) system of national vocational qualifications (NVQs) was first implemented in 1984–1987. The system has been commonly referred to as the NVQs, though the name today has been changed to the Regulated Qualifications Framework (RQF). It is interesting to note that with the election of Margaret Thatcher as prime minister in 1979, Britain began the painful process of moving from a government-controlled and planned economy to a more market-based economy. As a result, the 1980s were known for many strikes in the coal, steel, and shipbuilding industries, based on the expected numbers of people losing their jobs. Thus, the NVQ system was first established, in part, as a national effort to address the resulting social consequences of these dramatic economic changes.

The NVQ system introduced the term occupational framework as a way of extending the notion of an occupational standard to the entire national educational enterprise. That is, for the first time there was a common structure and accompanying sets of standards for all school levels, from kindergarten through higher education. The well-known O Level and A Level designations are educational certificates that one might receive at the end of one's schooling.

Today, most national occupational systems globally are based in some way on either the German system or the British system. The German dual work-learning system has attracted the interest of many countries to serve as a model, as the notion of combining academics with actual work experiences has made a profound impression. Even in the United States during the William Clinton presidency in the 1990s, educational policy makers implemented the school to work programs, which were based on the dual system. But the adoption of the German system has been hampered by three major issues.

First, it requires agreements of cooperation across the various social partners—businesses, education, chambers of commerce, guilds—and sometimes the agreements are not always in the best interests of each partner. For instance, when a business takes on apprentices, it incurs much expense, and the apprentice may decide to leave at the end of the learning period, and even work for a competing organization. This often occurs in the banking and financial services sector.

Regardless, most countries, other than the German-speaking ones, do not have a history of social cooperation among their major stakeholders, making the dual system in all its aspects difficult to implement. Related to this is the sometimes harsh management of access to occupations. It is sometimes difficult for young people to "follow their dreams" in an occupation, simply because the occupation may be considered saturated, and the market cannot absorb any more entrants.

Second, the German dual system is often perceived to be complex and oftentimes inflexible. That is, when other countries consider adopting the German dual system, they realize that all components should be included, and that everything takes time to plan and implement. For instance, the following story was told to me about 20 years ago, regarding the emergence of the job title of Web Master. Employers were informed that it would take nearly five years for government officials to analyze the job, publish the standards, and establish the apprenticeship system. In the United States at the same time, many individuals, even teenagers, were learning to be a Web Master on their own, without much formal instruction. And what happens when the software changes?

Finally, there has been limited access to understanding the German system simply because of language issues. Until recently, most documents issued by the Federal Institute for Vocational Education and Training (BIBB) https://www.bibb.de/en/, which guides national workforce policy making, have been published in German. Now with partnerships with many similar global research and development organizations, more and more reports from BIBB are available in both German and English. However, most of the core documents of interest, such as the actual documents describing the occupational standards, are available in the German language only.

In a relative sense, the British system has influenced the policies of many more countries globally than the German dual system, for two major reasons. First, the British system has either been adopted by or has greatly influenced the workforce development policies of most members of the British Commonwealth and former British colonies. As a result, most of these countries have devised their own unique systems, such as in Australia, New Zealand, Singapore, and Malaysia, which have become famous in their own right.

The overall influence of the British NVQs cannot be underestimated. Indeed, an entire consulting industry has emerged to help developing and near-developed countries adopt the NVQ system. Consider that nearly every country in the Arab Middle East, in Africa including South Africa, and many countries in Asia have based their own system of NOSs on the NVQs, even though many use the term "dual system" as a means to brand their use of the NVQs. For instance, while Kuwait and Saudi Arabia were never British colonies, they use the British system as their benchmark for their educational and workforce development systems.

Second, the British NVQ system can be found in most English-speaking countries, or countries that have English as a predominant second language such as in the Arab countries and Malaysia. The prevalence of English as the global business language, and the amount of resources published in English, makes it easier to acquire and share information about the NVQs.

Beyond the national workforce development systems from Germany and the United Kingdom, several other countries have adopted what might be considered blended systems, which draw aspects from both national systems. For instance, government policy makers from the Human Resource Development Service of South Korea have begun to use the term dual system for describing their national workforce development system. More than most other countries, South Korea has developed what might be called a hybrid system, taking elements from the U.S. educational system, the British NVQs, and the German dual system.

In brief, from the United States, South Korea has established an extensive community college and postsecondary technical education system. From the British NVQs, South Korea has established the NCS, starting in 2002. In addition, South Korea has implemented a tax reimbursement scheme, similar to what is used in many other countries to provide an incentive to companies to provide training to their employees. And from the German dual system, South Korea has required companies to take on apprentices, especially for technical occupations within larger companies, such as LG, Samsung, and Hyundai-Kia. The common-sense approach used in South Korea has resulted in this country becoming a benchmark for many other countries to follow, such as several in the Middle East and Africa.

Japan and the United States

Finally in this discussion of the history of NOSs, no mention has been made of Japan and the United States. In some respects, the systems in Japan and the United States have developed on their own. For different reasons, neither nation has a national system of occupational standards, but typically rely upon a patchwork of standards derived from trade associations, the private sector businesses such as the Microsoft certifications, and educational institutions such as community colleges, trade unions, and professional societies. In Japan, most occupational training occurs in postsecondary institutions, such as community colleges and technical schools. The secondary high schools tend to focus more on academic subjects. A national concern now is that many young people at age 18 do not have employable skills. In essence, the Japanese education and workforce training system has not served in any sense as a global benchmark. Few delegations from other countries visit Japan to study its national workforce development system.

Part of the reason for this has been the Japanese tradition of lifelong employment which, until recently, allowed a more long-term perspective on preparing individuals for the workforce. Occupations could be learned over time on the job. That is, individuals were hired directly from schools or universities with the expectation that the new hires would remain in the same company, especially the automobile companies Toyota and Honda, for many years, usually for their entire work lives. Clearly, the economic events of the past decade have tested this assumption, causing some education officials to begin to examine other options for increasing workforce flexibility.

As stated, it is generally agreed that the United States does not really have a formal national workforce development system, primarily because of the unique national culture and political system. Most planning about workforce development is assumed to occur within the individual states, not the federal government. The major national legislation in this regard is the Workforce Innovation and Opportunity Act (WIOPA), from the Employment and Training Administration of the Department of Labor, which provides funding to the states for certain activities related to supporting regional and community economic and workforce development.

While the United States does not have a system of NOSs, some occupational standards do exist as they have been established and managed through the efforts of various interested entities, but not by a regional or national governmental body. For instance, the National Council of Examiners for Engineering and Surveying, an independent, nonprofit organization, has established the requirements and tests for individuals seeking to become a licensed engineer across a number of different engineering specialties. Having a license from this organization is generally recognized as being an important criterion for employers seeking to hire an engineer.

The closest that the United States has in terms of an NOS is through the well-known O*NET resource, which was introduced in Chap. 2 as a major source of information when conducting a work analysis. O*NET was originally established in 1938 during the time of the Great Depression by the Department of Labor, and provides relatively comprehensive descriptions of over 1000 occupations. O*NET was initially intended as a reference guide to assist workers find employment.

The result was the publication of a quite thick book, much like an encyclopedia, which listed occupations and accompanying information for each occupation, called the *Dictionary of Occupational Titles* (DOTs). Updates to these volumes were published approximately every five years and distributed to every local public library for public access. In practice, individuals would use the book at the library as a resource to find jobs of interest. Unfortunately, there was no search capability, other than the table of contents, and there was no way to link the information to the local educational opportunities.

The online version of the DOTs was first made available in 1997 and, because of its ease of use and wealth of information, it is now used by educators, HR staff, and government officials globally. The format that originated with the print version to describe each occupation was carried through in the online version. The format does not necessarily conform to any format used by any other resource on occupations.

It is difficult not to overstate the influence of O*NET. Nearly every HR manager, on a global basis, is aware of this resource and uses it on a daily basis to identify job titles, write job descriptions, and specify job expectations. For instance, once, while this author was consulting with a petrochemical company in the eastern province of Dammam, in Saudi Arabia, O*NET was observed, for different reasons, to be on the screen of every staff member in the HR department. O*NET is often the starting point for conducting any research about a job or an occupation. For instance, many technical and vocational school educators globally, such as in China, make frequent use of O*NET in their curriculum planning.

A final note about occupational standards in the United States: The military branches for one have historically been well known for their well-developed skills development systems. In fact, many individuals enter military service as a means to acquire skills that might be useful later on in civilian life at the conclusion of their military commitment. Recently, the U.S. military—most notably the U.S. Navy—has instituted a system of occupational standards for many of the jobs held by enlisted military personnel. The documents are quite comprehensive and focus mostly on technical occupations. The standards appear more like the format of an NVQ and are primarily intended for training and promotion purposes.

Finally, based on interest in standardizing information about occupations, the International Labor Organization (ILO) established the International Standard Classification of Occupations (ISCO), originally in 1957, for the purpose of maintaining statistical information about occupations. The ISCO categorizes occupations into ten classifications. Now the classification system has the expanded purpose of providing a model for organizing occupations for those countries that have not developed their own national classifications.

Developing National Occupational Standards

A general four-stage process was presented in the previous chapter as a general guide to conduct an occupational analysis. Because of its implications at the national level, developing an NOS requires use of an expanded process, more involved than what might be used for more limited occupational analysis situations. An adapted version of the process used to develop NVQs is presented here. The development of most NOSs follows a similar process as the one presented here. The general suggested phases of the process are the following:

1. Conduct research on the business sector and the occupation or area of competence within the business sector to be analyzed.
2. Review the existing documentation of the occupation or the area of competence.
3. Gather information about the occupation or the area of competence, often using Developing a Curriculum as the primary method of gathering the information.
4. Prepare a draft of the national occupation standard using the approved format.
5. Seek out approvals of the draft NOS from a range of stakeholders and future users of the information.
6. Develop proof of concept examples of how the information will be used in practice.
7. Establish a means to conduct ongoing scans of the occupation or area of competence to ensure that the information is up to date over time.
8. Establish a management system for disseminating the standard to ensure its awareness by potential users.
9. Conduct follow-up research and evaluation studies on the accuracy, usefulness, and impacts of the NOS.
10. Release the NOS into the marketplace for reference by users.

As can be readily surmised from this list of phases, the process of developing an NOS is often a lengthy and somewhat involved undertaking, involving the participation of a number of professional staff to derive the intended outcome. This amount of effort is appropriate, given that so much is at stake with the resulting information. Literally, the NOS may influence the actions and decisions made by a variety of individuals across a nation, so errors cannot be made at the outset.

The National Competency Standards (NCS), as developed through the leadership of the HRD Service of Korea, Ministry of Employment and Labor, is a prominent example of an NOS. The NCS is a relatively large database of occupational standards based on the analysis of entire occupations. The HRD Services of Korea provides a wide range of workforce development policies and services to serve educational institutions, organizations, and individual job seekers. The NCS was established in 2002 and, since that time, both the HRD Services of Korea and the NCS have become benchmarks for many other countries to consider.

Each occupational standard of the NCS has the following basic components:

Occupation title. The general name of the occupation that includes as many instances of the occupation as possible.
Industry. The name of the business sector in which the occupation is part of.
Occupation. These are a list of the relevant occupations that would be included in the analysis.
Competency units. These are the broad sets of outcomes related to the occupations, based on the occupational analysis.

The NCS has a number of intended uses. Community colleges can use the information to design a curriculum, identify individual course titles, and even prepare lessons from this information. Organizations can use the information to inform themselves about the content of various jobs related to the relevant occupations. Individual job seekers can use the information as a basis for making an occupational choice and determining how best to prepare to enter the occupation.

Figure 8.1 shows the logic model of the NCS, showing how it can be used to develop individual lessons within community college settings. The figure serves as an example of a proof of concept, showing how seemingly broad sets of information with the Industry Sector can be progressively narrowed down so that the information can be used for developing a learning topic for a lesson.

As stated, the intended purpose of NOSs is to develop employment skills among job seekers and ensure a match between those skills with the needs of employers. There are other, often unstated, purposes of NOSs as well. For instance, from a societal perspective, NOSs provide the basis for more equitable employment opportunities across all sections of a society. That is, they make it possible for all individuals, regardless of their particular situations, to enter an occupation and to eventually make a good wage, to a greater extent

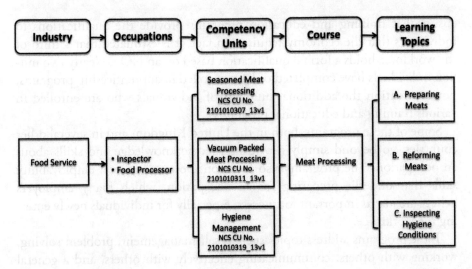

Fig. 8.1 Example of the structure of the National Competency Standards (NCS), South Korea

than what might be expected otherwise. So there are definite societal benefits to be expected from NOSs in terms of employment accessibility and wage levels, outcomes that are highly desirable for maintaining the economic health of any community.

At the same time, NOSs influence management practices and expectations, suggesting that NOSs help address gaps in skills within companies. Most readers of this book are likely aware of reports that raise alarms about global skills gaps among critical occupations. From a more personal perspective on this issue, most readers have likely heard or experienced a situation in which there was limited availability of properly prepared individuals for a certain job. In this sense, NOSs can be used strategically to promote entry into occupations in which there is higher demand than supply of individuals who possess the appropriate sets of skills.

Finally, the use of NOSs, especially when they are part of a broader national educational qualification framework, has served to influence education reform. In this sense, NOSs tend to make educational institutions more accountable as to the outcomes they are achieving in regard to the broader educational enterprise. In addition, such accountability makes it possible to compare different national systems with greater accuracy.

Comment

There is no doubt that NOSs have yielded many benefits to those nations that have invested resources to design and implement such systems. In the United Kingdom alone, over the past 25 years, it is reported that NOSs have helped ensure that training and education programs provide the qualifications to individuals that the economy requires. In fact, it is estimated that a third of the workforce holds a formal qualification based on an NOS. Nearly two million individuals have completed or have enrolled in apprenticeship programs, not to mention the additional numbers of individuals who are enrolled in various training and educational programs.

Some of these programs, both in the United Kingdom and in several other countries, go beyond simply providing specific knowledge and skills about an occupation. The programs also focus on the more general employability skills that underlie preparing for an occupation, which many employers believe are just as important for success, especially for individuals newly entering the workforce.

These programs address topics such as self-management, problem solving, working with others, communicating effectively with others, and a general understanding of the global economy and business issues. Thus, NOSs have often provided a more comprehensive set of programs focusing on preparing individuals to enter the workforce and meeting the needs of employers.

Given the espoused noble goals of NOSs, one might expect that they would be readily accepted within the countries that invest in them. NOSs have faced at least four issues of concern that have been raised about their use.

NOSs require an extensive amount of resources to gain the initial acceptance of all stakeholders, devise the specific supporting legislation and policies, obtain the necessary budget resources, recruit the administrative and professional staff, develop the information communication systems, and maintain relationships with stakeholder groups. And this list does not even include the resources required to conduct the actual occupational analysis studies.

Needless to say, many countries may express a desire to implement such a system, but once the amount of resources required is discovered, making it actually occur is often daunting and fraught with constraints. The question faced by many policy makers, especially in developing nations, is whether there are sufficient social benefits at that time for the amount of resources invested to achieve the benefits.

Organizations that employ the graduates are one of the primary intended audiences of NOSs. Information from an NOS should be used in the design of various employee development programs. In practice, while organizations readily agree when asked to participate in the process of conducting the occupational analysis, many employers are hesitant to make use of the standards once they are completed. Thus, the acceptance of NOSs in organizations is often not what might be expected.

Two related concerns seem to be expressed by managers in organizations. First, managers may raise questions about the relevance of the information within their specific work contexts, especially in those situations in which job content may be volatile and subject to frequent change. Second, many HRD practitioners in organizations are simply unaware of how to use the information from an NOS for the design of training programs. That is, no examples have been provided to show them how to actually adapt the information from the NOS. It is for this reason that a proof of concept component is included in the processes presented for each of the work analysis techniques.

In the same sense, educational institutions are also a primary audience of NOSs. And in the same sense, many educational institutions may not use the information from NOSs as they might be expected. The information should be used to help plan and implement educational programs based on the content of the occupations.

In practice, many educators acknowledge the importance of NOSs in a broad sense, but they have difficulty actually adapting the information at the more detailed level of lesson planning. In addition, educational institutions serve the employers in their immediate region, and the information in the NOS may not be altogether relevant to those employers.

The final issue of concern focuses on the underlying philosophical perspective of NOSs. For instance, in many countries, even ones that have well-regarded NOSs such as Australia and South Africa, concerns have been expressed about whether NOSs are in fact consistent with the values of a democratic, open society. Indeed, NOSs provide a reliable means to enter a particular occupation, especially for youth. At the same time, NOSs appear to predetermine the destiny of individuals toward technical occupations that may have limited career opportunities in the future. In a sense, NOSs are viewed as fostering a two-track society: those who learn an occupation through the NOS, and those who attend a university and eventually enter a profession.

Reflection Questions
1. To what extent have you been familiar with NOSs before the discussion in this chapter?
2. To what extent do you think that NOSs are an effective way of ensuring a prepared workforce?

3. Do you believe that national standards can be identified for occupations that are relevant across a wide segment of society?
4. Do you believe that it is possible to develop a set of occupational standards for all professions?
5. To what extent do you believe that the issues about national occupational systems are accurate, in terms of creating a two-tiered society of workers?

Reference

Drucker, P. (1957). *Landmarks of tomorrow*. New York: Harper.

9

Critical Incident Technique

Many human resource development (HRD) professionals, not to mention many managers, may wonder how it might be possible to analyze work that is mostly cognitive in nature. That is, work that expressly requires critical thinking as the major part of completing the task. Can work analysis actually be used to document what occurs inside your mind? For many, work analysis techniques are believed to be better suited for work that is more straightforward and observable in nature, simply because that is the way most techniques have been used in the past.

But as has been pointed out in this book, work has undergone much change, becoming more complex and requiring greater demands on individuals doing the work. In response, work analysis techniques should be available to respond to those changes.

For instance, consider the situation in which a production manager is expected to develop a production plan to meet a customer's need for an expedited delivery. In this case, the task statement would be: Develop a production plan for expedited products, and this task is clearly complex in nature. The outcome of the task would logically be the development of the completed production plan. What is the best way of analyzing this task and ones similar to it?

This chapter focuses on the critical incident technique, a technique that was first introduced in the 1950s by John C. Flanagan, a well-known and respected researcher and consultant in the field of industrial psychology. Now the critical incident technique seems even more important as a means to document the behaviors required to perform certain complex, knowledge-based, units of work.

© The Author(s) 2019
R. L. Jacobs, *Work Analysis in the Knowledge Economy*,
https://doi.org/10.1007/978-3-319-94448-7_9

It may be difficult for some to consider that thinking is a form of work, since thinking cannot be readily observed. It almost harkens back to the common joke frequently told about what professors do for a living. That is, they sit in their offices and think! But to be useful, even professors should follow their thinking with decisive action, which is informed by the thinking. In this sense, understanding the thoughts that precede the actions is the essence of knowledge-based tasks. Earlier in the book, it was suggested that tasks that require more thinking now occur across almost all jobs today, including many frontline jobs, not just for higher-level managers and professionals alone. The critical incident technique is uniquely suited to analyze those instances of work that involve critical thinking and doing as well.

Critical Incident Technique

As stated, the critical incident technique was first introduced in the literature by John Flanagan, in 1954, in a now-famous article in the journal *Psychological Bulletin*, aptly entitled The Critical Incident Technique. For some HRD professionals, this article simply represents a reference for a set of early ideas, before there was even a definable HRD field. For others, including this author, the article represents much more than simply a commonly used citation. The article in fact represents rigorous scholarship on a highly-useful research methodology, also appropriate as a work analysis technique as well. In this sense, the article represents a model on how HRD research and practice can in fact work together. That is, the article describes research studies showing how the technique was used, and also describes the practical organizational issues that the research studies sought to address. The sound research and the useful practice are linked together. At a time today when there are continuing discussions about how to make HRD scholarly research more relevant to practice, the article continues to serve as an exemplar on how to actually make this happen—though the article was published almost 70 years ago.

There is an inspiring story on how the critical incident technique was developed. The technique was first developed to address issues related to military flight training during World War II. John C. Flanagan, a psychologist in the U.S. Army Air Force, first conducted a number of studies investigating the effective and ineffective behaviors of pilots and crew members as part of the selection and classification of aircrews. Too many pilots in training were making critical errors, often leading to catastrophic results. The military believed that perhaps the training was not emphasizing the correct information, so there was a need to find out what additional training content should be included.

In 1944, Flanagan and his colleagues conducted a number of studies investigating how to identify the components of combat leadership. That is, what were the leadership qualities of an effective officer in the field? The researchers interviewed a large number of combat veterans to gather specific incidents about effective and ineffective behaviors with respect to this specific leadership activity. After analyzing several thousand individual incidents, the researchers were able to identify categories of combat leadership.

After the end of the war, Flanagan and his colleagues established the American Institutes of Research, from which they conducted more studies using the critical incident technique, continuing to focus on the critical behaviors of flight crews, both military and civilian. It is during this period that the studies specifically identified the critical incident technique as a form of job analysis, since the information had implications for pilot selection, training, and evaluation. Each of these studies entailed collecting several hundred to several thousand individual critical incidents, or short stories. That is why the critical incident technique has been described as the way to get the subject-matter experts (SMEs) to "Tell me a story".

In 1950, Flanagan conducted a series of research studies for the Delco-Remy Division of General Motors, to develop a performance rating instrument for hourly employees, based on critical incidents that were gathered from supervisors. Following these various studies has come a large number of published articles and doctoral dissertations on the critical incident technique that address questions across a wide range of occupations. These studies showed that the critical incident technique could focus on issues away from military and flight-training situations, and instead on everyday civilian jobs as well.

Since the early 1950s, the critical incident technique has since become one of the most widely used methods for research and development. There is a common-sense attraction to the technique, since the information comes directly from those individuals who have the experience of doing the task. And everyone likes to tell and hear a good story from informed individuals, as represented by the critical incidents. For instance, this author used the critical incident technique to study the effective interpersonal behaviors of supervisors in a post office setting. Critical incidents were gathered from experienced supervisors who were known for getting along with their subordinates (Jacobs, 1986). The resulting categories, drawn from the critical incidents, formed the basis of a supervisory training program and provided the content for a series of video clips that were used as part of the training program.

In addition, this author conducted an unpublished study for the Ohio Civil Service Employees Association, the union representing employees in the state of Ohio, to find out the dimensions of effective study approaches used by employees who had used their tuition assistance funds to enroll in college courses. For many employees, this was the first time in many years that they were back in a formal classroom setting, and there were management concerns about how well the returning students could set aside time and space to complete their readings, prepare their assignments, and prepare for tests. All of this represented new challenges for many of these individuals.

The prompt question for the critical incident interviews was the following: Tell me a time when you were effective as a student? Several hundred critical incidents were gathered and their underlying dimensions identified. The dimensions were used as part of an awareness training program to help better prepare individuals enrolled in future courses. The following are some examples of critical incidents gathered during the study:

- In the first course, I was asked to write a short paper. I had no clue initially, then I talked with the professor and he gave me some general ideas. This helped me focus on the assignment after that and I started to collect all the materials relating to it. I felt more motivated to complete the paper successfully after this. And the result was I got 10/10 for the paper. I really felt that I have accomplished something.
- I felt successful as a student after giving a presentation to a class as part of a final group project. My group was at a disadvantage because we only had two students as opposed to three or four students in all the other groups. But the two of us worked well together and we stayed in touch, even though we both had families and worked full-time. Not only did we receive an "A" for the project, but the professor asked us if she could use our presentation as an example for a future class.
- I was determined to find a quiet place in our house to study, so I made a corner of the family room that was only for me. I put up a curtain so I had some privacy from everyone else and a small table and chair. I could hide in my study place and do what I had to do. I think the kids were impressed by my dedication.
- There was one semester, actually my first in college, and had registered for a biology course. The first day of the class I learned that this course was actually used as the pre-med weed-out course, and it was terribly difficult. I had the chance to get out of this course and take an easier version to fulfill my GEC requirements. But I know I would have disappointed myself, even if my grades were higher, for taking the easier course. I was one of only three non-biology majors in the class, and got an OK grade. Now I am always proud that I stuck with the course and met this challenge.

The literature shows that the critical incident technique has been used to study a wide range of jobs and occupations, such as school principals, dentists, emergency room nurses, police officers, firemen, managers, and supervisors, among many others. The critical incident technique has also been found especially useful for analyzing certain behaviors among first responders and other professionals who have to make immediate, often highly consequential, decisions under stress.

Currently, two of my students at the University of Illinois are doing doctoral dissertations using the critical incident technique. One of the studies is investigating the learning strategies of designated expert employees in Korea and the other is on investigating certain decision-making behaviors of HRD managers. These studies will hopefully make a contribution to understanding expert behavior and HRD management, and will also continue to expand the use of this method. Soon, these studies will be completed and available in the literature.

The critical incident technique is based on the principle that gathering actual stories about a certain activity that have led to both effective and ineffective outcomes can provide unique insights about that activity in general. For instance, consider the following task expected of regional managers in a regional furniture company: Provide coaching to store managers on how to improve their store's financial performance. To document the components of this coaching task, the analyst might consider two basic approaches for gathering the information:

1. Ask experienced regional managers directly about the steps of the process they use when coaching a store manager
2. Ask experienced regional managers to relate specific incidents when they were effective or ineffective in coaching a store manager

At first glance, there may not seem much difference between the two approaches. They differ much in their basic approach to finding out the information. The first approach might be considered a deductive approach, since the regional managers being interviewed are in effect just relating what they do—or what they think they do—when they coach another manager.

On the other hand, the second approach might be considered more of an inductive approach, since the regional managers being interviewed are not offering their opinions, but are telling actual stories, from which meaning will be drawn from the stories. It is from the underlying meaning of the stories that the regional manager coaching process would emerge.

When doing an analysis of such a task, some might ask what is the real difference between the two approaches? After all, the resulting information might appear the same, more or less, anyhow. There is nothing fundamentally incorrect in using the first approach, but the second approach—involving the use of the critical incident technique—has the following unique benefits in terms of the information gathered:

- The information is anchored to the actual coaching behaviors of managers, not their perceptions of what they do.
- The information suggests the insights into coaching that would not be revealed otherwise.
- The information is based on both effective and ineffective use of coaching behaviors.
- The information serves as the first level of data, from which the analyst and others might use other methods and sources to find out more information about the coaching process.
- The information can have multiple uses, as the incidents can be used to analyze the components of the task on hand, develop scenarios grounded in practice for training purposes, and construct instruments for evaluating the coaching behaviors of supervisors on the job.

The critical incident technique seems best suited to document knowledge-based tasks with certain attributes. First, the task should have both a non-observable aspect, the thinking, and an observable aspect, the action, to it. This attribute is common across most knowledge-based tasks, but it is the thinking aspect that forms the essence of the task. For instance, when a supervisor is confronted with a problem situation, the action should follow only after the thoughts about how to address the problem.

Second, the task should have varying antecedents, suggesting that whatever happens beforehand that generates the need to perform the task cannot always be predicted. It is for this reason that the critical incident technique has been used to analyze decisions by occupations such as police officers, who need to determine under what circumstances to use deadly force, and emergency room physicians, who suddenly need to make decisions when confronted with a patient's life-threatening situation.

Third, in a related sense, the critical incident technique should be used with tasks for which there is a consequence of importance if an error is made. There are a number of sequences in the 1983 film *The Right Stuff*, which was based on Tom Wolfe's 1979 book of the same title, about the dangers encountered by the Project Mercury astronauts. The film graphically illustrates situations in which test pilots faced specific uncertain dangerous situations, such as loss of power in midflight, and how they responded to them, sometimes with disastrous consequences.

The consequence of error may not always involve life or death decisions, but the error may lead to consequences of a nature that are still important, such as failing to meet a customer's quality requirements, exceeding a cost estimate on a proposal, or experiencing delays in completing an assignment. All of these constitute important consequences of not performing the task correctly.

Finally, the action aspect of the task may not constitute a prescribed set of known actions, but the actions may constitute an altogether unique combination of actions. That is, there may be some individuality in the actions taken. In fact, studies of expert behavior suggest that these individuals spend much more time in thinking about a problem than engaging in the actions afterward. In this sense, the critical incident technique often seeks to determine the principles that lie beneath the actions when thinking, and not necessarily just the actions themselves.

Using the Critical Incident Technique

Using the critical incident technique is deceptively simple. At first glance, it seems that the technique is merely about asking certain individuals to relate a story from their experience, and then writing down what they say. Done! As a result, there are many studies in the literature that purport to use the critical incident technique, but upon closer inspection one wonders how the technique was actually used and how the results were derived. Obviously, the critical incident technique involves much more than doing the interviews alone. In fact, generating the incidents is not the end goal of using the technique. The goal in all instances is to derive meaning from a collective of the incidents.

The following summarizes the process of using the critical incident technique to analyze tasks. As a reminder, the process is part of the broader work analysis process. A review of the process shows that a number of decisions should be made along the way.

1. Plan to Use the Critical Incident Technique

Of importance in planning to use the critical incident technique is to specify the task in explicit terms and to identify how the information from the analysis will be used. Knowing this information is crucial for constructing the prompt question for the interviews later on.

As discussed, the critical incident technique is best suited for analyzing knowledge-based tasks. One can say that the critical incident technique is an example of a cognitive task analysis. Some example task statements appropriate for the critical incident technique are the following:

- Troubleshoot the location of missing parts from inventory.
- Deliver a presentation to management about weekly sales totals.
- Conduct a performance review session with a subordinate employee.

2. Select the Subject-Matter Experts

Selecting the SMEs is an especially important consideration when using the critical incident technique. In most instances, being considered an SME is relative to the level of experience of other employees around them. In some instances, some individuals may be considered as an SME, but in reality they have been on the job only for a few months. So it is quite likely that the individuals may be considered experienced, but not actually an expert.

In contrast, the critical incident technique requires that the SMEs have a relatively high level of experience with the task, both in terms of the length of time and the depth of engagement. It is important to remember that the SMEs are not just being selected for their knowledge of the task, but also for their ability to reflect on what they did, and then generate stories based on experience. Having stories to tell can only be done when SMEs have extensive experience, to an extent greater than when using other work analysis techniques.

Determining the number of SMEs to interview is difficult to recommend in most instances. Of foremost importance is to have enough SMEs to provide a sufficient number of incidents for analysis. From experience, most SMEs can usually generate around six to eight incidents each. Related to the number of SMEs is the desired number of incidents that should be gathered. There is no established rule on what is the desired number of incidents. The number often depends both on the availability of SMEs and the extent of the analysis that will be done afterward. From practice, in principle the number of incidents should represent a critical mass of stories that represent the possible ways that the task has been carried out. If an exact number is desired, experience suggests that the minimum number of incidents is likely to be around 36 or so.

Most sources on using qualitative research methods suggest that there is a point of saturation, when the topic is completely covered, from which adding more respondents would not be necessarily productive. Also, there is the notion of circularity, in that essentially the same incidents begin to reappear. In general, it seems prudent to recommend that as a benchmark, from 10 to

12 SMEs should be interviewed, if this is possible. Again, there are no rules in this regard, only guidelines. Fewer SMEs may be sufficient but, again, it depends on the richness of their experience from which they can generate incidents. The number of SMEs may be viewed as a limited factor for using the critical incident technique. Most analyses using the critical incident technique are not research studies per se, so the overriding goal is the relevance of the information, not necessarily the rigor of the method.

3. Gather the Critical Incidents

Gathering the critical incidents is the core of using this method. The interviews can be conducted using a small group of SMEs, similar in respect to a focus group setting, or the interviews can be done one on one. In practice, one-on-one interviews are preferred because they allow individuals to reflect on their experience, without being distracted from the comments of others. On the other hand, being in a small group might generate a more welcoming atmosphere and help jog the memory of the SMEs about situations from the past.

Before the interviews it is necessary to inform the SMEs about the purpose of the interview, and suggest they begin to reflect on the prompt question before the actual interview occurs. For instance, the following example passage might be sent to the SMEs beforehand:

> We need your input in developing a training program for future managers on how to provide feedback to subordinates about their performance. We will require about three hours of your time total, over two to three sessions. To prepare for our meeting, we ask that you reflect on your experiences in providing feedback to your employees about their work performance, even thinking of specific sessions that stand out in your memory. We will be asking about these in particular. These sessions might have turned out well or perhaps not so well in the end. We are interested in both situations. Thank you in advance for your time to participate in the interviews.

The prompt question at the beginning of the interview is especially important as it establishes the boundaries of interest. In practice, it is suggested that the analyst begin by helping the SMEs generate a mental image of the situation being analyzed. This is important to reduce any confusion about the focus of the analysis. In some situations, a video clip might be shown to reinforce an understanding of the situation. The analyst can use the images as a springboard for recalling the specific incidents related to this situation. For example, the following statement might be suggested:

I'd like you to think about the situations in which you provided feedback to a subordinate employee about their work performance. As a manager, I know that you have done this many times. Can you remember the last time you conducted one of these sessions? Tell me about that situation. Based on all your experiences, reflect back on all the times you've provided feedback to a subordinate, can you tell me what happened during some of these sessions?

In practice, most SMEs have some initial difficulty thinking of specific stories, and likely need some probing by the analyst. Some SMEs have even initially stated that they really can't think of any situation in particular, but it often occurs that after the first story, others will come to be remembered. Getting SMEs to tell stories is somewhat like using an old water pump—you know that there is information below the surface, and the SME just needs to have their memory jogged a bit for the information to come out. There are usually more stories than the SME would initially believe existed.

Throughout the interview, the analyst should keep raw notes about what the SME is saying. Recording the interview is appropriate as a fallback from the notes, but may be done only with permission of the SME given in advance. The recording might provide additional richness to the incidents being gathered, which might be lost otherwise. After the interview, the analyst can begin to edit and format the incidents gathered. Editing is done to remove extraneous information, without influencing or changing the content of the story itself.

Formatting the incidents is an important consideration as all the incidents should have a parallel structure. In a sense, by specifying a format for the incidents, the analyst is imposing an artificial structure on the incidents at the risk of losing some of the spontaneity of the SMEs' comments.

Formatting provides the analyst with a template for gathering the information, suggesting what information should be gathered and in which areas the analyst should probe for more information. Formatting also ensures greater reliability when analyzing the incidents, since the stories will have more or less the same structure. In practice, the following describes the four parts of the format used to gather the critical incidents:

- *Context.* This information is about the background of the incident: Where did the incident occur? What was the occasion for the subsequent action to occur? Was there a problem to solve? A decision to be made? A process to follow? Who else was involved? What other information can help establish an understanding of the situation? The context is the set-up to the response that will follow.

- *Response*. This information is a rich description of the SME's understandings, thoughts, and actions in response to the context. This information distinguishes the critical incident as being important and likely makes it memorable to the SME.
- *Results*. This information is about what happened as a result of the SME's response to the context. The results might be reported from a number of different perspectives. How did the SME perceive the situation? How did others perceive the situation?
- *Reflection*. The final part of the format is often combined with the Results or it can be a separate category. The information is about what the SME thought about the situation after it was over, from the benefit of time and additional deliberations. An example of a critical incident, with all the categories included, is the following:

> As regional manager, I had scheduled the individual monthly performance reviews with each of our store managers, and I knew beforehand that these sessions would likely not go well. Sales goals on large ticket pieces of furniture had been increased and just a few of the stores were able to meet them. I took extra care when I met with the store managers, trying to be as understanding of their situations as possible, knowing that many of them would be immediately defensive when we discussed why they hadn't achieved their sales goals. I was pleased that I took a softer approach that time, because I learned about some issues related to our advertising flyer and delayed delivery schedules. Later, a few of the managers commented that they also dreaded having the meetings with me, but they commented how much they appreciated my approach to the meetings. It really reduced much of the tension.

As stated, using a standard format helps guide the analyst and makes it easier to conduct the required deeper analysis of the critical incidents in the next phase. It is worth repeating the difficulty at times in gathering critical incidents. It takes some discipline on the part of the analyst to keep the SME focused on relating a story, and probing for further information when the story is being told. The critical incidents are meant to report actual stories, not opinions or perceptions about an event.

4. Derive the Underlying Behaviors from the Incidents

As stated, the incidents are not in themselves the desired end product from using the critical incident technique. The incidents are the raw data from which the deeper collective meanings can be derived. In this sense, it is the information that lies beneath the surface of the critical incidents that is of most value to the analysis. In the context of work analysis, the critical incident technique is used to derive the underlying behaviors that exist within the task statement.

Admittedly, analyzing the collective of the critical incidents in search of their deeper meanings, or the components, is not a particularly exact process. Some analysts prefer to use computer proprietary software programs designed to analyze qualitative data, especially when there are an extremely large number of incidents to analyze. Most software programs have the functions to tabulate word frequencies, some level of text interpretation, coding of similar sets of ideas, and visual mapping capabilities. These functions are often helpful as a first stage in identifying the components. A number of well-known computer programs that have been proved useful are listed at the end of this chapter.

Experience suggests that the most tried and true method remains the process of induction—that is, the analyst simply reads and reviews each incident, begins to get a sense of the particular information in the incident, and then sees if there is a link between the content in that incident with the content of other incidents. The analyst reviews the incidents and then seeks out other incidents from which initial groupings of incidents can begin to take form. This requires that the analyst continually generates some impromptu hypotheses about what makes the content of the incidents in the grouping similar to each other.

To conduct the analysis in this way may require that each incident be written or printed on a 3″ × 5″ index card, and the cards be spread out on the floor or a large table top, or posted on a wall. In that way, the analyst can easily review each incident and then move the incidents around into provisional groupings. Each grouping should have a sufficient number of incidents to appear as a complete set of ideas. Groupings should have about the same number of incidents in them.

To achieve some consensus, it is advisable to have more than one analyst involved in the process. The analysts can work alongside each other or at a separate time. When working together, the analysts can discuss the meanings of the incidents as they proceed in the analysis, and seek to find common ground. When working alone, the analysts can compare their respective independent ways of grouping the incidents after each has completed their own grouping. A discussion should follow to achieve some level of agreement.

From practice, it does not seem to matter whether the analysts review the incidents together or apart from each other. In fact, when conducting the analysis together, the analysts seem to have a greater opportunity to discuss and make explicit each other's thoughts about what they are perceiving in the incidents. In addition, once a draft grouping of the incidents has been assembled, it may also be appropriate to invite one of more SMEs to review the groupings of the incidents, and confirm that they make sense. In the end, of most importance is the generation of meaningful information derived in a relatively reliable way, all of which is anchored to the incidents.

Once the groupings appear robust, that is, each of them seems complete and mutually exclusive from the other groupings, then the analyst can begin to generate a label or theme that represents the essence of the grouping of incidents. As stated, from a work analysis perspective, the label should be considered similar to the individual behavioral components of a task. Beyond the assignment of the label, each grouping should also be operationally defined. That is, a statement that makes clear the meaning of the label in this instance.

The following example shows the labels of the task components and operational definitions that were derived from an analysis of the task introduced earlier in this chapter:

Task Name: Provide coaching to store managers on how to improve their store's financial performance.

Task Components:

A. *Follow a coaching process.* When delivering a coaching session, regional managers should use a process which will guide them on how to conduct the session with store managers.

B. *Be aware of store manager's responses.* During the session, regional managers should be aware of verbal and nonverbal information coming from the store managers.

C. *Conduct the session in an appropriate setting.* Regional managers should identify a meeting location that is conducive for conducting the coaching session with each store manager.

D. *Use data to support comments.* Regional managers should be careful to support all comments based on actual financial data, not on perceptions or hearsay.

E. *Provide follow-up after the coaching session.* At the conclusion of the coaching session, regional managers should send a follow-up message to store managers about what was discussed and items that require action.

From this information, a decision was made to develop a standardized coaching process for use by managers in the organization, based on the task components. In this sense, the analysis of the critical incidents resulted in deriving five task components, which formed the basis of a standardized coaching process, which, in turn, became the content for a future management training program.

5. Prepare the Final Report

The final phase of using the critical incident technique is the preparation of the final report. From experience, a draft version should be prepared first, and reviewed by the various stakeholders, including SMEs, senior management, and HR, among others. From experience, the final report should include the following sections:

- Title page
- Executive summary
- Brief statement of the business problem
- Brief description of how the critical incidents were gathered
- Representative examples of the critical incidents
- Presentation of the results, including the task statement, the behavioral components of the task, and the operational definitions
- Statement about how the information was gathered

Comments

The critical incident technique has enjoyed much attention among researchers and practitioners alike since it was introduced in the 1950s. It has sufficient flexibility for a number of different purposes. From the perspective of work analysis, the critical incident technique is used as one way to analyze the components of knowledge-based tasks. Knowledge-based tasks were discussed in depth in Chap. 1, and refers to units of work that involve employees thinking before they act. The critical incident technique may not be appropriate for the analysis of all knowledge-based tasks. The information it provides is unique from any other work analysis method.

Reflection Questions

1. Do you understand the unique aspect of the critical incident technique, which calls for the analyst to identify stories, or incidents, instead of the opinions of SMEs?
2. The critical incident technique depends on both gathering the critical incidents and then identifying the common categories across the incidents. Have you ever tried to induce such information from a set of information before, and what issues did you face?
3. To what extent might the critical incident technique be appropriate to analyze tasks that you perform now or have performed in the past?

4. How difficult do you think it might be to conduct critical incident technique interviews, in terms of prompting the SMEs to remember a sufficient number of stories from their past experience?
5. Can you recognize the ways in which the critical incident technique differs from conducting a typical structured interview with an SME? How would you continue to prompt the SME to remember incidents from the past?

Reference

Jacobs, R. L. (1986). Use of the critical incident technique to analyze the interpersonal skill requirements of supervisors. *Journal of Industrial Teacher Education,* *23*(2), 56–61.

10

Work Process Analysis

Perhaps no other principle has influenced management practice more than the emphasis now being placed on work processes. Managers are now keenly aware that work processes in effect define how all organizations actually function. As presented in Chap. 1, a work process is defined as the series of human actions and technology-based events that occur over time, often taking place across functional boundaries and involving diverse groups of people, which convert inputs into outputs.

Authors in the quality management literature first began discussing the importance of work processes in the late 1970s and early 1980s. For instance, the highly popular book *The Goal*, by Goldratt and Cox (2004), introduced the basic principles of work processes in the form of an engaging parable.

Work processes became part of the human resource development (HRD) literature primarily through the ground-breaking book by Gary Rummler and Alan Brache, *Improving Performance: Managing the White Spaces on the Organizational Chart*, first published in 1990 and then followed by revised editions in 1995 and 2012. In brief, the book proposed that organizations should be viewed as complex systems, and that all organizations have three system levels: the organization, the process, and the job performer. Each of these levels can be understood from their respective goals, design, and management. The resulting combination of variables forms a nine-celled arrangement that is now used by HRD professionals and managers alike for planning organizational systems and diagnosing performance issues.

At the core of the nine cells is the focus on work processes. The authors point out that the process level is the one at which most performance issues in organizations tend to occur and where there is the greatest opportunity for

© The Author(s) 2019
R. L. Jacobs, *Work Analysis in the Knowledge Economy*,
https://doi.org/10.1007/978-3-319-94448-7_10

improving organizational performance. So, if HRD professionals are truly interested in improving the performance of their organizations, beyond the rhetoric of simply espousing this goal, then they should be critically aware of this aspect of the organization.

In practice, the book has been instrumental in transitioning HRD practice to a more strategic proactive perspective, rather than a more traditional reactive perspective. Even so, many HRD professionals continue to doubt whether an interest in work processes should be part of their practice, as they have focused more of their efforts on designing and delivering training programs for individuals only. And, at first glance, work processes seem to be more the concern of line managers working with the quality or engineering departments in their organizations, rather than the HRD or human resource (HR) departments. Regardless, many HRD professionals have now been challenged to expand their frames of reference about the scope of their work.

Of note, a quick glance suggests the different ways that the term *process* is used in the HRD literature. Process is used when referring to the performance improvement process, the learning process of trainees, and the training design process, among several examples. To ensure clarity and to avoid confusion, the more complete form of the term *work process* will be used throughout this discussion. As stated, a work process is an actual set of events that occur over time that produce an outcome.

Work Processes

As stated, a work process focuses on how a series of work events get done across individuals and functional areas of organizations. That is, the focus is more on understanding the coordination of the various events to achieve the outcomes, not just on the behaviors of individuals in doing their work. Since work processes involve more than one person, group, or function, nearly everyone in an organization is part of several work processes at the same time. In that sense, everyone contributes to achieving the intended outcomes, oftentimes through what is known as throughputs. Throughputs are the outcomes that occur during the work process, as opposed to the outputs that occur upon completion of the process. Throughputs are the results that occur along the way.

Work processes can be understood by the names used to define them. That is, a statement that establishes the boundaries of the work process. For instance, the following are examples of the names of work processes from different organizations:

- Distributed item order fulfillment process (a company that distributes industrial parts to commercial customers)
- Patient intake information gathering process (a medical clinic)
- Store-level financial performance review process (a regional retail chain)
- Commercial customer broadband sales process (a company that provides broadband services to businesses, not to residences)
- Telecom network design process (a company that manufactures and installs large telecommunications systems)
- Management trainee selection process (an HR process in a global accounting firm)

Each statement describes a single work process of importance within these particular organizations. Of course, many other work processes exist in these organizations as well. How to identify and prepare such statements will be discussed later in this chapter. Logically, one can envision groups of people engaged in their respective duties which together contribute to achieving the intended outcomes of each of the work processes listed. Understanding and documenting work processes has become critical for many organizations competing in the global economy. How did organizations come to realize the importance of work processes?

Addressing this question requires some understanding of the changes most organizations have undertaken in the past several decades. An emphasis on work processes derives from principles first introduced in the quality management literature, beginning in the 1970s. In the United States, there was an emerging realization that many products and services were not competitive in the global marketplace. Saying that U.S. businesses and industries have now embraced a broad-scale revolution in their management practices to become more competitive, over the past 40 years, would be an understatement.

It might be helpful to present an illustrative example to better appreciate the challenges faced by organizations some time ago. Consider that in 1980, a year that many view as a defining moment in the survival of many U.S. companies, consumers interested in buying a compact front-wheel-drive car might have considered purchasing either a Honda Civic or a Chevrolet Citation.

At the time, though the Honda brand was relatively less well known than the Chevrolet, consumers were initially attracted to the Civic by the perceived cute styling—some people playfully thought it looked like a tennis shoe—and the apparent quality of its fit and finish, the overall reliability ratings, and its gas mileage. In that year, the Honda Civic sold relatively well in 1980, about 140,000 units, which was considered promising given that as a foreign brand many consumers were not entirely familiar with it. Today, the

Honda Civic continues to be a successful model by Honda that is sold world-wide, and several variations of the model are in fact assembled at a large manufacturing facility in central Ohio of the United States. Seventy percent of the parts in today's Honda Civics are made in the United States.

The history of the Chevrolet Citation started out extremely promising, but unfortunately had a disappointing ending. In 1980, as a new model, the Chevrolet Citation became the best-selling car model of that year, with over 800,000 units sold. It was a clear signal that many consumers were looking for a smaller car in the context of the on-going oil crisis of the time. Yet, because of continuing quality issues and repeated recalls to address engineering and design defects, sales dropped to under 100,000 units in 1983. By 1985, sales had fallen even further and General Motors' senior management eventually decided to discontinue production of the model altogether. Today, almost no one remembers that Chevrolet once had a promising model that was intro-duced in 1980 named Citation, and what its fate was in the marketplace. It was a good idea, but not well executed.

There are many reasons why a car model might succeed or fail in the mar-ketplace. In retrospect, it became apparent that quality was now an important consideration for consumers, more so than cost alone. The Citation was a slightly larger car than the Civic and had a lower sales price by over one thou-sand dollars, which was a significant amount of money at that time. The Civic met the needs of an emerging demographic of young professionals who recog-nized the relationship between quality and value in the long run.

The case study illustrates that being competitive in the global marketplace meant that American management practices had to change in dramatic ways. In fact, there was no possible way that management practices at the time, especially in the United States, could achieve the three crucial goals of the global economy at the time and which continue to be important today: high volume of production, high levels of quality, and low competitive cost.

How to achieve these goals at the same time, often believed to be nearly impossible by many managers, received much commentary in the quality management literature, including from a number of important voices includ-ing W. Edwards Deming (Demings, 1986), Joseph Juran (Juran, 1992), Armand Feigenbaum (Feigenbaum, 1991), and Phillip Crosby (Crosby, 1980), among several others.

Each of them differed somewhat on which management practices were most critical and should be changed, based on principles taken from the Toyota production system, as was first devised by Japanese industrial engi-neers starting in 1945 (Liker & Meier, 2006). Yet, one point among all the authors involved in the quality movement was their common focus on how the work was actually arranged, or the importance of the work processes used in organizations. From their work came the term process management, that is, managing with a focus on work processes instead of functional areas, and the term process improvement, that is, seeking ways to improve work processes. It is now indisputable that work processes have become the core focus of most efforts to improve organizational performance.

Some additional context might be helpful in understanding this point. Through the 1980s, most organizations arranged their work on the basis of what is known as a push production system. That is, arranging work with an emphasis on high volume, intending to produce or deliver as many copies of a product or service as possible, based on market estimates of likely customer demand. Hopefully, the product or service would hit the market at the right time and consumers would be satisfied. This basic approach worked out well for many years, including how the Chevrolet Citation was conceived and produced. That is, this approach worked until consumers began to notice that some other brands of cars had fewer quality issues, for about the same price.

The opposite perspective from the push production system is known as the pull production system. The pull production system calls for production to be much more sensitive to ongoing changes in the marketplace. It recognizes that customers might be fickle, and organizations should be responsive to these changes based on consumer demand, all the while maintaining high levels of quality throughout. The pull production reduced costs since it eliminated much of the waste associated with the push production system, and dictated that whatever quality issues arose should be addressed immediately, avoiding the cost of rework once the product had been assembled.

The 1980 model of the Honda Civic, then produced in Japan, was basically designed and assembled using a pull production system, resulting in its relatively higher levels of quality and reliability ratings. The Honda Civic could not compete with the Citation in terms of price, but it could excel in terms of its value.

For most U.S. organizations, moving toward a pull production system required a dramatic realignment of organizational resources, including how the production or the service delivery actually occurred. For instance, in a production environment, no longer could the same pieces of equipment be grouped together, such as having all the stamping presses that formed rounded shapes from flat steel, or be arranged in a neat row. Now there was a need to arrange the equipment into what is called focused subassemblies, with teams of employees working together to make a completed product, instead of making many duplicate copies of the same component part. Similarly, in a service-delivery environment, no longer could similar job titles be grouped together in large numbers—such as auditors—separated from their internal customers.

Organizations of all sizes and across all business sectors have now adopted quality management principles derived from the pull production system. In fact, there has evolved a technology of management practice that forms a common language among nearly all global managers, and seems the only possible way to achieve the three crucial goals necessary to compete in the global economy.

As stated, at the most fundamental level, successful implementation of the quality management principles depends on an emphasis on work processes. Most organizations today engage in organized efforts to continuously improve their quality, which is based on their ability to systematically analyze current work processes, and then to determine how to make those work processes become less wasteful and inefficient, often involving the workers involved to help uncover the issues and solve the problems. Most efforts today to document work processes are based on the need to use the information as part of some performance improvement process.

Analyzing and improving work processes were activities once considered of most interest in the manufacturing and production business sectors only. Yet, interest in work processes is now pervasive across all business sectors. For instance, when a financial services company provides quick feedback to a customer seeking a business loan, that commonplace occurrence is in fact an example of how managers of the financial services company understood the importance of streamlining their work processes, where possible, to achieve this competitive advantage. And, many health-care delivery organizations, such as hospitals and clinics, have been among the most aggressive adopters of these principles.

Types of Work Processes

So far this discussion has provided a context for understanding the importance of work processes. In practice, every organization can have many different work processes that, in an everyday sense, cross over its functional boundaries. These work processes may not always be entirely visible, but they exist in all organizations nevertheless. Indeed, their existence becomes apparent only when something of importance doesn't go as planned. Then everyone involved realizes something was not done at all or was done inadequately along the way. Many companies have learned this lesson when they pay for the cost of rework before the product leaves the organization or of recalls after the product has hit the market. How is it possible to make sense of all the work processes that occur in organizations?

Table 10.1 summarizes the four types of work processes that commonly occur in organizations and provides some comments about understanding each type from the perspective of the analyst. Knowing that these different types exist and what each type means helps inform analysts about the basic structure of the work process and insights on how the work process should be analyzed.

Table 10.1 Types of work processes

Type	Definition	Comments
Specific to the organization	Work processes that specifically support the mission in terms of producing the products and delivering the services of the organization. These work processes make the organization unique from other organizations.	The analyst may be unfamiliar with the content of the work process. Yet, the analyst should be aware that all work processes have the same basic arc of activity: input, process, and output, which can be used as a guide.
Common across organizations	Work processes that occur in many organizations, such as sales, marketing, contracting, and purchasing. Though these work processes occur in different organizations, they logically have many aspects in common.	Every organization may have its own unique work processes, which are considered as being common. Yet, the analyst should draw upon what was done in previous situations to provide a guide for the basic structure of a common work process
Support in most organizations	Work processes that support the ongoing operations of the organization, such as recruitment, selection, hiring, and even training. Again, these work processes occur in different organizations, but they are often identical with some expected variation.	The analyst can draw upon previous experience to know what to expect when analyzing support work processes, and to provide a basic structure. Support work processes should be among the easiest to analyze.
Administrative	Work processes that are often the least apparent, but involve planning, decision making, and managing. These work processes likely involve people meeting together and working as a group to achieve an outcome.	The administrative work process is really about how information is processed among a group of people, and what they do with the information. Sometimes, administrative work processes are difficult to analyze, because they may have an emergent quality to them. Yet, all administrative work processes have a basic set of phases.

Specific Work Processes

Logically, every organization has many work processes that specifically support the mission of the organization. That is, these are the work processes that make it possible to produce the products and deliver the services that are unique to the organization. These work processes make the organization distinct from other organizations, and are often the focus of most performance improvement efforts. Many specific work processes may be considered proprietary in nature, as they represent a part of the intellectual property of the organization, and should remain confidential.

Organizations typically comprise many specific work processes, and they vary depending on the nature of organization. For instance, the specific work processes in an electronics manufacturing company logically differ from those work processes in an information technology (IT) services consulting firm. The work processes in each organization are geared to achieving their respective missions. The electronics company has work processes that result in a completed product—namely circuit boards. The IT consulting firm has work processes that result in a service provided to a customer—namely a plan to address the needs of the customer. At first glance, there would seem little in common between the two work processes used in this example. Yet, upon closer examination, the two specific work processes do have at least one important characteristic in common.

All work processes share an underlying structure based on the system theory elements of inputs, processes, and outputs. That is, regardless of the content of the work process, all work processes follow this basic arc of activity: there are a set of actions at the beginning that serve as the inputs, which then inform the activities in the middle of the work process, which result in the outcomes at the end of the work process.

Experienced analysts begin to recognize that this pattern exists and often keep this principle in mind when analyzing specific work processes, in particular. Analysts are usually content-free, and an understanding of the basic structure of work processes, irrespective of their content, provides a handy beginning point in almost any situation. In this sense, to the informed analyst, there are no specific work processes that appear totally unique.

Common Work Processes

Another type of work process comprises what are called common work processes. From experience, these work processes represent the same activities that might be found in many organizations, such as those found in the sales, marketing, contracting, purchasing, and other similar organizational functions. Logically, the nature of the work processes related to these functions will differ to some extent across organizations—for instance, the sales process used in a retail furniture store differs markedly from the sales process used in a telecom company—but there are enough parallel components of the two work processes that make it possible for the analyst to understand what the work process might look like in a basic sense.

One of the most frequently occurring common work processes involves customer service. The number of organizations that are engaged in this activity is seemingly endless, from providing IT support by a software company to troubleshooting monthly billings by a natural gas utility. While the nature of the service might differ, the observant analyst will likely find similarities in the flow of the work process used to provide the customer service, from the initial greeting, to the problem identification, to the problem resolution. Obviously, the extent that there is a transfer from the information in one work process to another varies across situations. But analyzing a common work process in one organization likely provides a head start when analyzing a similar work process in another organization.

Support Work Processes

The third type of work process often found in organizations is the support work process. Again, these work processes occur in most organizations and have the purpose of maintaining the ongoing operations of the organization. Examples of support work processes include recruitment, selection, hiring, and even the design and delivery of training programs.

Support work processes represent the basic, often essential, activities found in all organizations. They do not focus on the production of products or delivery of services, such as the specific work processes, but they are critical to organizations nevertheless. Again, there will likely be differences across organizations in their support work processes. But there is a sufficient parallel structure among them that will benefit the observant analyst. For instance, every organization recruits new employees, so the basic elements of the recruiting work process used by most organizations will likely appear similar in many respects. Or, the training design process may be the same in general, but differ in situations based on the intended nature of the programs—technical or managerial in nature.

Logically, there will always be differences in the support work processed based on each organization's requirements. Yet, having an experience with one, say, work process that involves recruitment and selection enables the analyst to bring to the project some knowledge about what to expect in the next situation.

Administrative Work Processes

The final type of work processes often found in organizations is the administrative work process. These work processes are the least apparent compared to the other types and, as a result, they are frequently overlooked. In fact, many analysts might not consider them to be work processes at all, since they differ from the others so much. In practice, administrative work processes often appear more like meetings among managers or discussions among selected individuals, not like a work process per se. Yet, administrative processes do occur when individuals come together for the purpose of engaging in a planning activity, solving a problem, or making a decision, among other group-based activities. The work process represents what actions the group will take to achieve the intended outcome.

Administrative work processes are similar to common work processes, because they occur across all organizations. It is just now that such goal-oriented group activities would be considered as a formal work process, and that the components of the work processes should in fact be analyzed. Perhaps the most frequent administrative work process is when organizations engage in a strategic planning activity or develop a guiding master plan.

The four types of work processes presented here represent a synthesis of the author's experience. Other analysts might identify other types altogether. Regardless, the basic purpose for identifying types of work processes is to provide the insights necessary to make analyzing any given work process more efficient and effective. That is, analyzing the work processes with less wasted time and more accuracy. The analyst can generalize from past experiences to any new situation at hand.

Analyzing Work Processes

This section presents the steps for analyzing work processes in the context of human resource development practice. As stated, in most instances, analyzing a work process is done for the purpose of some planned performance improvement activity. These are variously known in organizations as corrective action teams, performance improvement meetings, or even as part of an organized Kaizen event. Kaizen, the Japanese word for change for better, is a specific approach that has been adopted by many global organizations for the purpose of making incremental improvements, on a continuous basis, and requiring a broad base of employee participation. During the Kaizen event, employees examine a particular issue of importance, such as addressing why there are unusually high defects in an area or a number of missed delivery schedules, and then to review and figure out how to improve the work processes involved in achieving those outcomes.

The steps for conducting the analysis of a work process are a sub-part of the broader work analysis process. The following discussion explains each step.

1. Identify the Name of the Work Process

Perhaps the most important step in analyzing a work process is the first step—knowing what is the work process in the first place. Identifying a name for the work process involves developing a carefully worded statement that defines the work process, and requires some careful consideration. A work process statement should include four points:

- Context or focus of the work process
- Action word that best describes the ongoing activity of the work process
- Any qualifying words that distinguish the work process from other similar ones
- Using the word *process* at the end to clarify that the statement describes a work process, not a task or a duty

The statement should be carefully worded so that it includes these four points. In too many instances, the analyst does not identify in explicit terms the name upfront, and stakeholders may be uncertain about the focus of the analysis. Embedded in the name is the understanding that boundaries exist for all work processes, where each one begins and ends, and that there is an outcome of the work process.

For instance, consider the following statements that name a work process:

- New graduate engineer technical sales recruitment process
- Small business IT fiber network design process
- Subassembly production area defect reduction problem-solving process

Each of these statements come from different organizations and include the four points that have been identified. A careful review of the statements suggests that the outcomes, respectively, will be: a list of recruited newly graduated engineers for technical sales, a document that presents a network design of a small business, and defects reduced in a particular subassembly production area. It is important that the statement makes it clear that an outcome will occur from engaging in the work process.

An additional insight into work processes is that many of them begin and end within the organization itself, which is how people most often think of work processes. Yet, consider the more complex situations today in which work processes may originate with a supplier, external to the organization, and even end external to the organization, with the customer. For instance, consider the following statement: Dedicated supplier product warehouse restocking process. This statement suggests that the restocking of the products actually starts with actions taken by suppliers and ends with the restocking of the products in the organization's warehouse. Situations in which the work process extends beyond the boundaries of the organization have become more and more commonplace.

2. Determine the Format of the Analysis

Work processes can be analyzed using at least three formats. Each seems better suited based on how the information will be used later on.

Text. In Figs. 10.1 and 10.2, examples of the most common format are shown. In Fig. 10.1, the text is presented simply as a list of steps. In Fig. 10.2, the text is shown as a page from a training manual. In the text format, the information is presented as a detailed, sequentially ordered list of steps. It should be noted that the way of presenting the steps has a certain recommended format as well. That is, given that work processes involve handoffs from suppliers to customers, each step, to the extent possible, is written to follow that same pattern.

Each step begins by naming the supplier or who initiates the action, followed by the verb that describes the action, and then followed by who or what receives the action. This approach may seem complicated but, when completed, the final document has a better flow and is easier to follow. Again, the goal is for clarity and simplicity in presenting the information, but without losing the complexity of the content.

Swim lanes. As shown in Fig. 10.3 of an administrative work process, the swim lane format lacks the apparent details of the text format, but it does provide an immediate overview of the work process, showing the various actions of the work process over time and across functional areas. The term swim lane format has been commonly adopted in the quality management literature as a visual way of denoting how the work process moves across formal boundaries. The boundary lines are similar to the floating ropes one might find in a swimming pool. The example shows a combination of the list of steps and the swim lane formats.

1. Customer places order with Customer Service Representative.

2. CSR enters order on Customer Information System.

3. CSR inspects accuracy of order.

4. CIS identifies which items are in stock.

5. CSR informs customer of inventory status.

   For items not in stock:
   1. CSR informs customer
   2. CSR places backorder with supplier.

   For items in stock, go to next step.

6. CSR confirms order with CIS.

7. CIS sends order information to Accounting Clerk.

8. CIS send order information to Shipping Clerk.

9. CIS deducts order items from inventory.

10. Shipping Clerk picks order from warehouse.

11. Shipping Clerk packs order.

12. Shipping Clerk inspects shipment information with order information.

13. Shipping Clerk inspects shipment to ensure package meets requirements.

Fig. 10.1 List of steps: distributed-item order fulfillment process

In practice, because of its visual approach, the swim lane format is especially useful for small groups of employees seeking to identify the location of performance issues, such as bottlenecks or wasted actions, in the current work process. Then, they might rearrange, add, or delete steps that would represent the desired version of the work process. The text format is usually done first to ensure that all the information is complete; then the information is transferred to the swim lane format afterward.

Visual display. As shown in Fig. 10.4, the visual display may have the least detail but it often has the most appeal and ease of understanding. The visual display could be shown as a simple line drawing or a visual with more detail in it. The visual display is useful in providing a summary of the work process—that is, what actually happens in an overall sense, with just enough explanatory information. The example presented in Fig. 10.4 shows through the arrows the movement of the production of a part in a work area, starting in the top left-hand side of the display with an unshaped piece of metal, then proceeding forward in a U shape, until the completed part exits the work process from the lower left corner.

158   R. L. Jacobs

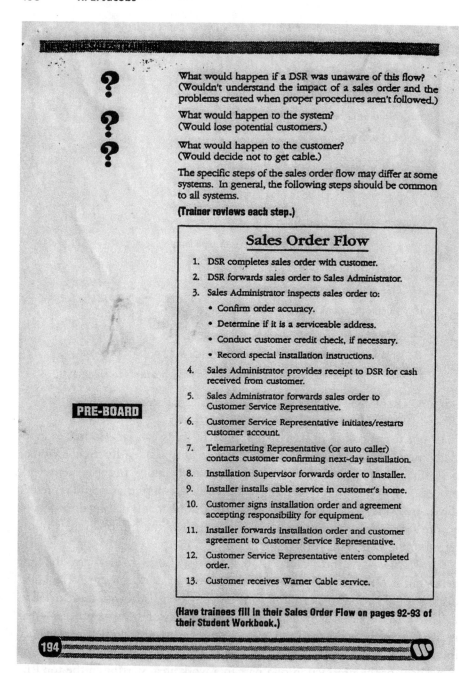

What would happen if a DSR was unaware of this flow? (Wouldn't understand the impact of a sales order and the problems created when proper procedures aren't followed.)

What would happen to the system? (Would lose potential customers.)

What would happen to the customer? (Would decide not to get cable.)

The specific steps of the sales order flow may differ at some systems. In general, the following steps should be common to all systems.

(Trainer reviews each step.)

Sales Order Flow

1. DSR completes sales order with customer.
2. DSR forwards sales order to Sales Administrator.
3. Sales Administrator inspects sales order to:
   - Confirm order accuracy.
   - Determine if it is a serviceable address.
   - Conduct customer credit check, if necessary.
   - Record special installation instructions.
4. Sales Administrator provides receipt to DSR for cash received from customer.
5. Sales Administrator forwards sales order to Customer Service Representative.
6. Customer Service Representative initiates/restarts customer account.
7. Telemarketing Representative (or auto caller) contacts customer confirming next-day installation.
8. Installation Supervisor forwards order to Installer.
9. Installer installs cable service in customer's home.
10. Customer signs installation order and agreement accepting responsibility for equipment.
11. Installer forwards installation order and customer agreement to Customer Service Representative.
12. Customer Service Representative enters completed order.
13. Customer receives Warner Cable service.

(Have trainees fill in their Sales Order Flow on pages 92-93 of their Student Workbook.)

PRE-BOARD

194

Fig. 10.2 List of steps: customer sales order process

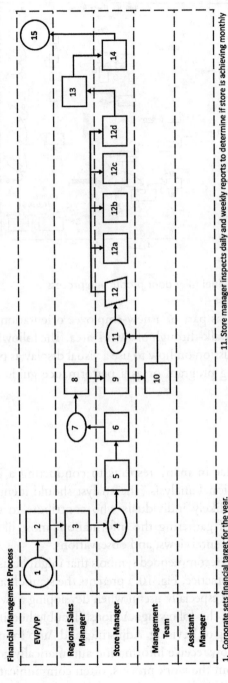

Financial Management Process

1. Corporate sets financial target for the year.
2. EVP/VP sends financial goals to Regional Sales Manager.
3. Regional Sales Manager sends financial goals to Store Manager for review.
4. Store Manager reviews financial goals.
5. Store Manager revises financial goals.
6. Store Manager sends revised goals to Regional Sales Manager for approval.
7. Regional Sales Manager reviews revised financial goals.
8. Regional Sales Manager send revised financial goals to EVP/VP for approval.
9. Store Manager notifies Management Team of monthly budget and financial goals.
10. Management Team informs sales office, and warehouse associates of budget and financial goals.
11. Store manager inspects daily and weekly reports to determine if store is achieving monthly financial goals, based on following items:
    - Sales volume
    - Payroll budget
    - Monthly profit
    - Customer traffic
    - Controllable expenses.
12. Store manager troubleshoot to identify potential solution to achieve financial goals.
    12a. Adjust work schedules
    12b. Ensure best practices are being used
    12c. Coach associates on critical tasks
    12d. Adjust inventory levels.
13. Regional Store Manager conducts monthly financial review with Store Manager.
14. Regional Store Manager informs Management Team of status of achieving monthly financial goals.
15. EVP/VP send P&L report to Store Manager.

Fig. 10.3 Example of a swim lane format with list of steps

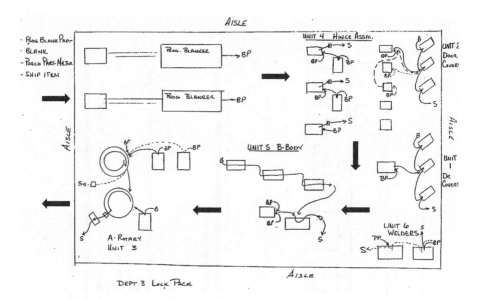

Fig. 10.4   Example of a visual display—fuel filler door production process

The visual display is often used as part of a new-employee orientation in which the employee experiences a walk-through of a work area. The following section of the book includes a discussion on how to use a visual display as part of a structured on-the-job training program or as a performance guide for reference.

3. Conduct the Analysis

Analyzing a work process is similar in many respects to conducting a job analysis or conducting an occupational analysis. The analyst should identify the sources of information, most likely individuals who contribute to the work analysis, and the methods of gathering the information, most likely through a group process, individual interviews, and observations.

Of interest to many analysts is the recommended symbols that might be used when analyzing a work analysis. In practice, Fig. 10.5 presents the symbols and their respective meanings, which are especially useful when developing a swim lane format. There are symbols for the following: Actions, Troubleshooting, Decision making, Inspecting, Editing or Revising, Adjusting, and Auto Inputs.

Of note, many work processes now receive information automatically generated from actions taken away from the work process, often communicated through information technology. This event is denoted in a work process analysis as an Auto Input. In addition, the arrows of a work process analysis

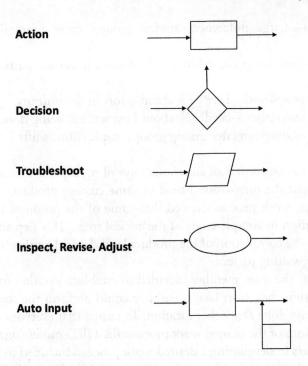

Fig. 10.5 Work process symbols

denote the direction of the relationship—that is, the origination of the step and the destination of the step. Another way of saying this is: Who does what for whom?

4. Use the Information

As stated, analyzing work processes is most often used as part of the performance improvement process, which could be facilitated by the HRD professional, a manager, or a quality staff member. The point of documenting the work analysis is to review the current situation and determine how best to address a recurring issue or problem that is preventing achieving the intended outcomes.

In this sense, using the work analysis is often in the context of soliciting suggestions on how to improve on the work process in some way, or respond to planned changes in the way the work is being done. Here are a number of issues that are often addressed when reviewing a work process:

- *Rework*—People must correct something at the end of the work process
- *Errors*—Mistakes done at certain points during the work process
- *Bottlenecks*—Stacks of work in particular parts of the work process

- *Variations*—Large differences among groups, cycle times of the work process
- *Idleness*—Downtime caused by a lack of work in certain parts of the work process
- *Customer complaints*—Feedback about errors in the outputs
- *Employee complaints*—Feedback about how work is being done
- *Conflicts*—Disagreements among groups, supervisors, shifts

For instance, customers of a manufacturer of orthopedic devices expressed concerns about the turn-around time of some custom products. An analysis of the current work process showed that some of the products were sent to another location to complete one of the critical steps. This step added at least one week to the completion of the product, and delayed getting an expedited product to a waiting patient.

As a result, the team members decided to establish a station for expedited products within their own facility, so they could perform the step as needed that was always done at another location. To ensure that everyone understood the implications of the desired work process, the HRD professional facilitated team members in developing a desired work process. Included in this version of the analysis was a decision point as to whether the product should be considered expedited or could be sent out to the other facility. The desired work process was carefully documented and a proposal was made to management and the quality staff for their input and approval.

Comments

This chapter makes the point that work processes have now become a critical focus for many HRD professionals. Further, the chapter provides an introduction to the knowledge and skills to conduct an analysis of a work process. There often seems a disconnect in organizations between the nature of the HRD practice and efforts related to improving quality. HRD professionals assert their interest in improving performance as a professional goal, but in practice they typically have limited involvement in the activities that have the most impact for achieving that outcome. Part of the issue, as discussed here, is that many HRD professionals likely do not possess an understanding of work processes or the skills to actually conduct an analysis of a work process.

How to become more involved in the quality improvement efforts of their organizations would seem to be an aspirational goal for many HRD professionals. In practice, viewing work processes from an HRD perspective is often more responsive to the needs of organizations than the perspective necessarily taken by an industrial engineer or even a quality staff member. Viewing work processes from an HRD perspective helps to keep in mind throughout how the information will be used in the end. There is always an end-user perspective that can be associated with HRD practice.

Reflection Questions

1. Have you considered the understanding of work processes as part of your professional responsibilities?
2. What is the relationship between work processes and individuals performing their respective tasks?
3. Can you identify the types of work processes in an organization in which you now work, or have worked in the past? Do they fit the definitions as presented here?
4. Which format of presenting a work process seems best suited for helping stakeholders improve the work process?
5. Do you agree that the work process is the most important aspect of organizations to focus on when implementing a performance improvement process?

References

Crosby, P. (1980). *Quality is free: The art of making quality certain*. New York: Signet.

Demings, W. E. (1986). *Out of the crisis*. Boston: Massachusetts Institute of Technology, Center for Advanced Engineering Study.

Feigenbaum, A. V. (1991). *Total quality control* (3rd ed.). New York: McGraw-Hill.

Goldratt, E. M., & Cox, J. (2004). *The goal*. New York: Routledge.

Juran, M. (1992). *Juran on quality by design: The new steps for planning quality into goods and services*. New York: The Free Press.

Liker, J. K., & Meier, D. (2006). *The Toyota way fieldbook: A practical guide for implementing Toyota's 4Ps*. New York: McGraw-Hill.

11

Individual Competencies

The next two chapters focus respectively on understanding individual competencies and then on conducting a competency analysis, which is the work analysis technique used to identify and describe individual competencies. Individual competencies represent a relatively large set of information, and separating all of it into two chapters provides an opportunity to more fully develop the various topics. It should be noted again that the following discussion departs from the previous chapters in an important way conceptually.

Each of the previous chapters of this section introduced work analysis techniques that addressed the first underlying question: What is the work that people do? That is, the focus has been on the work, not on the people doing the work. Analyzing the work that people do is relevant across many organizational situations, and constitutes a major part of the practice of work analysis in the context of human resource development (HRD).

There is now a need to address the second component of work analysis: What are the characteristics of the people who are effective in doing the work? Understanding the nature of the people in the context of their work has a growing number of implications. For one thing, this question connects with the broader strategic planning issue in organizations of determining what type of individuals would be best suited for the future. Given the rate of change in many organizations, many global managers are now asking more fundamental questions about the people doing the work, beyond whether the people possess the specific knowledge and skills to meet job expectations. Thus, the characteristics of the people, in the form of individual competencies, have emerged as a critical aspect of work analysis.

© The Author(s) 2019
R. L. Jacobs, *Work Analysis in the Knowledge Economy*,
https://doi.org/10.1007/978-3-319-94448-7_11

As discussed in Chap. 1, there are important implications that follow each of the two underlying questions, and combining them together in this book is a departure from most other resources on the topic of work analysis. The emerging needs of organizations demand that HRD professionals have the knowledge and skills to use a wide range of work analysis techniques, including ones that address both underlying questions. Increasingly, HRD professionals now have job titles such as manager of talent development or talent management, suggesting an emphasis on the characteristics of individuals.

It should be made clear that individual competencies should always be considered in the context of an identified job role, not just simply an understanding of the individual in isolation from any context. Instruments such as the popular Clifton StrengthFinder Test (Buckingham & Clifton, 2001), seek to measure individual personality characteristics, which are typically not grounded to any particular job role or organizational context. As a result, the instrument has uncertain value as a tool for work analysis, and is more suited to simply provide information to individuals about themselves for their own purposes.

One of the continuing issues about individual competencies has been how to define them precisely, especially given the different ways that the term competency itself has been used in the literature. Some sources are quite inclusive, referring to a competency as being all the knowledge and skills related to a job. Other sources somehow align competencies with job analysis. Still other sources consider the terms competency and competence as having the same meaning. In addition, individual competencies have been equated as an organization's core competencies. Finally, some have associated the term competency-based instruction with individual competencies.

To be clear, as used here, an individual competency identifies the characteristics of individuals who are effective in a particular job role. Individual competencies should not be identified through a job analysis, but through a competency analysis, which will be discussed in the next chapter, Chap. 12. The outcomes of a job analysis and competency analysis are quite different.

In addition, for clarity, the term competence does not have the same meaning as competency, though to many they appear to be similar or even the same. In fact, the term competence refers to a person's relative level of ability in a particular area of endeavor, such as whether the person is a novice, specialist, experienced specialist, expert, or master (Jacobs, 2003). Care should be taken to ensure that the two terms—competency and competence—are not mistakenly considered as synonyms.

Further, individual competencies should not be confused with an organization's core competencies, as originally introduced by Prahalad and Hamel (1990). Core competencies identify the multiple resources available to organizations to continually develop and innovate its products and services. Indeed, an organization might even identify the specialized knowledge and skills of its employees as a core competency. Finally, competency-based instruction comes from a totally different theoretical perspective than does the term individual competency, which is originally derived from the mastery learning movement and has a behavioral theory perspective. In brief, competency-based instruction calls for the alignment of the training objectives, training content, and the training evaluation.

The HRD literature is replete with differing perspectives on how to define its many terms, and the term *competency* is certainly a prime example in which one can find a multitude of definitions. Unfortunately, many of the definitions offered in the literature are proposed without ever considering the broader context of the term, such as how defining one term logically fits with the definitions of other terms. Too often, definitions are presented in isolation from related terms. The following two chapters define individual competencies in a way that, admittedly, may be narrower than the definitions proposed by other authors. As stated, it makes little sense to define a term without having the definition to be consistent with related terms and, in addition, without a clear, concrete referent from practice available to support its proposed meaning.

Background of Individual Competencies

Table 11.1 briefly summarizes the differences in focus between the two major components of work analysis: a focus on the work and a focus on the person doing the work. The summary shows that focusing on the person refers to those characteristics, such as personality traits, that are considered critical for success in a particular job role. Individual competencies have been used

Table 11.1 Comparing the two basic perspectives of work analysis

	Focus on the work	Focus on the people
Goal	Document the work behaviors and additional information.	Identify the underlying personality traits and characteristics of people who are best at doing the work.
Assumption	If we know the work, we can design training that allows almost anyone to learn the information and be successful.	If we know what type of person is the best fit, we can help individuals acquire the characteristics required to be successful.
Context	Long history in industrial settings of documenting jobs and processes, based on industrial psychology.	More recent considerations of what makes an employee successful, based on personality psychology.

mostly for individuals at the professional, management, and executive levels of organizations. A job role refers simply to the way a person contributes in an organization. For instance, individuals in a management job role generally contribute by overseeing and directing the work of others. Individuals in that role have in fact different job titles and areas of responsibility, such as manager of marketing, manager of information technology services, manager of customer service, and so on. A job role is a way of understanding the broad responsibilities of individuals who perform similar kinds of work.

Understanding individual competencies seems even more prescient today given the emergence of knowledge work. As discussed, work continues to undergo change toward greater levels of complexity. It seems important to emphasize that organizations should systematically respond to these changes and ensure that employees possess high levels of knowledge and skill to perform their jobs. But that information is not necessarily static, and will likely change as the requirements of the work change. Indeed, in the long term, possessing specific areas of knowledge and skill may be less important than possessing the characteristics that enable a person to be successful in performing the work in the first place.

Individual competencies first emerged in the management literature in the 1960s, and the subject has grown in interest and importance in both the scholarly and popular literature from that point forward. Individual competencies emerged from the concerns that there was an overreliance on using intelligence tests for selecting managers and executives and that job analysis, as was practiced at that time, was too limited by its focus to provide useful information about the nature of the best managers and executives. A number of scholars who were interested in the workplace began to ask whether interest should be shifted from the work to the nature of the workers themselves as individuals.

One of the most prominent of these psychologists was the well-known scholar and professor of psychology, David McClelland. In 1963, McClelland established the McBer Consulting Company, as a means to put his ideas about personality and motivation into practice. Seeking ways of finding practical uses for research was a unique occurrence among scholars at the time. McClelland is responsible for introducing the original notion of individual competencies, which he defined as any characteristic of a person that differentiates performance in a specific job, role, culture, or organization.

From McClelland's perspective, competencies could be derived from a broad range of sources, including an individual's knowledge and skills, motives, as well as their personality traits. Personality traits seem to be the major component of individual competencies. He resisted making individual competencies appear too similar to that of a duty, as has been defined earlier in this book. Instead, he viewed competencies to be more like life clusters that defined the individual, not the specific work the person was doing.

In 1973, McClelland published an especially influential article entitled "Testing for Competence Rather Than for 'Intelligence'", in which he expressed in strong terms his frustration with the use of IQ tests for selection. In the article he stated somewhat metaphorically that if you are hiring a ditch-digger, it doesn't matter if his IQ is 90 or 110—what matters is whether he can actually use a shovel. This article presents ideas about human performance that even today should be considered part of the foundational principles of the HRD field and, along with Thomas Gilbert (2007), have had a major conceptual influence on the field.

In his last published research article, McClelland (1998) reported a study entitled "Identifying Competencies with Behavioral-Event Interviews". In the article, which continues to influence the competency literature, McClelland reported using the behavioral-events interview method, which he adapted from the critical incident technique, to identify 12 management competencies. In doing the study, McClelland purposely used the behavioral-event interview technique with individual managers to reveal each manager's thoughts, feelings, and actions when engaged in each of the competencies, irrespective of the task at hand.

Later, Richard Boyatzis, a professor at Case Western Reserve University and earlier a colleague of McClelland, further refined the notion of competencies in his important book *The Competent Manager: A Model for Effective Performance* (1982). Boyatzis conducted an impressive large-scale study among 2000 managers across 12 organizations to identify what comprises the basis for managerial talent.

Boyatzis suggested that since individual competencies constitute an underlying construct of individuals and since the constructs should be considered as abilities, it seemed logical to assume that individuals might be able to acquire the behaviors associated with them, given the appropriate development opportunities. Boyatzis identified a number of personal characteristics for managers, such as:

- Team Orientation
- Sensitivity to Others
- Trust Building

Together, these constructs form a model of individual competencies. Underlying the work of McClelland and other psychologists interested in individual competencies is the notion of personality psychology, even though, as stated, personality traits may constitute just one of several aspects that comprise an individual competency. In general, personality psychology is the branch of psychology that studies both how people differ and how they are the same. Personality can be defined as the internal traits that influence how people think, act, respond, and feel in various life situations. Personality also influences how people think of themselves as well, or their self- perceptions. Personality psychology emerged from the need to more systematically learn about ourselves as unique individuals.

Needless to say, understanding personality has fascinated scientists, artists, writers, and everyday folks alike since the beginning of time. In the arts, perhaps there has been no more insightful person who showed insights in the vagaries of personality than the famous playwright from the early 1600s, William Shakespeare. Who else in history has explained with more clarity the reasons why an individual should descend into madness than Shakespeare in his tragedy *King Lear*, written in 1605?

Understanding personality in the context of the workplace has perplexed managers since early times as well. One can only imagine the quandary of the master tradesman in the Middle Ages somehow trying to size up the potential of a young apprentice seeking to be taken on. More than a few masters must have posed the following question: How do I know that this person has the right stuff to eventually become a master tradesperson himself? Similar to managers of today, the master craftsman was interested in finding apprentices who could not only learn the craft, but also carry on the culture that surrounds the craft. Otherwise, investing in the novice would be a waste of his resources.

Several theoretical perspectives of personality psychology exist, including psychoanalytic, behaviorist, social cognitive, and humanistic. Each of these perspectives has contributed in different ways to our understanding of people and their behavior. Of most relevance to individual competencies is the perspective of personality psychology that comes from the trait theory perspective of personality psychology.

Gordon Allport is considered a pioneer scholar in identifying personality traits, whose groundbreaking work continues to inform our understanding of individual competencies (Allport, 1968). As a faculty member at Harvard University in the early and middle part of the twentieth century, Allport moved in a different direction from another psychologist interested in traits, the famed gestalt psychologist, Sigmund Freud. In general, Freud sought to understand the traits of individuals through intense contact with them, from which he might reveal the meaning of their past experiences as a means to explain their actions today.

Instead, Allport focused more on identifying those traits that exist in the present, and which might be generally applied to almost all people. In taking this perspective, Allport focused on identifying types of human traits that more or less remain with us during our lifetime. Along with his colleagues, Allport identified three categories of traits that define a person's personality.

Cardinal traits are the broadest set of characteristics that a person might possess, and they tend to dominate and shape a person's basic behavior toward most aspects of life. Allport used the term cardinal as a way of signifying that these traits are fundamental to a person. In fact, the more common understanding of cardinal traits is that these are a core part of the person's personality.

Cardinal traits are not likely to change much over a person's lifespan, and may be the result of early teaching from an influential person or source, and may not become fully developed and be manifested until later in life. Cardinal traits are part of a person's basic makeup as a person. For instance, a child learns to be honest through the ongoing teaching of his or her mother. Then the child begins to carry forward those small lessons through adolescence and adulthood, and then generalizes them into a broader mature perspective. In this regard, honesty might be considered an example of a cardinal personality trait.

Central traits differ from cardinal traits, and are those that Allport theorized that all humans possess. Central traits are also broad in nature, but are more immediate to guiding our everyday actions than cardinal traits. In a sense, they form the basic foundations of a person's personality that is observed by others. For instance, some examples of central traits can include honesty, sociability, perseverance, and anxiousness, among others. Central traits may overlap with cardinal traits to some extent, but central traits are most often used to describe a person as a whole, in a more holistic sense. For instance, we might say that a particular person is honest, friendly, or kind.

Allport posited that people typically possess five to ten central traits. To this end, the number of traits present in an individual and the extent to which they can be measured will vary across people. Consider how a personality scale might be used to ask a large number of individuals to rate themselves on their sociability, from Always Sociable to Seldom Sociable.

Finally, Allport identified secondary traits, which appear only in the presence of certain circumstances, such as when an individual expresses a preference for doing one action or another. In an everyday sense, these are the traits that become most apparent to others on a regular basis, though they may not always be consistent across all situations. For instance, some people enjoy riding roller coasters when they visit an amusement park and purposely seek out that thrilling experience, while others are fearful of them and avoid the experience altogether. So thrill seeking might be considered a secondary trait, based on its context.

In the same way, a manager in an organization might be considered to possess the secondary trait of self-directedness, because she addressed a troublesome quality situation on her own, without being told to do so. But, given another problem situation requiring attention, the manager might not engage in the same self-directed problem-solving behaviors. Secondary traits appear to be much more context-based than central or cardinal traits.

Secondary traits are especially important for understanding individual competencies, as they appear to be the most malleable and subject to change of the personality traits that were identified by Allport. That is, the secondary traits might be developed or enhanced based on some systematic intervention. Could a training program or talent development experience of some kind be devised to increase self-directedness, if this trait was of value to the organization and to the job role?

The discussion about personality types, as proposed by Gordon Allport, provides a background for understanding individual competencies. As stated, Allport's work seems relatively well suited for understanding individual competencies since it identifies a type of trait that matches up, more or less, with individual competencies. In understanding Allport's work, at least three issues should be considered.

First, though Allport's work has had much influence and has some common-sense logic, none of his work was based on empirical validation. That is, no studies were ever conducted to establish the construct validity of the traits. They are presumed to exist. As a result, when considering the use of individual competencies, caution should be exercised to determine whether the individual competencies are in fact based on secondary traits as intended. How to clearly articulate the various traits, and adapt the information into a contemporary work setting seems a continuing issue when considering the use of individual competencies.

Second, related to the preceding issue is the fundamental question about whether a secondary trait can, in fact, be changed or developed in individuals. Some observers simply believe that people are who they are, with no real possibility for influencing the nature of their personalities. Assuming that at least some personality traits can be changed underlies the notion of using individual competencies.

Finally, Allport's work and many recent authors do not fully differentiate between a trait, which is believed to be a stable characteristic, and a state, which is believed to be more transitory. Stability is a critical issue for those interested in individual competencies from a measurement perspective. They would ask: How can the trait be measured if it is subject to change?

In practice, the point of individual competencies is that since they can presumably be learned and changed, stability may not be entirely desirable. As a result, organizations appear to be more interested in the notion of personality states. For instance, the Myers-Briggs Type Inventory (MBTI) (Myers, 1995), a well-known personality scale used in many organizations, is often given to employees to identify one or more of 16 combinations of their personality types, based on the work of the psychologist Carl Jung. Such an instrument is used primarily to help individuals know more about themselves.

In conclusion, individual competencies emerged from an interest in knowing more about the people doing the work, instead of the work itself. Individual competencies seemingly provide greater insights about what type of people are most successful in a particular work context, information that would be of great benefit to the organization. For many organizations, individual competencies now include personality constructs and other relevant personal characteristics as well. The importance of individual competencies has raised the issue of which is more important for organizational success—whether employees should simply have the knowledge and skills to do their jobs or should employees have the appropriate personality traits and characteristics? Proponents of each side of the issue can make compelling arguments from their perspective. As stated, the perspective of this book is based on the practical needs of societies and organizations. There is no reason to necessarily value one side of the issue over the other, as each may be appropriate based on the problem to be addressed.

Using Individual Competencies

In practice, many organizations today use individual competencies for a number of different reasons, including recruitment and selection, promotion, performance management, human resource planning, and employee development.

Recruitment and Selection

Including information from the individual competencies in position announcements and as part of published job requirements. As a result, new hires in the organization would likely be better matched with the characteristics of their future job roles.

Promotion

Determining whether individuals possess the individual competencies required for success in an upgraded position. As a result, organizations can use the individual competencies as potential criteria for consideration, and individuals can plan for future promotions by considering how to acquire individual competencies.

Performance Management

Establishing the acquisition of individual competencies as goals for individuals. Individuals can identify ways of acquiring individual competencies as part of their personal development plans.

Human Resource Planning

Determining what will be the likely individual competencies required of employees for the future. Organizations can include individual competencies as part of strategic planning processes.

Employee Development

Designing programs as a means to help individuals to acquire individual competencies. Organizations make it possible for individuals to acquire the individual competencies, and individuals can participate in the programs as they seek improvement in their current job role or if they want to be considered for a future promotion. This is the essence of competency development, which comprises the programs used to help employees acquire the individual competencies.

Logically, HRD professionals should lead in designing competency development programs. As will be discussed in Chap. 17, these programs typically focus more on experiential learning activities, reflection, and feedback as a means to promote change. In practice, the challenge of these employee development programs is to match the most appropriate learning experiences with the individual competency.

The program does not necessarily introduce training content per se. Instead, the program typically provides a series of challenging situations for individuals to respond to, and be observed in the process. Structured feedback is often provided at the end of the experience.

In this sense, acquiring an individual competency basically comes from the increased awareness of the individual competency, feedback from others on the level of performance on the challenging situation, reflection on what the individual competency means in a personal sense, and finally expressing a commitment toward making a change.

Today, a sizeable number of authors continue to focus their attention on individual competencies as they relate to specific job roles, such as HR (e.g., Ulrich, Younger, & Brockbank, 2012) and especially leadership (such as, Donahue, 2018). Books and articles about individual competencies related to leadership continue to attract much attention in organizations.

In addition, numerous management consulting firms worldwide provide a thriving set of services to client organizations in the form of archived sets of competencies, from which the clients can select which ones would seem most appropriate in their particular situations. The consulting firms provide further service by helping to operationally define the individual competency and describing the behavioral indicators within the context of the client's organization.

The use of individual competencies has expanded by separating them into various categories. For instance, it is not uncommon today for organizations to identify distinct categories of competencies. General competencies usually apply to almost all levels of supervisors, managers, and executive-level employees of the organization regardless of their role, such as the following:

a. Achievement Orientation
b. Analytical Thinking
c. Conceptual Thinking
d. Customer Service Orientation
e. Developing Others
f. Flexibility
g. Influencing Others
h. Information Seeking
i. Self-Directedness
j. Sensitivity to Others

Leadership competencies usually apply only to those employees who serve in roles in which they direct the efforts of others, such as the following:

a. Analyzing Problem Situations
b. Decision Making
c. Managing Execution
d. Adapting to New Situations

Functional competencies usually apply to employees in select roles across the organization, such as the following:

a. Business Process Knowledge
b. System Thinking
c. Managing Change

d. Labor Laws
e. Quality at the Source
f. Safety Regulations

Even the most cursory review of these lists suggests that competencies now typically include a mixture of personality traits (Achievement Orientation), areas of knowledge and skill (Project Management), and sets of important information (Safety Regulations). It is no wonder that the meaning of an individual competency—originally meant to be based mostly on personality traits—has confused many managers and HRD professionals alike.

In practice, many of the so-called individual competencies now used in organizations can actually be interpreted as representing duties or even the prerequisites of a job, more than anything else. In his original thinking, McClelland sought to be inclusive in conceptualizing an individual competency. That inclusiveness has invited subsequent authors to add more and more to the concept, to the extent that the boundaries of individual competencies have become particularly blurred, so that any given individual competency might well be considered as a job duty or task in another situation. It is for this reason that the meaning of an individual competency is kept relatively narrow in this discussion.

One of the most famous early case studies demonstrating the use of individual competencies was in 1985 by the Mazda Motor Corporation. At that time, Mazda decided to open a new plant along with Ford, in Flat Rock, Michigan, at the site of Ford's Michigan Casting Center. The new facility would produce two mid-sized cars, which became known as the Mazda 626 and the Ford Probe, starting in 1987.

Mazda decided that it could not simply hire individuals from the existing workforce, without knowing more about the people and their abilities, in the context of the new work approach being implemented. The new work approach involved people working together as a team instead of working alone, as was mostly the case in the past. As a result, Mazda conducted an extensive analysis of the jobs and tasks in the new facility, and they also identified the required individual competencies of employees, the most prominent of which was the competency of teamwork.

As a result, Mazda implemented a series of role-play exercises and in-basket simulations, as a means to help determine whether individuals who sought employment possessed the competencies that had been identified. Employees were observed and rated as they participated in these various activities, and final hiring decisions were based in part on this information.

The case study was one of the first case studies to show how individual competencies might be used with frontline employees instead of managers. Of note, the joint production venture between Ford and Mazda continued until 2012, at which time Ford took over the facility and, after a major refitting, used it to produce the Ford Fusion.

Comment

Readers may not have realized another distinguishing aspect for understanding individual competencies. That is, individual competencies expressly focus on generating models that represent the behaviors of the most successful or the most effective employees in a particular job role. In the previous chapters, which described how to analyze specific units of the work, the focus has been on documenting what is considered best practice, but best practice is usually understood in the context of individuals at the beginning points of their learning.

As will be discussed in the following chapter, that difference has practical implications for how individual competencies are identified and described. In many organizations, uncertainty about what constitutes effective behaviors in their context has led to some reliance on external sources for that information, with the assumption that this information has some transferability across organizational settings.

Reflection Questions

1. Individual competencies addresses the second major component of work analysis. Do you agree that understanding the person, as opposed to the work, has merit for analyzing what people do in their jobs?
2. Do you believe that there are, in fact, distinct characteristics that make some people more effective in a job role than others?
3. Do you believe that personality characteristics of people can be changed through an employee development program?
4. Many organizations invest considerable resources to identify the required individual competencies in their organizations. Do you think this investment is wise, in terms of a return to the organization in better productivity, lower turnover, and greater instances of promotability?
5. From your own work experience, can you discern differences in the personality of your colleagues, and do you believe these differences may influence their effectiveness on the job?

References

Allport, G. W. (1968). *The person in psychology.* Boston: Beacon Press.

Boyatzis, R. (1982). *The competent manager: A model for effective performance.* New York: John Wiley.

Buckingham, M., & Clifton, D. O. (2001). *Now discover your strengths.* New York: The Free Press.

Donahue, D. E. (2018). *Building leadership competence: A competency-based approach to building leadership ability.* State College, PA: Centrestar Learning.

Gilbert, T. (2007). *Human competence: Engineering worthy performance.* San Francisco, CA: Pfeiffer.

Jacobs, R. L. (2003). *Structured on-the-job training: Unleashing employee expertise in the workplace.* San Francisco, CA: Berrett-Koehler Publishers.

McClelland, D. (1998). Identifying competencies with behavioral-events interviews. *Psychological Science, 9*(5), 331–338.

Myers, I. B. (1995). *Gifts differing: Understanding personality type.* Mountain View, CA: Davies-Black Publishing.

Prahalad, C. K., & Hamel, G. (1990). The core competence of the organization. *Harvard Business Review, 68*(3), 79–91.

Ulrich, D., Younger, J., Brockbank, W., & Ulrich, M. (2012, July). HR talent and the new HR competencies. *Strategic HR Review, 11*(4), 217–222.

12

Conducting a Competency Analysis

This chapter discusses how to conduct a competency analysis. The focus here is on using competency analysis to identify which individual competencies are critical for success in a certain job role, and then to develop a competency model that describes in detail each of the identified individual competencies. A competency model includes an operational definition of each individual competency, the levels of behavioral indicators, and presents the relationships among the individual competencies. A competency model is the outcome of conducting a competency analysis. Competency analysis might also be used to identify organization-wide core competencies or function-specific competencies, but those usually entail different analysis processes.

Most human resource development (HRD) professionals have had limited experience in conducting a competency analysis. Even so, many HRD professionals have now become more and more involved in their organization's talent management initiatives in which individual competencies play a key contributing role. Talent management typically involves the coordination of a broad range of activities, including recruitment, selection, development, and promotion (Arp, 2014). In many instances, managers realize that such a broad-based set of activities requires a critical analysis of the organization's mission statement, resulting in the development of a detailed plan related to the management of the organization's workforce in general. Needless to say, talent management has become a major influence on determining the strategic human resource (HR) policies of many organizations. As stated, individual competencies play a key contributing role, as they provide the basis for almost all activities related to talent management.

© The Author(s) 2019
R. L. Jacobs, *Work Analysis in the Knowledge Economy*,
https://doi.org/10.1007/978-3-319-94448-7_12

Many HRD professionals likely have some awareness of individual competencies in general, but to have any experience in actually conducting a competency analysis seems another matter altogether. Because of its perceived complexity, many organizations simply rely upon a consulting firm to provide this service. Given the continuing interest in individual competencies within many organizations, it makes sense for HRD professionals to have knowledge and skills in actually using this work analysis technique. Having at least an understanding of the process often distinguishes individuals in terms of their potential contributions to an organization.

Not surprisingly, the term competency analysis itself has been used to denote other meanings related to HRD practice as well, besides the way it is used here. For instance, a few references use competency analysis to describe when an organization-wide audit is conducted of the current and future knowledge and skills gaps across critical jobs. Used in this way, this activity seems more akin to the process of training needs assessment. Again, the terms used in this book may have multiple meanings elsewhere, but the meanings presented here seek to have a logical and consistent relationship among all the other terms presented and in the context of HRD practice.

Issues in Analyzing Individual Competencies

Many managers have been attracted to using individual competencies, as the reasoning behind them seems compelling. As presented in Chap. 11, individual competencies can be used to achieve a number of different purposes, the most prominent of which is to use them as the basis for designing employee development programs that enable employees to acquire the characteristics related to the identified individual competency. It is assumed that once individuals possess these characteristics, they will be more successful in their job roles, leading to greater organizational effectiveness.

Logically, before individual competencies can be used, regardless of the purpose, they must first be identified and understood. When embarking on the process of analyzing individual competencies, issues of concern invariably arise that should have been anticipated beforehand. Otherwise, the effectiveness of using the individual competencies will likely be hindered to a large extent. More than a few organizations have invested considerable amount of their resources in conducting a competency analysis, only to realize later on that something obstructs their use, which could have been avoided in the first place.

The following discussion presents four issues of concern that often arise when conducting a competency analysis.

Involvement of Senior Leaders

Individual competencies are based on the characteristics of successful employees in a certain job role. Clearly, such individuals should be involved in the competency analysis process, if they in fact exist in the organization. Involving a wide range of stakeholders in the competency analysis process is critical to ensure success. But who exactly are the stakeholders? Are they just the individuals directly involved in the competency analysis process, such as the successful employees in the job role who will serve as subject-matter experts? Are they the immediate managers of the employees in the job role?

More than any other work analysis technique, competency analysis requires the commitment and involvement from a broad range of stakeholders, especially the senior leadership of the organization. Involving senior leaders is especially critical for two reasons. First, because individual competencies draw from a strategic perspective of the organization, these individuals will be able to provide their perspective about the individual competencies, keeping in mind the organization's mission and vision statements. Second, in a practical sense, using the individual competencies later on will require an allocation of resources, and senior leaders should be involved in making decisions about their use along the way.

In practice, this means that HRD professionals should be prepared to conduct one-on-one interviews with key senior leaders, such as the vice president of HR in their corporate offices, the division directors of the functions in which the job role exists, and even the president of the organization. All of their voices should be included in identifying and describing the individual competencies. As stated, no other work analysis technique requires as much involvement of senior leaders in the process. Experience suggests that even if the information from these individuals does not necessarily differ from the information gathered from other sources, the mere fact that they were involved in the process can make it easier when seeking their assistance on some related issues later on.

Relationship with the Mission Statement

When identifying the individual competencies for a job role, stakeholders can often lose sight of the organization's mission statement as the context. That is, the issue is that stakeholders may select those individual competencies that appear consistent with their own perspective of the job role, apart from any other consideration. In some instances, the individual competencies selected may in fact be inconsistent or not entirely supportive with the mission statement.

For instance, a relatively large regional bank sought to use individual competencies with its branch managers in the retail division. Having the individual competencies was believed to be helpful in identifying individuals who might be eligible for promotion from senior teller to assistant manager and from assistant manager to manager in the retail area. Considering individuals for such promotions is a critical decision for the bank. The individual competencies would also be used to guide future efforts in its internal corporate university.

At the same time, in response to competitive pressures in some of its markets, the bank's senior leaders decided to revise its mission statement, as a means to reinforce the importance of service to its customers. Clearly, employees in the various branch manager roles are keenly aware of the importance of customer service, since they interact with customers daily. As such, the original individual competency identified, Customer Orientation, was viewed as not emphasizing customer service sufficiently.

As a result, the individual competency was renamed as Serving Our Customers, and a revised operational definition and behavioral indictors had to be prepared. The case study illustrates not only the need for the individual competencies to reflect the mission statement, but also to ensure that all senior leaders are involved in the process.

Relationship with Job Expectations

Perhaps the most frequently occurring issue is reconciling the relationship between the individual competencies with specific job expectations. Since individual competencies typically focus on a certain job role, the expectations of a job may in fact conflict in some respects with the individual competency. In practice, when individuals realize the disconnect between the two sets of information, the validity of the individual competencies immediately comes into question.

For instance, a large information technology (IT) consulting firm sought to implement individual competencies for its many project managers, who serve clients globally. In this way, the organization could use the individual competencies as another set of criteria to identify promising project managers for future development and promotion. One of the individual competencies identified was Sensitivity to Others, which is often identified as an individual competency across many management job roles.

The disconnect occurred when some project managers, who are typically under immense pressure to accomplish project milestones for their clients as part of their job expectations, are also being asked to acquire a characteristic that focuses them on being more sensitive to the feelings of others around them. Being sensitive to others is a laudable characteristic for all managers. But in the turbulent world of consulting firms involved in software design and development, there are points in time when forceful and emphatic discussions must occur between the project managers and the software engineers back at the home office, and that sensitivities may seem less important than getting the project accomplished. It is no wonder that when attending the employee development program, several of the project managers questioned how they might actually do both: achieve challenging project goals within established budgets and also exhibit the characteristics of being sensitive toward others along the way.

Expectation of Change

As stated, many organizations expend considerable resources to identify and use individual competencies. Often, after the employee development program is delivered for the first time, there is a sense of satisfaction that the entire cycle has been successfully completed. What occurs next is often perplexing to many managers and HRD professionals. That is, in spite of the success of the first cycle, some aspect of the job role or the organization may have unexpectedly undergone change, affecting the nature of the individual competencies.

Of course, revising the employee development program based on feedback from the first time it was delivered would be naturally expected. What is meant here is the issue that some aspect of the organization has undergone change—such as, a merger or acquisition, a new culture adopted, a revised mission statement, new customer requirements, new products or services, revised work requirements, change in work methods—which now calls into question the individual competencies in the first place. Individual competencies are especially sensitive to such changes.

The issue is not to be fearful of such changes, as they are inevitable in today's uncertain environment. Rather, the issue is how to expect change to occur and to conduct the competency analysis with this fact in mind, instead of them being considered a rigid edifice that would be expected to last for an extended period of time. How to avoid locking in on a certain cluster of individual competencies only, and considering them flexibly is an important issue for many HRD professionals. Part of the issue is that many organizations rely upon the services of a consulting firm to provide the individual competencies for the organization to use, without also providing the knowledge and skills to the client organization on how to make the necessary changes on their own. Change occurs regularly and often without any advance warning.

For instance, a medium-sized regional bank was using individual competencies to guide the development of all management-level employees. Then, as is happening on a frequent basis throughout the financial services industry, the bank was acquired by a much larger regional bank, which had its own set of individual competencies and approaches for developing managers.

In fact, much of the competency model that was used eventually required much extensive revision. For instance, the acquired smaller bank wanted its managers to have the characteristics of an entrepreneur, based on the individual competency of Respond to Customer Needs. Managers of this bank were known to provide service to customers even after business hours, say, to ensure that a credit card was unblocked for a known customer, who was soon departing for an overseas business trip. Once the smaller bank was acquired, managers were now much more bound to follow established rules and policies, so that the definition and behavioral anchors of Respond to Customer Needs had taken on a much different meaning.

There are numerous potential issues for analyzing and using individual competencies. From experience, the four issues discussed earlier can often be anticipated in advance. In summary, the issues focus on involvement, relationship with other sets of information, expecting changes to occur, and being able to respond to them.

Competency Analysis Process

As stated, when seeking to analyze individual competencies, many organizations simply decide to contract with an external consulting firm that specializes in this area of practice, and then follow the suggested process used by the consulting firm. Consulting firms have typically gathered an extensive database of individual competencies, based on their experience in other organizations and the literature. Some refer to this database as a competency dictionary or a competency bank.

The information about individual competencies is assumed to have transferability across organizational settings, because of the basic similarity among many job roles. For instance, the individual competencies for a middle manager job role are likely the same, with some expected variation across companies, even though the companies may represent different business sectors. Nevertheless, the ways that these individuals do their work has much in common. The information provided by a consulting firm is likely considered proprietary, and is used by the client only with permission.

There are some good reasons to use a consulting firm to conduct a competency analysis, especially as a means to make the overall project more efficient. As stated, the firms typically have an established set of individual competencies which otherwise would need to be generated in the organization. The client organization is able to review the list of competencies, and select the ones that appear most appropriate for individual use by the client.

There are also some reasons to not rely entirely on an external consulting firm, and instead to conduct at least part of the competency analysis in-house. For one thing, there is value to the organization for engaging in the competency analysis process itself. The competency analysis process requires that fundamental questions be asked about the nature of the organization and the type of individuals best suited to work in it. In a sense, though not planned for this to occur, the competency analysis often brings with it time for reflection and discussion among stakeholders, as they begin to realize that individual competencies are a reflection of the organization. Few managers have ever had time to think about the organization in this way.

In addition, as discussed, conducting at least some of the process in-house also increases the capacity of the organization, which may be important when updates will be made to the information, which invariably occurs. Without seeking to be critical of consulting firms, most of them will insist on doing the project work themselves, and are not necessarily willing to transfer their knowledge and skills to the client, for use at a later time. In general, in too many instances when working with consultants, the client may receive an acceptable product from the consultant, but the client has not learned much about doing the work themselves. The client organization should have some in-house abilities to carry on after the consultant finishes.

As a result, it is recommended that organizations seeking to conduct a competency analysis consider the following suggestions:

- Engage an external consulting firm to help make the process less cumbersome for the organization, especially in terms of identifying the original individual competencies for the selected job role.
- Stipulate in the agreement with the consulting firm that staff from the client organization will work alongside the consultants as part of the project as a means to help build this same capacity in the organization.
- Participate in developing the competency model, especially the components that involve the operational definition and the behavioral indicators for each individual competency.
- Lastly, propose to the consultant that the steps of the competency analysis process used will be identified together, so that it reflects the specific needs of the organization.

These suggestions assume that the organization has the staff available who are willing and able to actively participate in the process. The following discusses the suggested phases of conducting a competency analysis:

1. Assemble a Blended Project Team

After the decision has been made to use individual competencies, it is recommended that a project team be assembled composed of both internal staff members and, if appropriate, external consultants. The following internal team members are suggested:

- HRD manager
- HR representative
- One or more employees who serve in the job role
- One or more managers who oversee the job role
- A senior manager who has a perspective of the organization's mission and vision
- Another manager or staff member who has a perspective on the job role or on using individual competencies

It is suggested that a team leader be appointed, and that the HRD manager would be an appropriate person to serve in this role. The stakeholders of the project include a wide range of individuals, most likely including corporate leaders and division managers.

2. Identify the Name of the Job Role

The first item of business for the project team is to name the job role that is the focus of the project. There was likely some idea of the name of the job role when the decision was made to use individual competencies. But this is a time to name the job role with more precision, to ensure a common understanding. The team should be reminded that the job role represents a number of different job titles, but all the job titles are grouped together since they represent common contributions to the organization.

For instance, an organization might have individuals who lead projects across several different functions, such as IT, marketing, and production. Thus, project management would be the suggested job role.

The following list suggests some names for job roles:

- Human Resource Management
- Middle-Level Management
- Project Management
- Front-Line Supervision
- Product Leadership
- Service Leadership
- Quality Leadership
- Safety Leadership

After naming the job role, it is recommended that an official statement be generated that specifically presents the name of the job role, the job titles that comprise the job role, and the strategic importance of this job role, providing a rationale for why this job role is the focus of the project. This information should be distributed to all stakeholders of the project.

3. Identify the Individual Competencies

Obviously, this is a critical step in the process. Individual competencies can be identified using the following sources and methods:

- Review the literature for articles and case studies that report the use of competencies in organizations.
- Search the Internet for lists of competencies as made available by consulting firms and other organizations.
- Generate an original set of individual competencies based on one-on-one interviews, small-group interviews, and even a modified version of the Developing a Curriculum (DACUM) technique. DACUM can be adapted for this purpose.

In each of these, the sources of information would be senior leaders, managers, and job incumbents. The following is the recommended prompt question for data gathering:

Reflect on the job role of _____ as it appears in several jobs throughout our organization. Think about the individuals who you have known who were successful in this job role. Do you have this person in mind? Now tell me what were the personal characteristics of this person? I'm not interested in the things they did on their jobs. I'm interested in knowing more about them as a person. Can you tell me what was it about them that made them successful?

From these sources and methods, a list of potential individual competencies can be generated for review. Individual competencies should be formatted in a certain way, so that when they are reviewed, they are presented in a consistent way. Individual competencies are not duty or task statements, so there is no need to present them in that format, starting with an action verb and an object to the action. Instead, individual competencies represent a construct, or an abstract concept. As such, the statement representing each individual competency should represent a distinct idea, often with an action orientation, which is complete in its meaning. The following are some suggested examples of statements representing individual competencies:

- Service Quality to Customers
- Sensitivity to Others
- Focus on Client Needs
- Solving Problems in a Team Setting
- Leads Others
- Adaptable to Project Changes
- Networking among Colleagues
- Self-Confidence with Subordinates

In too many instances, the names given to individual competencies seem vague and incomplete, such as Adaptability, Networking, or Influence. Clearly, these names would be open to interpretation and make it more difficult to use the individual competency in practice.

4. Select the Individual Competencies

From the list of identified individual competencies, the stakeholders should be asked to help select which ones—preferably from about five to eight individual competencies—best represent the job role. In practice, it is unlikely that more than eight individual competencies would be any more useful, and would rather be an overwhelming number when designing the employee development program. The following are the recommended criteria to be used:

- Is there a consensus among the stakeholders?
- Can the stakeholder envision someone actually performing the individual competency?
- Are the individual competencies exclusive from each other?

- Do they together represent a set of information, which appears comprehensive?
- Are there any ideas that might be missing or not adequately represented?

Having stakeholders select the individual competencies might be done in a group setting, such as putting the name of each individual competency on a $3'' \times 5''$ card, and then having the group members rank them in order. Experience suggests that there will likely be consensus among the stakeholders.

Another approach would be to use a web-based survey instrument, when there are many potential respondents who may not be in the same location. The stakeholders can rank order the individual competencies, or they can rate each individual competency in terms of the following:

- Importance of the Competency
- Frequency in Using the Competency
- Opportunities to Observe the Competency

5. Prepare Operational Definitions

In practice, this step could occur after the individual competencies have been selected, or it could occur at the same time. Having the operational definitions available may be helpful when stakeholders review the list of individual competencies, and then they select which ones are the most important. An operational definition is defined here as an agreed-upon way of understanding something, within a particular context. In this sense, operational definitions of the individual competencies are important as they clarify the meaning of each individual competency, so that there are no misunderstandings about their meanings.

The first draft of the operational definitions should be written by just a few staff who are closest to the process. There is no need to involve every stakeholder at this point. The following are some recommended criteria for writing the operational definitions:

- The definitions should be based on a synthesis of information from a review of the literature, descriptions of case studies, and from the consulting firm.
- Of importance, the definitions should be ultimately based on the context of the organization, which may result in the statements having a different emphasis from those found from other sources.
- Each definition should refer to one individual competency only, with care being taken that the definition has clear boundaries from other definitions.

- The definitions should be written in parallel form, with as many similarities in structure as possible across the statements.
- The definitions should add to the meaning of the name of the individual competency, not simply repeat the words.
- The definitions should clearly communicate their intent, possibly having some quick reviews by others to provide feedback to the writers, since they will eventually be used as part of the employee development programs.

The following are some examples of individual competencies and their operational definitions:

- *Sensitivity to others*—Having the ability to perceive how another person might be reacting to a situation, through their verbal or nonverbal communications.
- *Service quality to customers*—Anticipating the requirements of those receiving our services and meeting those requirements in a way that exceeds their expectations.
- *Focus on client needs*—Recognizing that when interacting with clients, understanding their situations should take priority over simply explaining our services.
- *Solving problems in a team setting*—Using a planned process to solve production problems that engages all the team members, not just doing it alone.

6. Generate Behavioral Indicators

This step is sometimes considered the most important part of the process. To this point, each individual competency is understood by its name and operational definition. What is required now is a set of different behavioral indicators that provide an anchor for understanding the individual competencies in a practical way.

Some sources refer to these statements as levels of demonstration, others refer to them as performance indicators, and still others refer to them as behavioral anchors. The term used here is behavioral indicator, since it seems most descriptive of its meaning. Regardless, all seem to describe the same set of information, more or less. For instance, Table 12.1 shows an example of a competency, Achievement Orientation, having three levels of demonstration associated with it.

At first glance, given that the levels are numbered, it might be reckoned that the numbers have some kind of meaning. That is, the numbers might represent

Table 12.1 Example individual competency and levels of demonstration

Individual competency: Achievement orientation
Operational definition: Demonstrates behaviors that seek to accomplish outcomes of importance
Levels of demonstration:
Level 3: Takes calculated risks to achieve desired outcomes
Level 2: Specifies goals that often go beyond expectations
Level 1: Seeks out ways of working more efficiently, to accomplish the same goals

increasing levels of complexity or that the numbers somehow represent the abilities of individuals performing at different levels in the job role. In addition, the literature lacks much guidance on clarifying the meaning of this information as well, as there seems no agreed-upon approach for organizing this information other than simply stating that there is a recognized need for having such statements.

Unfortunately, HRD practitioners are often uncertain how they should generate this type of information, the format to use, and their ultimate purpose. From practice, the following comments should be considered.

Groups of experienced practitioners often debate which format for the levels of demonstration are best, without ever seeming to achieve any conclusion. In actuality, of most importance is how the information will in fact be used later on. To this end, the resolution comes back to a basic principle from system theory: Start at the end first. That is, practitioners should determine how the levels will be used to achieve the goals of their project, then design the levels of demonstration accordingly.

For the most part, the levels can become inputs for the design of the employee development program. The levels are also used as ranges within what is called an instrument used to evaluate employee performance, called a behaviorally anchored rating scale (BARS).

In practice, a somewhat modified version of the critical incident technique, as discussed in Chap. 9, is typically used to generate the levels of demonstration. The information is gathered from individuals who have experience in the job role or have observed others in the job role. The prompt question for the critical incident technique is the following:

Consider the competency _____. Do you know how we are defining this competency for people who serve in the _____ job role? Let me briefly explain the definition so that you are clear about this. When you consider this competency, tell me about some actual actions on the job that you've done or observed someone else doing that show this competency in practice.

The responses that result from this prompt question are analyzed for their meaning, and then synthesized into distinct groupings of action. The levels of demonstration are derived from these various groupings of action. In practice, there are limitations in the number of actions that respondents can typically recall. Consider that during the critical incident technique interviews, the levels of more than one individual competency may be addressed.

In practice, it is recommended that identifying at least three distinct levels of demonstration should serve as the goal, although more might be possible, but not always necessary. In addition, the levels of demonstration might be flexibly organized depending on the nature of the individual competency in the following ways:

- The levels might describe behaviors that are completely unrelated to each other, as they simply describe instances of behaviors that support individual competency. The following are examples of these behaviors:

  Individual competency: Leads others
  Behavioral levels: Empowers others to make decisions; gains trust through honesty; encourages others to succeed

- The levels might describe behaviors that are related to each other, as they describe parts of a process or activity. The following are examples of these behaviors:

  Individual competency: Solves problems in a team setting
  Behavioral levels: Gathers information about the problem; involves others in identifying the causes; identifies alternative solutions to the problem

- The levels might describe behaviors that are related since they occur in a particular work context. The following are examples of these behaviors:

  Individual competency: Is adaptable to project changes
  Behavioral levels: Responds to information from client; identifies options for action; develops updated project plans

One of the issues in generating the behavioral indicators is that some might in fact be perceived as a separate individual competency itself, and not as a behavioral indicator. In practice, this process may have revealed an individual competency that had not been considered beforehand. More likely, the behavioral indicator should be revised to ensure it is actually describing behavior supporting the competency.

7. Develop the Competency Model

As stated, in this instance, a competency model presents the various sets of information about the individual competencies and a visual representation of the relationships among the individual competencies. Competency models can be represented in a variety of ways. Readers are urged to search the Internet for the many formats that might be found. For instance, Fig. 12.1 presents a simple competency model for the role of project manager.

Comment
This chapter introduced the process of competency analysis, which in retrospect may appear relatively complicated. Competency analysis typically involves at least three major cycles of data gathering:

1. Identifying and selecting the individual competencies
2. Confirming the operational definitions
3. Identifying the various behavioral indicators that support each individual competency. How to manage the competency analysis process, taking into account all the various stakeholders involved, can be a logistical challenge.

Fig. 12.1   Example competency model of project manager

In the end, many organizations undertake a lengthy process to use individual competencies, and then realize that the same information was somehow intuitively known beforehand. That is, when considering the individual competencies of the management job role, it makes sense to have predicted upfront that problem solving will be a part of the individual competencies upfront. As stated, the ultimate value of the competency analysis process is often the process itself. That is, the process forces stakeholders to reflect deeply on the nature of the organization and really become immersed in its meaning.

Finally, in some organizations, a trend has appeared to extend the meaning of individual competencies, certainly beyond its original intent. Individual competencies are intended to describe the characteristics of successful employees in a certain job role. Increasingly, organizations have identified the category of Technical Competencies as well, which, in practice, appears much more like a focus on the components of the job, not a focus on the people. Clearly, organizations can decide how to label their efforts in ways that suit their needs. It seems prudent to ensure that managers and HRD professionals understand the implications of those decisions.

Reflection Questions

1. What are your initial thoughts about the competency analysis process? Does it appear logical? Does it appear practical?
2. Competency analysis follows some different data-gathering phases. Can you envision yourself undertaking and managing such a complex process?
3. The results of a competency analysis process are often dismissed as merely representing common-sense information. In spite of this concern, what are the benefits of conducting a competency analysis? To the organization? To individual managers?
4. The usefulness of the individual competencies depends on identifying the operational definition and the levels of behavior. How difficult do you think it will to identify this information in practice?
5. The competency model represents the product of the competency analysis process. What are the benefits for individuals and the organization from such a representation?

Reference

Arp, F. (2014). Emerging giants, aspiring multinationals and foreign executives: Leapfrogging, capability building, and competing with developed country multinationals. *Human Resource Management, 53*, 851–876.

Part III

Using Work Analysis Information

In Part III, the chapters show how to use, in a practical way, the information that results from conducting a work analysis. The chapters present information that is most relevant for human resource development practice.

13

Task Statements and Training Design

Consider the following situation in an organization after a job analysis has been conducted, including an analysis of selected tasks identified from the job analysis. In practice, the human resource development HRD professional now wants to know how to use the information from the task analysis to design a training program? There are many resources that provide in-depth information about designing training programs, especially when the programs will be delivered for a group of trainees in a classroom setting. Most of these resources describe the general phases of the training design process, and provide skills in certain aspects of importance. One of the most commonly used training design processes is called Analysis, Design, Develop, Implementation, and Evaluation (ADDIE).

Upon closer review, few of these resources, including ADDIE, do not explicitly address the question of how to design training programs based on information from any aspect of a work analysis. The question might be posed: What value these training design processes might actually have for HRD practice if this important set of information is omitted?

As stated, few resources address how to design training programs based on a job analysis. The Systematic Curriculum and Instructional Design (SCID) (Norton & Moser, 2007) and the Training for Performance System (Swanson & Holton, 2009) are noteworthy exceptions to this somewhat blanket observation. Part of the issue is the continuing misconception that task analysis is best suited for analyzing work that is relatively simple, procedurally based, and technical in nature. How many academic courses or professional workshops on training design have used or still use, for instance,

© The Author(s) 2019
R. L. Jacobs, *Work Analysis in the Knowledge Economy*,
https://doi.org/10.1007/978-3-319-94448-7_13

the simple tasks of preparing a peanut butter sandwich, assembling a flash-light, or constructing a paper airplane, as nonsensical illustrative examples a task analysis? So the belief is that designing training programs for such training content is relatively straightforward, and likely not worthy of much attention.

As discussed throughout the book, even though work continues to have action aspects to it, work has become much more knowledge-based, requiring much more critical thinking along with the action. So the understanding of tasks and task analysis has now progressed far beyond these simple, nonrepresentative, examples.

This chapter will not address the entire training design process, which would require an entire book unto itself. Instead, this chapter will only cover two aspects of particular importance when designing training programs: deriving training objectives from task statements and organizing the knowledge components of tasks, which often represent the prerequisites of the task, along with the learning of the task itself.

Adapting Task Statements as Training Objectives

Is there a more overworked topic of discussion in the training design literature than how to prepare training objectives? That said, for review, training objectives are simply statements prepared at the beginning of the training design process that describe what is expected of trainees in terms of their learning outcomes at the end of the training program. The value of training objectives comes for trainees as a way of informing them of their learning expectations. The value also comes for the designers of the training as a means to help guide the planning process. Training objectives are another example of the system-based principle of starting at the end, first.

Most resources differentiate between those training objectives that are knowledge-based and those that are performance-based. Knowledge-based training objectives are often associated with the levels of Discriminations, Concrete Concepts, and Abstract Concepts, as described by Robert Gagne, when he identified Intellectual Skills as one of five major types of learning outcomes. Most HRD professionals use the two-part format of knowledge-based training objectives when designing their training programs.

Of interest here is how to specifically adapt a task statement to a performance-based training objective, such that the training objective will be useful in the design of the training program. These objectives are often considered as the target training objectives, or the objectives that describe what is expected from the trainees at the end of a unit of training. Such information is the beginning of the process of making the task information useful. Consider the following list of task statements, taken from the same duty, from a job analysis conducted of a telecommunications engineer:

a. Conduct an inspection of the Internet protocol network components.
b. Prepare the Internet protocol network inspection report.
c. Develop the Internet protocol network preventive maintenance plan.
d. Implement the Internet protocol network preventive maintenance plan.

Each of these task statements represents unique sets of complex work, likely requiring several days or more to complete each task. The tasks are critical for ensuring that the broadband service to customers using their mobile telephones is not interrupted because of a hardware or software issue. All of the tasks will be included in a training program for a group of new hire telecommunications engineers.

Figure 13.1 shows an example how a task statement can be converted to a target training objective by adding two more components to it: a statement of the conditions and a statement about the standard. As stated, a target training

Task Name
Resolve supervisor-employee conflict situations

Target Objective
Given a set of ten situations describing supervisor-employee conflict situations, each trainee will specify how to resolve each conflict situation. The resolution must meet the following criteria:

a. Include all steps of the ABC Conflict Resolution Process
b. Result in a win-win situation
c. Consistent with company policies
d. Determined to be not detrimental to work performance

Enabling Objectives
a. State what is meant by conflict
b. Distinguish between conflict and non-conflict situations.
c. Define what is meant by a supervisor-employee conflict situation
d. State the components of the ABC Conflict Resolution Process
e. Given a set of situations in work settings, trainees will classify them as being examples or non-examples of supervisor-employee conflict situations
f. Given a set of supervisor-employee conflict situations, trainees will assign the appropriate ABC Conflict Resolution technique for each situation without error

Fig. 13.1 Example adapting task statement to training objectives

objective identifies what the trainee will be able to know and do at the end of a unit of training, such as a lesson or series of lessons. From the target training objective, the enabling training objectives can be identified, which describe the outcomes that should be accomplished during the training program, that are necessary to achieve the target training objective. In a sense, the enabling training objectives are prerequisite to the target training objective.

The format shown here is consistent with the format presented by Robert Mager (1997), in his classic book, *Preparing Instructional Objectives*. Adapting task statements requires an understanding of the following principles:

- Each task statement represents what might be considered a target training objective. That is, what would be expected of trainees at the end of the delivery of a considerable amount of training content.
- The task statement provides the behavior component of the training objective.
- The two additional components are: (1) a statement of the conditions of what will be provided to trainees at the time that they are tested and (2) the standard of how well the behaviors should be conducted, in terms of the amount of time, the degree of accuracy, and quantity of things to be done within a period of time.
- The standard component of the training objective should represent the expectations of performance at the end of the training, not the performance expectations later on when the employee has experience in performing the task. The standard component at the end of the training cannot possibly be the same as the job expectation.

Adapting task statements to training objectives has a symbolic importance, as this is one of the first steps for making information from a work analysis useful. In this sense, training objectives begin to make the task analysis information useful. By itself, the information from a work analysis has no practical value.

Identifying the Knowledge Components of Tasks

Given that training objectives have been prepared from task statements, a common follow-up question is the following: How do we identify the knowledge components that are embedded in the tasks? Many HRD professionals intuitively understand that knowledge components exist, but may be uncertain regarding how to identify this information.

The knowledge components of tasks should in fact be considered as the areas of prerequisite knowledge and skills that enable individuals to perform the target training objective, as derived from the task statement. In a sense, the target training objective allows the designer to start at the end first—that is, what the trainee will be expected to do at the end of the training—and begin to identify the enabling objectives to achieve the target training objective.

Consider the following target training objective that has been derived from a previous task statement:

Given an operating simulator of a back-office telecommunications system, vendor technical specification manual, and locally developed inspection report form, trainees will conduct an inspection of the Internet protocol network components, meeting the following standard:

a. The inspection must be completed within one hour.
b. All the inspection points must be identified and named correctly.
c. All inspection points much be reviewed and given a rating of GO, NO GO, or UNCERTAIN.
d. All inspection points must include a comment to support the rating.

Given this target training objective, one can ask the following question: What are the areas of knowledge and skill that are necessary for individuals to learn first, before they can achieve the target training objective? The response to this question might result in identifying the following concepts:

- Telecommunications
- Telecommunications system
- Back-office telecommunications system
- Internet protocol
- Internet protocol network
- Internet protocol network inspection

Based on the entering knowledge and skills of trainees, enabling training objectives could be constructed for each of these concepts and would be included in the training program. As shown in the unrelated simple example in Fig. 13.2, the content of each concept would be identified through a concept analysis. A concept analysis is the means to generate an operational definition of each concept, the fixed attributes, the variable attributes, and examples and close-in non-examples of the concepts that align with the various attributes. As stated, this information forms the knowledge component of the training program.

Concept: Chair

Definition: A specific kind of furniture that allows a person to sit down, upright.

A. Critical Attribute
   1. Room for one person to sit down

B. Variable Attributes
   1. Number of legs
     a. Four
     b. Three
     c. Two
     d. One
     e. None

   2. Side arms
     a. Present
     b. Absent

   3. Size of back
     a. High
     b. Medium
     c. low

Example 1:	Wooden school chair
Rationale:	A1, B1a, B2a, B3b
Example 2:	Egg Chair
Rationale:	A1, B1e, B2b, B3a
Non-example 1:	Sofa
Rationale:	Lacks A1
Non-example 2:	Hammock
Rationale:	Lacks A1
Non-example 3:	Bar stool
Rationale:	Lacks B3

Fig. 13.2 Example of a concept analysis

Comment

This chapter introduced two important aspects of training design that are based on the use of task statements. Adapting a task statement to the format of a training objective is the first aspect, which many HRD professionals have not done as part of their practice. Making the transition from simply a task statement to a training objective begins the process of making the information useful. From the training objective, the prerequisite areas of knowledge and skill—mostly concepts and principles—can be identified.

In a training situation, the value of learning concepts and principles comes not from the satisfaction of learning this information alone. The value of the learning comes from the realization that the concepts and principles are necessary for learning how to perform the task itself.

Reflection Questions

1. What experiences have you had in writing training objectives? Have you ever considered that the basis of the training objective should be adapted from an expectation of the job?

2. What are the implications of the approach suggested in the chapter in terms of writing training objectives? Do you think this approach might address concerns about the lack of training transfer from many training programs?
3. Target training objectives identify trainee expectations at the conclusion of a set of training. What is the role of enabling training objectives in this case?
4. The chapter suggests that the knowledge components of a training program are actually the prerequisites for performing the task. Do you believe this is a reasonable perspective when considering the design of training programs?

References

Mager, R. F. (1997). *Preparing instructional objectives: A critical tool in the development of effective instruction* (3rd ed.). Atlanta, GA: The Center for Effective Performance.

Norton, R. E., & Moser, J. (2007). *SCID handbook* (7th ed.). Columbus, OH: Center on Education and Training for Employment, The Ohio State University.

Swanson, R. A., & Holton, E. F. (2009). *Foundations of human resource development*. San Francisco, CA: Berrett-Koehler Publishers, Inc.

14

Structured On-the-Job Training Modules

Structured on-the-job training (S-OJT) is defined as the planned process of having an experienced employee train a novice employee on a unit of work in the actual work setting or a setting that closely resembles the work setting. S-OJT is the only training approach that makes use of a planned process for its design and delivery, occurs in the actual work setting, and has the direct involvement of a trainer.

More typically, most of the on-the-job training that occurs in organizations can be considered unstructured in nature. That is, trainees learn through a process of engaging in a series of trial and error on their own, watching others perform the task without any guidance, or being trained by someone who may not be fully qualified or prepared to be a trainer. As a result, research has shown that unstructured on-the-job training takes longer and achieves outcomes that are lower than S-OJT. There is a compelling reason for investing in S-OJT, when the task to be learned has importance to the organization.

Perhaps no other training approach is as dependent on using information from a task analysis as is S-OJT. The task analysis provides the content for the training and, as a result, forms the core aspect of an S-OJT module.

S-OJT modules are the instructional materials that accompany S-OJT programs. An S-OJT module is an organized package that contains all the information necessary to deliver the training. Like a lesson plan, an S-OJT module

---

Parts of this chapter are based on information that was presented in Jacobs, R. L. (2003). *Structured on-the-job training: Unleashing employee expertise in the workplace.* San Francisco: Berrett-Koehler. All rights reserved.

documents the training content, based on a task analysis, and guides the delivery of the training. S-OJT modules are more comprehensive and more self-contained than a traditional lesson plan.

In practice, S-OJT modules are the documents that both the trainers and trainees have in their hands when the training is being delivered. Trainers use the modules as they get ready to deliver the training, as reference when they deliver the training, and as they rate the performance of trainees after training. Trainees use the modules as they prepare for the training, receive the training, and perform afterward to demonstrate that they have in fact learned the content. When S-OJT modules are used in these ways, they play an important role in ensuring the success of the training.

Components of an S-OJT Module

The basic components of almost all S-OJT modules include the following:

- *Title.* The title presents the content of the module in explicit terms. To promote consistency and clarity, the module title should follow directly from the task name or the information on which the training content is based.
- *Rationale statement.* The rationale statement tells the trainee why the training is important by stating what the trainee can do with the information that he or she acquires in the training. The rationale statement should also focus on the importance of the information to the development of the individual employee or the organization's effort to attain long-term goals.
- *Training objectives.* The training objectives specify what the trainee should know or be able to do as a result of the training. This component is sometimes omitted as the task statement itself suggests the outcome of the module.
- *Training prerequisites.* Training prerequisites are the area of knowledge, skills, and attitudes that trainees must possess upon entering the training session. The prerequisites also include what previous training programs should have been completed. Trainers use these prerequisites to determine the readiness of trainees for training. It also helps trainees determine their own readiness for training.
- *Training resources.* Since the training occurs in the work setting, trainers should gather together any data, equipment, tools, and instructional materials that training calls for. The scheduling of S-OJT often depends on the availability of resources. Resources used in ongoing work of the organization will have to be taken offline so that training can be conducted. Specifying the resources needed for training in the module itself helps limit interruptions in training while a trainer looks for, say, a document or a tool.

- *General safety and quality.* This component states the general safety and quality requirements associated with the task. Embedded within the task analysis are specific areas of safety and quality that should be addressed, during the actual performance of the task. This information includes a statement about the overall safety or quality perspective of the organization. Typically, a trainee will already know this information, but including it in the module links the more general statements to a specific unit of work.
- *Training content.* This component of the module is the task analysis itself, often formatted in such a way to be more useful in practice. In this sense, the training content and the task analysis are basically the same documents.
- *Training events.* How should training be delivered? This is the question that trainers most often ask. Understandably, for them it is the most visible part of S-OJT. Training events describe how to deliver S-OJT to trainees in the most effective way. The delivery of the S-OJT module typically involves five training events:

  1. Prepare the trainee
  2. Present the training
  3. Require a response
  4. Provide feedback
  5. Evaluate performance

- *Performance tests and feedback forms.* At the conclusion of training, the trainer should make certain that the trainee has successfully achieved the training objectives. Thus, modules should include a performance check, such as performance-rating scales, product scales or process scales. A module can also contain forms that document the completion of training and provide summative feedback certifying that the training objectives have been achieved.

Organizations use this information in different ways. Some organizations purposely integrate this information as part of the employee's developmental plan and require that the information be maintained in a formal way. Other organizations use the forms only for employee feedback. An increasing number of organizations use the feedback forms for personnel planning and employee development.

Examples of S-OJT Modules

The Appendix of the book presents four complete S-OJT modules that focus on the following knowledge-based tasks:

- Optimize process unit product yield
- Develop the IP network preventive maintenance work plan
- Conduct inspection of components before welding
- Prepare IP network health check report

As stated, each of these example S-OJT modules is based on tasks that are complex in nature, involving knowledge-based tasks. That is, tasks that require the trainee to recall knowledge from previous learning, and to use that information to perform a set of work. In this sense, simply performing the actions called for in the S-OJT module would be insufficient, without the ability to recall or have access to the previous knowledge.

Comment

This chapter introduced how to use task analysis information for the preparation of S-OJT modules. S-OJT, as a training approach, has often been considered as being best suited for presenting tasks that are relatively simple, and mostly involve learning physical actions. It is true that most these characteristics would be an accurate description of on-the-job training in the past.

Yet, as work has become more complex, there is a growing sense that what was true in the past cannot be the same today. The chapter is mostly about showing how more complex, knowledge-based tasks were addressed through S-OJT.

Reflection Questions

1. Are you familiar with the extent of the on-the-job training used in an organization that you are familiar with?
2. To what extent would you say that the on-the-job training in the organization mentioned earlier is structured or unstructured in nature?
3. Can you recognize the importance of conducting a task analysis for preparing an S-OJT module?
4. Can you understand how the requirements might differ for learning a relatively complex knowledge-based task as opposed to a simple task, involving physical actions only?
5. What issues might arise in using this training approach for knowledge-based tasks?

15

Performance Support Guides

All of us have used a performance support guide in some way or another in our daily lives. As shown in Fig. 15.1, the next time you put fuel in your car or truck, you will see a list of steps for the user to follow. All fuel pumps provide a brief set of instructions on how to insert your credit card, select the type of fuel you wish, and whether you want a receipt. The prompts are sometimes continued on the screen on the pump. Some prompts even ask if you wish to purchase a car wash as well! Sometimes this information is presented completely with icons or simple pictures, in other instances it is presented as text, and in others as a combination of icons and text.

Now that more cars are being powered by electric motors, electric recharging stations will also need to present a performance support guide to ensure that users know how to connect the charging station to their car's outlet. Most of these users are doing this task for the first time, so that error is always a possibility, and doing it properly is critical for ensuring the recharge has occurred.

Refueling or recharging our cars is a simple task that many of us perform on a regular basis, perhaps weekly. One would think we could just remember how to do it, and the information would be unnecessary. There remains the need for providing a performance support guide of some kind, to ensure that the intended activity is done correctly. Without it, there's always the probability of making an error, and suffering some kind of unwanted consequence.

Performance support guides are documents, printed or electronic, that include all the information necessary to ensure that people are reminded to carry out a task and know how to do it. That is, what should be done and how to do it. In

© The Author(s) 2019
R. L. Jacobs, *Work Analysis in the Knowledge Economy*,
https://doi.org/10.1007/978-3-319-94448-7_15

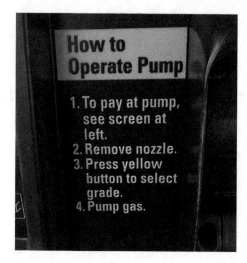

Fig. 15.1   Steps to use the fuel pump

this sense, performance support guides are dependent on information provided by a task analysis. That is, the task analysis provides the core set of information from which the performance support guide can be developed.

In practice, performance support guides are known variously as work instruction sheets, job guides, or standard operating procedures (SOPs). Performance support guides can be used as a means to replace training, or as a means to complement training. In either case, performance support guides are designed and used in the following combination of situations:

- People already know the task, but may require a constant reminder
- People do not need to learn the task, just to know how to perform it when required
- People might find the task relatively easy and not requiring any formal training programs, but there are aspects that might be forgotten without some kind of reference
- People do this task within the context of performing other tasks, so there is a concern about overloading the person with information
- People know how to perform the task, but there may be some specific aspects that require additional attention
- People might find the task to be especially complex or difficult, and may not remember all the components
- People might make errors at certain points, which require some additional information

- People know how to perform the task, but are required to use a performance support guide when performing the task, based on a legal or policy requirement
- People know the task, but if the task is not done completely and reliably, there is likely a high consequence of error

Human Error

Since the beginning of time, there have always been individuals in the workplace who have written down information for themselves, as a means to reduce error. In fact, in my own experience, an illustrative example of this occurred several years ago, when a highly skilled technician at a power generating station of an electric utility company was retiring. On the last day on the job, he surprised all around him by producing a set of documents that he had kept hidden in his desk drawer, and he pronounced that he wouldn't be needing them anymore. Unbeknown to anyone else, over the years the technician had written down, in his own way, and collected in a thick folder, critical information that he had gathered during the various planned shutdowns and maintenance activities that had occurred. Included in the documents were measurement settings, steps of procedures, and comments and observations about special instances he had encountered over the years. In a sense, the technician had produced his own set of performance support guides.

For some reason, he had thought that keeping this information was somehow not appropriate, since it was not authorized by anyone in authority in the company. The information was just for his own personal use, believing that if he shared it, he might actually be in trouble for doing so. Why he would believe this to be true is another matter. But it does suggest misunderstanding about the need to document work, and also provides some insight into this individual's valiant effort to prevent him from making errors in the future. That was the core rationale for keeping all this information because, as an expert, he could not simply remember all the details of his work, and wisely wrote down information he believed was important.

Human error is among us all the time. People make mistakes all the time and in most cases the consequences are of small importance. A product is shipped a day later than scheduled. A customer is given some misinformation and the vendor apologizes. A product requires some simple alterations to meet the customer's final expectations.

Human error may also lead to consequences that are of high importance. A ferry boat's hatch is mistakenly left open, and water pours in during unusually stormy weather with high waves, and the ship sinks with great loss of life, all because one person had forgotten to close the hatch on one particular occasion.

A particular lab test is conducted too late by a technician in a company that manufactures edible oils, and the technician makes the startling discovery that a critical additive has been omitted from the production process. As a result, several railroad tank cars filled with vegetable oil that were headed to a commercial bakery had to be emptied just before they were scheduled to leave for the customer's facility. Both of these actual situations illustrate that sometimes there are dire consequence of error.

George Miller (1956) famously wrote about human memory error in one of the most oft-cited articles in psychology entitled "The Magical Number Seven, Plus or Minus Two: Some Limits on Our Capacity for Processing Information". As a psychologist, Miller was originally interested in the natural limits of human memory, which he found for most people to be seven items in length, plus or minus two. Any longer than that would be problematic for memorizing the information. That is why telephone numbers in the United States are seven digits in length, excluding the area code, and why our social security numbers have nine digits, and are grouped in groups of three, two, and four. Miller said that chunking information in groups makes it easier to remember the whole. All of this makes sense from a memory perspective.

Miller also made some interesting insights into human behavior and error. He theorized that most human actions require the magic number seven, plus or minus two, in terms of the number of actions involved. And he found that more lengthy sets of human actions likely have multiples of seven, such as 14, 21, or 28 steps, and so on. In my own instruction, I often ask students to review their projects after they have analyzed a procedural task, and to report the number of steps in the analyses. Invariably, their task analyses consistently show multiples of seven, plus or minus two. It is an amazing demonstration of this principle, and it seems to never fail. As stated, human behavior, as documented in a task analysis, tends to follow a reliable arc of action, starting with a beginning, continuing with a middle, and culminating with an ending.

Further, Miller posited the most likely location where human error might occur, irrespective of the content of the task. That is, if the task was seven steps in length, he suggested that all things being equal, human error could be predicted at one point more than any other along the way. In fact, this point is around step number five.

Long ago, as an instructor of photography, I confirmed the assertion by Miller, but in a somewhat nonscientific way. I had made a set of reference sheets to help guide students through the procedure of developing black-and-white film, which would produce a negative, from which photographic prints could be made. With the advent of digital photography, many people today may be unfamiliar with the photographic process that was used until just a few years ago. Today, there is no need for a darkroom to make pictures, but a computer screen instead.

At that time, developing film required first the removal of the film from the 35mm cartridge, the loading of the film onto a metal reel, and the placement of the reel into a metal canister, all done in complete darkness. The reference sheets were intended to guide performance of students with the lights on, then with their eyes closed to simulate a darkroom, and then to practice in a completely dark room. For many students, this task was extremely difficult to master, and had a high consequence of error. The film could be affected if there was any light leakage, or streaks would be seen on the developed negatives if the film was not loaded correctly, or there would be bends or scratches on the negatives if the film was mishandled, making it difficult to make quality prints later on.

In retrospect, it became clear that students consistently made the most errors when performing this procedure around step five, all other things being equal. That is, about two-thirds of the way through the task, or at the two-thirds point of the second or third set of seven steps. The explanation for this is that the student's attention was likely heightened at the beginning of the task and at the end of the task, as the task was nearing completion. But it seems the student's attention seemed to wander, just around one-third of the way through the steps used to develop the film. In addition, consistent with Miller's suggestion, when analyzing most procedure tasks, the number of steps identified, invariably, was seven, plus or minus two, or a multiple of seven: 14, 21, 28, and so on.

The prediction and understanding of human error has much to do with performance support guides. The underlying goal of performance support guides is to reduce the probability of human error at the time of expected performance. That is, since error can be expected to occur in all that we do as humans, the question becomes how we can anticipate when errors will most likely be made, and what actions we should take to prevent them from occurring, to the best of our abilities.

Performance Support Guides

Performance support guides have variously been known over the years as job aids, job performance aids, and performance guides. The term performance support guides seems most descriptive of the various ways they appear today in the work setting. That is, they can now appear, for instance, as posters on the walls of production settings, as labels on service and delivery vehicles, or as embedded information that appears on a screen. The wide range of this information fulfills the common purpose of providing a guide to support an individual's on-the-job performance. As stated, in a complex society, performance support guides of some sort are around us all the time, helping to guide our behaviors and avoid errors. Here are some examples of performance support guides:

• Football quarterback who has the plays written on a wristband
• Take-off checklist/landing checklists
• Airplane safety information in the seat pocket in front of you
• Putting fuel in your car
• How to fill out a form
• The various components of a form
• Check-in kiosks at airports
• Check-out stations in a grocery store

There is an interesting, though somewhat tragic, history of the origination of using contemporary performance support guides. The story that is told is true, but whether it represents the true origination point of performance support guides can be debated. What is true is that performance support guides were used as a result of the story, and that it is the first instance in which use of such documents was mandated, even continuing today. This story occurs, as one might expect, in the aviation industry.

In 1934, several years before the start of World War II, the U.S. Army Air Corps invited several aircraft manufacturers to design and develop prototypes of a new multiengine bomber, and announced that there would be a competition to see which company's design would be awarded the contract. The requirements were that the airplane should fly at least 10,000 feet in altitude, for ten hours, with a top speed of at least 200 miles per hour. A fly-off was to be conducted at the Wilbur Wright Field in Dayton, Ohio, now known as Wright–Patterson Air Force Base. There were three finalists, and the Boeing B-17 airplane was deemed the favorite beforehand by the government.

The Boeing B-17 was named the "Flying Fortress" because it was capable of mounting machine guns on its top, at the bottom, and on the end tail, in addition to the large area inside to hold bombs. On October 30, 1935, the competitive fly-off occurred, with the Boeing B-17 competing with two other airplanes. The Boeing B-17 had been very impressive in flying all the way from Seattle to Dayton, Ohio. Unfortunately, as the airplane took off during the fly-off, with a highly experienced pilot and copilot at the controls, the airplane lifted from the runway, then unexpectedly plunged back down and crashed, killing all the crew members aboard, including Boeing's most experienced test pilot. Later, investigators discovered that the crew had forgotten to disengage the gust lock on the tail wing. The gust lock is engaged only when airplanes are parked on the ground, as a means to reduce the stress of wind on the wings while the aircraft is on the ground.

Since the prototype B-17 had crashed, it was immediately disqualified from the contract competition, even though it was the government's preferred design. Later, a legal loophole was found that allowed the government to consider the airplane again and, in the end, Boeing received the contract to produce the B-17. The first production of the airplanes was delivered in 1937, and by the end of World War II, there were over 4500 of these airplanes in service.

The story is part of U.S. aviation history, but it has some implications for work analysis as well. Afterward, it became apparent that even with a highly experienced crew, there was a likelihood of forgetting to do something of importance when flying this especially complex airplane. Unlike airplanes in the past, the B-17 had four engines and had in fact the most complicated set of controls of any airplane ever produced. With all that information to remember, the likelihood of forgetting even the smallest detail was greater than ever, even for these highly skilled pilots. From that time forward, a requirement was implemented that checklists should be prepared, part of which covered the preparation for take-off, and that the copilot would read each point on the checklist to the pilot. Today, that requirement continues as a routine safety practice, as mandated by the Federal Aviation Agency, for all commercial flights.

Thus, performance support guides originated from a tragic situation and loss of life, but over the years, the practice of reviewing a checklist before engaging in action that may also have potentially dire consequences has become standard practice. For instance, Atul Gawande, a surgeon, wrote a highly recommended book entitled *The Checklist Manifesto: How to Get Things Right* (2009) in which he extols the virtues of analyzing even the most mundane information, and generating a seemingly simple checklist to ensure that something of importance actually gets done. Indeed, the book explains in a simple and masterful way the essence of using a performance support guide.

Design Variables of Performance Support Guides

Performance support systems should be designed considering the following four considerations:

- *Location of the guide*—Where will the guide be located?
- *Nature of the behaviors*—What type of behaviors are involved?
- *Delivery of the message*—How does the guide communicate?
- *Users of the guide*—Who will be using the guide?

Location of the Guide

The location identifies where the performance support guide will be used, within the context of the work setting. Some options include the following:

- *External location*—The guide could be away from where the task is actually conducted, such as a poster, sign, or set of reference documents
- *Mobile*—The guide can be carried along with the employee, such as a booklet, set of reference cards, or small hand-held devices.
- *Embedded*—The guide has been engineered to be part of the task, usually involving virtual assistants, such as a help window, Siri on Apple devices, and Alexa on Amazon

Nature of the Behaviors

This consideration identifies the nature of the behaviors that will be presented on the guide.

- *Procedure*—Presenting the step-by-step way of doing something
- *Identify*—Showing the various parts and purposes of an object
- *Reference*—Making information available for access as needed
- *Intuitive*—Fixing something based on previous principles
- *Troubleshooting*—Matching a problem situation with causes and solutions
- *Inspection*—Guiding what to do when reviewing a process or product
- *Decision making*—Matching the possible options with decision considerations
- *Artificial intelligence*—Acquiring new patterns of understanding based on previous actions

Figure 15.2 shows how a procedure analysis was adapted for use as a work instruction sheet. Aside from being based directly on a task, the performance support guide might also be designed so that information can be accessed for reference, mostly from a database, such as a glossary of terms or set of technical information. In this sense, perhaps the most frequently used performance support guide of this type is called a parts and purposes table. As shown in Fig. 15.3, the analysis may also focus on the parts and the locations of the individual parts. Figure 15.4 shows an example of a parts and purposes analysis that defines the function of each of the parts. This approach is used to present the names of the parts of an observable object of some kind, such as a control panel or a computer screen. In the two examples, the parts and purposes analysis can be presented in visual or text form. Through the use of

Midwest Express Group	Doc Title	Pack the Skid		Type of Analysis	
				X Step By Step	Parts- Purpose
	Doc No.	2B Example	Page 1 of 4	Inspection	Process (Workflow)
				Troubleshooting	Information/Other

1. Locate part in put away location according to part number, quantity, and color from MEI Check Sheet.	• Ensure correct parts are packed on skid according to palletizing method • Part number, quantity, and color can be found on supplier label • Ensure that the correct part number will be palletized • FIFO procedure must be followed to ensure that parts are used in the order that they are received	
2. Begin palletizing parts according to layout	• Parts must be in proper location for ELP production • Containers will fit the dimensions of the skid when properly packed • Supplier labels must be visible • If it takes more than 5 minutes to locate proper part, call on team leader, then continue to palletize	• B and B2 containers and containers over 40lbs must be lifted by 2 associates; follow proper lifting techniques • Dollies should be used to help lift when possible • Parts must be securely nested on skids
3. Continue to palletize all parts on MEI Check Sheet using steps 4 and 5	If short parts, follow the Short Parts Procedure for a PSS Packing Associate	

Special Instruction & Protective Wear							Training		Revision		Approval	
Special Instruction						Prerequisite		Date		Production Team leader (AM)	
								Editor		Production Team leader (PM)	
Protective Wear	X	Cap	X	Glove	X	Sleeves	Qualified Trainer		Reason		Supervisor	
	X	Glasses	X	Shoes	X	Earplug					Manager	

Fig. 15.2 Example of a procedure analysis adapted as a performance support guide

pictures or line sketches, the location of the part is shown in relationship to the whole object, and a detailed description of the function of each part is also identified.

A parts and purposes analysis presents information that was gathered by analyzing the object, often with assistance of a subject-matter expert, much like what would be done with a task analysis. Many consumer products include such a table as a means to explain the object that they have purchased and an overview of its various components. This information is usually provided in the document before the steps are given, for instance, to assemble the object or install the software.

Delivery of the Message

This consideration is how the information in the guide will be presented. In most instances, the information from the task analysis should be converted in a way that best fits the purpose of the guide, including the following:

Task*: Part B: Identify the parts and purposes of the assembly station #1

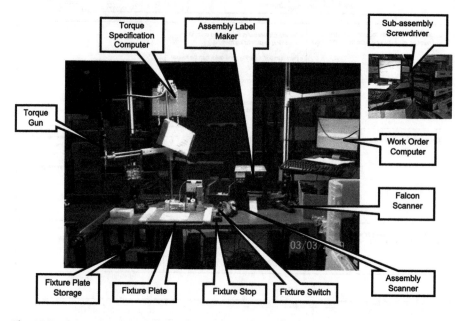

Fig. 15.3   Example of a parts and location analysis

Task*: Part B: Identify the parts and purposes of the assembly station #1 (Cont'd)

Part	Purpose
Torque Gun	To screw in and torque bolts to specification
Fixture Plate Storage	To storage the various fixtures used in the assembly area
Fixture Plate	To secure the bracket for each assembly during process
Fixture Stop & Fixture switch	To ensure that each assembly piece is complete
Assembly Label Maker	To print out individual labels for each assembly
Assembly Scanner	To scan each assembly
Falcon Scanner	To scan labels in receiving /shipping area
Work Order Computer	To maintain accurate control over each assembly work order
Sub-assembly Screwdriver	Part of assembly process before torque gun. (Used for part X000 only)

Fig. 15.4   Example of a parts and purposes analysis

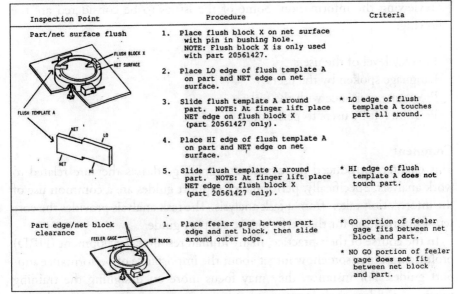

Gaging Tool HF1-62385
Parts 20561426 and 20561427

Inspection Point	Procedure	Criteria
Part/net surface flush	1. Place flush block X on net surface with pin in bushing hole. NOTE: Flush block X is only used with part 20561427.	
	2. Place LO edge of flush template A on part and NET edge on net surface.	
	3. Slide flush template A around part. NOTE: At finger lift place NET edge on flush block X (part 20561427 only).	* LO edge of flush template A touches part all around.
	4. Place HI edge of flush template A on part and NET edge on net surface.	
	5. Slide flush template A around part. NOTE: At finger lift place NET edge on flush block X (part 20561427 only).	* HI edge of flush template A does not touch part.
Part edge/net block clearance	1. Place feeler gage between part edge and net block, then slide around outer edge.	* GO portion of feeler gage fits between net block and part.
		* NO GO portion of feeler gage does not fit between net block and part.

Fig. 15.5 Inspection analysis adapted as a performance support guide

- *Text*—Using words to convey the message
- *Table*—Formatting the information into a table for reference
- *Figures with arrows and boxes*—Using directional arrows to suggest a sequence of activities
- *Icons, pictures, or drawings*—Using nonverbal information to convey the message
- *Combination*—Using a combination of text, pictures, drawings, and icons to convey the message

Figure 15.5 presents an example of an inspection analysis that has been converted into a performance support guide. Line drawings and arrows have been added to the guide to ensure users can identify the precise locations of the inspection points.

Users of the Guide

This consideration identifies who will likely be using the guide. It is interesting to note that the safety information provided in the seat pocket on many international airlines is presented as a series of drawings, instead of text, recognizing that passengers speaking different languages would likely be reviewing the information. Some of the issues to be considered are the following:

- Literacy level of the users
- Language spoken by the users
- Previous experience with the task
- Pressure felt by users to perform

Comment

This chapter introduced performance support guides as they are related to work analysis. Specifically, performance support guides are a common use of the information taken from a task analysis. The task analysis provides the core set of information for the performance support guide.

In the course of their practice, many human resource development (HRD) professionals may somehow forget about the importance of performance support guides. For instance, they may focus more on designing the training program, and lose their focus on what happens when trainees are required to perform what was learned after the training program. As a result, engineers, safety specialists, or quality staff members may be asked to develop the performance support guides when managers realize there is a need for one in the work setting.

HRD professionals are in a unique situation in this regard, given their understanding of the trainees and their ability to analyze work based on an understanding of the trainees. This statement does not propose that HRD professionals should be solely responsible for developing the performance support guides. But it does suggest that HRD professionals should have been the ones to propose the development of the performance support guides in the first place, and they can provide the task analysis information from which to base the documents, regardless of all those who are involved.

Reflection Questions

1. What are some of the performance support guides that affect your life?
2. How do these guides help reduce errors that you might make otherwise?
3. Reflect on a task analysis that you may have conducted, and consider how you would adapt the information for use as a performance support guide?
4. Which design consideration might be most important in your situation?
5. Consider what would be the consequences if a task analysis was not the basis for a performance support guide?

References

Gawande, A. (2009). *The checklist manifesto: How to get things right.* New York: Metropolitan Books.

Miller, G. A. (1956). The magical number of seven, plus or minus two: Some limits on our capacity for processing information. *Psychological Review, 101*(2), 343–352.

16

Performance Rating Scales

An area of practice of increasing importance to human resource development (HRD) professionals is the design and use of performance rating scales. Unfortunately, there seems much uncertainty about what constitutes best practice in this regard, especially when predetermined standards may not be available. Regardless, the analysis of tasks or individual competencies should underlie the design of all types of performance rating scales.

Performance rating scales have many different uses. For instance, managers use performance rating scales when they review a subordinate at the end of a review period. Individual employees use performance rating scales when they assess their own abilities relative to various individual competencies. And, HRD professionals use performance ratings scales to ensure that learning has occurred among trainees at the end of a training program.

Types of Performance Rating Scales

Performance rating scales are almost always used to measure some level of skill or the outcome of using the skill. Use of the term scale suggests that some behavior or product of the behavior is being measured. Performance ratings are not meant to be used to measure the extent of knowledge acquisition, as this would be more appropriate for cognitive test items, such as a test having multiple-choice-type items, matching-type items, or essay-type items. In a sense, measuring skills versus measuring knowledge can be distinguished by the following basic question: Who holds the pencil? For the most part,

© The Author(s) 2019
R. L. Jacobs, *Work Analysis in the Knowledge Economy*,
https://doi.org/10.1007/978-3-319-94448-7_16

performance rating scales involve a rater, who observes someone or something, and thus the rater holds the pencil. For cognitive test items, the individual taking the test holds the pencil.

The decision tree presented in Fig. 16.1, based on the work of my former colleague Bruce McDonald and myself, shows that the first question is whether knowledge or skills will be measured. For knowledge, cognitive test items would be most appropriate. For skills, a performance rating scale would be most appropriate, based on whether or not the rating would be based on predetermined standards. Having a predetermined standard means that the rater should refer to

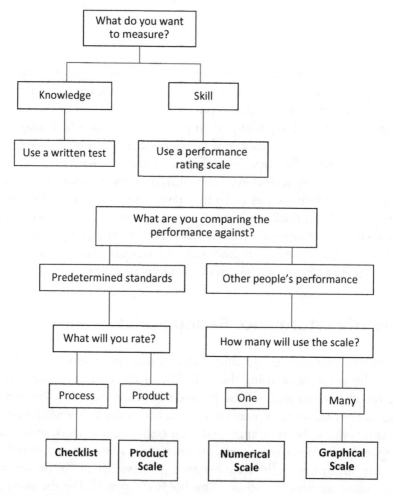

Fig. 16.1 Performance rating scale decision chart

an objective referent that serves as the standard. For the rater, the standard can be understood by one of the following methods: matching a text description and a real instance, matching a list of criteria with a real instance, or matching images or a model with the real instance. It is for this reason that Rummler and Brache (2013) call this performance requirement accuracy—the accuracy of the match between an actual instance and a standard.

Not having a predetermined standard also occurs with performance rating scales, and this frequently occurs when rating individual competencies. When a standard is not available, then raters must consider the individual competency and then provide a rating based on their own understanding of the individual being rated, often using other people as the standard. This is no different from the case when it is said that a cognitive test is graded on a curve, referring to the bell curve of a normal distribution. When using other people as the standard, it is more likely that there will be a wider distribution of ratings, which is preferable, since this indicates that there were individuals who were rated as being high, medium, and low, in a relative sense.

Not having a predetermined standard occurs in more instances than many HRD professionals might consider. For instance, many performance reviews do not have a predetermined standard, unless some measures of volume, rate, or productivity are included in the performance review.

When there are predetermined standards, the next decision point is based on what the rater will observe. One possibility is to observe a process, which is an ongoing activity of some kind. For instance, this might include observing a customer-service representative responding to a customer's problem, a manager conducting a performance review session, or a trainer delivering a training program.

The other possibility is to observe a product, which is something that could be a physical or virtual thing of some kind. For instance, this might include a completed design, a completed report prepared for management, or a set of software prepared to meet a customer's need. In each of these instances, there would be a predetermined standard comprising a list of attributes that the product should have.

The decision flowchart shows that if there are predetermined standards, and the phenomenon being rated is a process, then one should use a checklist. If there are predetermined standards, and the phenomenon being rated is a product, then one should use a product scale.

When there are no predetermined standards, then the next decision point is the number of people who will be serving as the rater. There are instances in which there might be just one person as a rater, such as when a person does a self-rating on a competency assessment. In some other instances, there might be one rater when a human resource staff member rates a candidate to be hired. It is more likely that there will be more than one rater, which then involves issues of calculating a coefficient of interrater reliability. This basically refers to the consistency across the various raters in their respective ratings of a person.

If there are no predetermined standards, and there is only one rater, then one should use a numerical scale. If there are no predetermined standards, and there is more than one rater, then one should use a graphical scale.

Designing Performance Rating Scales

As stated, there are four different types of performance rating scales. The types of performance rating scales are basically differentiated by whether or not the rater will be able to use a predetermined standard. Having a predetermined standard changes the nature of the information in the resulting document, and influences to a large extent the design considerations and the process. This section of the chapter describes the design components for each type of performance rating scale.

Checklists

Figure 16.2 presents a performance checklist that is located at the end of a structured on-the-job training module, and serves as an example of a checklist. Checklists measure an ongoing activity, and are usually based on information derived directly from a task analysis. Most checklists are based on the behaviors presented in a procedure analysis, though a checklist can be adapted from almost any pattern of work. As shown in the example, checklists should have the following components:

- Name of the task being observed
- Name of the individual being rated
- Name of the person doing the rating
- Date that rating occurred
- Listing of the behaviors of the task, based on the established standard
- Rating of each behavior, based on whether the behavior was observed and can be indicated by one of the following: Yes–No; Complete–Incomplete; Meets Criteria–Does Not Meet Criteria; Acceptable–Not Acceptable
- Final rating at the end of the document based on the ratings of each behavior

Task Name: Assemble the fuel canister (1730A-TK5-A000) **PERFORMANCE CHECKLIST**

	Step	Performance Criteria	Yes	No
1	Insert two fuel clips into canister bracket	Clips must be in correct position		
2	Move canister bracket to work station #1			
3	Engage fixture stop to lock bracket into place			
4	Remove canister from container and scan label			
5	Place canister assembly label to top of canister filter			
6	Use torque gun to attach bolts to assembly	Torque must be within specifications		
7	Remove quick disconnect stop on left side of tube			
8	Move canister to work station #2			
9	Push drain tube onto canister ports			
10	Push drain tube assembly onto canister port, aligning tube	Tubes must be aligned		
11	Install drain tube clip to drain holes	Drain tube clip must align with drain holes		
12	Install fuel tube assembly onto canister port	Clip must aligned with fuel tube		
13	Push pressure tube assembly onto canister port	White dot must align with canister		
14	Place canister into shipping container	Part must be oriented as specified		
15	Place cardboard lid on top of container			

Criteria: All steps must be completed without error

Employee: _____ **Date of Rating:** _____

Name of Rater: _____ **Overall Rating:** Complete/Not Complete

Fig. 16.2 Example of a checklist

Product Scales

Figure 16.3 presents a product scale that is used to inspect a completed bill of lading form, an important document whenever products are shipped. Not having the bill of lading completed accurately can lead to missed schedules and even legal consequences for supplier organizations. Product scales measure the attributes of a physical or virtual thing. In practice, product scales are often used as part of evaluating whether a product has achieved an acceptable level of quality, derived from the information from an inspection analysis. As shown in the example, product scales should have the following components:

- Name of the product being rated
- Listing of the attributes of the product, based on the established standard

Task Name: Inspect completed bill of lading form.   **FORM INSPECTION**

Inspection Point	Criteria	Yes	No
a. Name, address, and contact information of carrier	• Written legibly • Match with invoice information		
b. Name, address, and contact information of consignee	• Written legibly • Match with invoice information		
c. Shipment identification number	• Match with shipper's purchase order		
d. Name, address, and contact information of shipper	• Written legibly • Match with shipper's purchase order		
e. Truck trailer number	• Match with actual trailer number		
f. Name, address, and information where to send bill	• Written legibly • Match with purchase order		
g. Number of shipping units	• Match with purchase order		
h. Description of each article	• Match with purchase order		
i. Special handling remarks	• Specified as required		
j. Weight of each article	• Match with shipper's order		
k. Rate of each article	• Match with purchase order		
l. Total fees to be collected	• Exact match between funds owed and collected		
m. Shipper's signature	• Written legibly		

Criteria: All inspection points must be complete

Employee: _____ **Date of Rating:** _____

Name of Rater _____ **Overall Rating:** Complete/Not Complete

Fig. 16.3   Example of a product scale

- Rating of each attribute, based on whether the attribute was observed, as indicated by Yes–No; Complete–Incomplete; Meets Criteria–Does Not Meet Criteria; Acceptable–Not Acceptable
- Final rating at the end of the document based on the ratings of each attribute
- Name of the rater
- Date that the rating occurred

Numerical Scales

Numerical scales differ from the two previous types of performance rating scales, because they are intended to be used when there is no predetermined standard and they are used by only one person. Numerical scales measure the perceptions of one person when rating another person. Or a numerical scale can be used when individuals rate themselves. Perhaps numerical scales are used most often as a diagnostic tool when individuals are asked to rate themselves about whether they possess a set of abilities or behaviors, such as individual competencies. In this sense, graphical scales—the next type of scale discussed—should always be preferred over the use of numerical scales. Graphical scales reduce the possibility of misunderstanding the meaning of the behaviors to be rated.

Figure 16.4 presents an example of a numerical scale, based on having a manager rate another manager along a set of individual competencies.

Job Role: Manager   **NUMERICAL SCALE**

Employee:_____ **Business Unit:** _____

Name of Rater: _____ **Date of Rating:** _____

Instructions: To the best of your ability, rate the manager on the following individual competencies:

A. Builds Trust with Peer Managers

1	2	3	4	5
Unacceptable		Meets Expectations		Exceeds Expectations

B. Collaborates with Peer Managers

1	2	3	4	5
Unacceptable		Meets Expectations		Exceeds Expectations

C. Takes Initiative on Assignments

1	2	3	4	5
Unacceptable		Meets Expectations		Exceeds Expectations

D. Customer Focus

1	2	3	4	5
Unacceptable		Meets Expectations		Exceeds Expectations

E. Communication Skills

1	2	3	4	5
Unacceptable		Meets Expectations		Exceeds Expectations

Fig. 16.4 Example of a numerical scale

In practice, the individual competencies may be presented along with an operational definition. Two points of importance arise when designing and using a numerical scale. First, the behaviors to be rated do not require additional descriptions or behavioral anchors, since there is only one rater. It is assumed that the one rater clearly understands the meaning of each behavior. Thus, no further description would be required. Second, because there is only one person doing the rating, there is no need to be concerned about the reliability, or consistency, of the ratings.

In practice, numerical scales tend to have limited usefulness, but it is important to know that they exist, largely because they are often misused. In many instances, numerical scales are mistakenly used when there is more than one rater, such as the situation with graphical scales. As shown in the example, a numerical scale should have the following components:

- Name of the job role
- Instructions to the rater
- Name of the person doing the rating
- List of behaviors or competencies to be rated
- Ranges for the rater to select, such as Numbers from low to high; High, Medium, Low; Can Perform, Can Perform with Help, Cannot Perform; Not Difficult, Somewhat Difficult, Very Difficult

Graphical Scale

As stated, graphical scales are used when there is no predetermined standard and more than one person will be doing the rating. In this sense, graphical scales measure the perceptions of a set of individuals who rate another individual's abilities or characteristics. The raters review each behavior on the scale, review the anchors that define the ranges of the behavior, and then provide their best rating of the behaviors. For instance, a group of managers might be asked to rate whether an individual possesses the individual competencies required for a possible promotion.

As shown in Fig. 16.5, a graphical scale is similar to a numerical scale, but with the addition of statements that serve as behavioral anchors assigned to each scale range. At first glance, the statements may appear to be a minor addition to the document. The addition of the statements entails much planning to ensure that they meet the following criteria:

Job Role: Manager   **GRAPHICAL SCALE**

Employee:_____ **Business Unit:** _____

Name of Rater: _____ **Date of Rating:** _____

Instructions: To the best of your ability, rate the manager on the following individual competencies:

A. Builds Trust with Peer Managers

1	2	3	4	5
Does not follow through on commitments, closed manner when dealing with others		Follows through on commitments, open to giving information		Role model of consistency in meeting commitments, sharing information

B. Collaborates with Peer Managers

1	2	3	4	5
Seldom reaches out to other managers, unwilling to help others succeed		Spends time to get to know other managers, seeks assistance when needed		Develops relationships with other managers, open to suggestions from others

C. Takes Initiative on Assignments

1	2	3	4	5
Seldom takes responsibility, even when asked,		Responds to requests to complete assignments		Seeks out ways to ensure the work gets done

D. Customer Focus

1	2	3	4	5
Misinterprets customer requests, waits to be contacted by customer		Keeps customers informed, delivers on commitments, responds to needs		Anticipates needs, follows up to ensure satisfaction, solicits feedback

E. Communication Skills

1	2	3	4	5
Shows little interest in what what others say, unprofessional speaking or writing		Shares information as needed, listens and asks questions, speaks to others using appropriate tone		Demonstrates ease in sharing information, asks questions and ensures understanding

Fig. 16.5 Example of a graphical scale

- Statements show a logical progression within each behavior
- Statements within each behavior are mutually exclusive from each other
- Statements can be based on sets of descriptive phrases or descriptions of actual instances, and both should be easily visualized by the rater
- Statements are consistent across the various behaviors

- Statements are valid, or grounded, within the context of the work setting
- Statements are written in parallel form, and carefully edited to ensure clarity

Many graphical scales are also known as behaviorally anchored rating scales (BARS), as was introduced by Campbell, Dunnette, Arvey, and Hellervik (1973), in their classic article entitled: The Development of Behaviorally Based Rating Scales. In the article, the critical incident technique is mentioned as the most commonly used way of generating the behavioral anchor statements.

An example prompt question for the critical incident technique might be the following: Tell me a time when you were effective or ineffective in performing this behavior? As one might imagine, identifying a set of distinct behavioral anchors for a particular behavior from this prompt question takes some skill, requiring a cycle of conducting the interviews, editing the responses, and having stakeholders review and approve the anchors afterward.

Figure 16.5 presents an example graphical scale related to a set of individual competencies. The following are the components of graphical scales:

- Job role
- Purpose statement of the scale
- Name of the person doing the rating
- List of behaviors or individual competencies to be rated
- Ranges for the rater to select, such as High, Medium, Low; Can Perform, Can Perform with Help, Cannot Perform; Not Difficult, Somewhat Difficult, Very Difficult
- Statements that serve as behavioral anchors that are attached to each scale range, which give meaning to the ranges

In practice, unfortunately, many graphical scales are not designed with the care required, for them to be both reliable and valid. Reliability in this instance means whether a rater consistently gives the same rating repeatedly, known as test—retest reliability, and whether groups of raters give consistent ratings, known as interrater reliability. Validity in this instance means whether the list of behaviors and the behavioral anchors for each behavior actually represent the requirements of the work—known as content validity.

One does not need to review many instances of graphical scales in organizations to find one of two major issues that exist with the documents. This fact is disheartening from the perspective of those seeking to ensure best practice. Many graphical scales simply do not have any behavioral anchors attached to the scale ranges and thus should be considered as numerical scales. And, if they do have behavioral anchors, the statements are brief and not descriptive of the intended behaviors, having been generated in an expedient approach, and not in a systematic way.

As will be discussed in the next chapter, graphical scales are a critical part of identifying and assessing individual competencies. In fact, the behavioral anchors identified for the graphical rating scale are the same set of information used to denote the levels of demonstration of individual competencies.

Comment

As stated, more and more, HRD professionals are being asked to design performance rating scales, for a wide range of purposes. Performance rating scales are an important way of using information directly from a task analysis or a competency analysis. Checklists are the most common form of rating scale used by HRD professionals. Increasingly, as HRD professionals become more involved with talent management and development initiatives, there is a greater need to understand instances when there are no predetermined standards, for the development of numerical and graphical rating scales.

Reflection Questions

1. Were you aware that performance rating scales could be differentiated by whether they had predetermined standards?
2. Which type of performance rating scale seems most useful in your own situation?
3. Can you differentiate the differences between a checklist and a product scale?
4. Can you differentiate the differences between a numerical scale and a graphical scale?
5. Can you identify an individual competency, and then reflect on a set of behavioral anchors for that competency?
6. What are some of the issues in identifying the behavioral anchors?

References

Campbell, J. P., Dunnette, M. D., Arvey, R. D., & Hellervik, L. V. (1973). The development of behaviorally based rating scales. *Journal of Applied Psychology, 57,* 15–22.

Rummler, G., & Brache, A. (2013). *Improving performance: How to manage the white space on the organization chart.* San Francisco, CA: Jossey-Bass.

17

Competency Assessment and Development

How do organizations actually use the individual competencies that were discussed in Chaps. 11 and 12? By themselves, the individual competencies do not have much usefulness. The most common way they are used is through the processes of competency assessment and competency development. In many organizations, competency assessment and development have become part of the broader topic of talent management, a topic that many human resource development (HRD) professionals have become more involved in. Talent management is considered the entire process of selecting, recruiting, developing, and retaining the best individuals in organizations.

Discussions about talent management often include revising the organization's mission statement and considering whether an alternate perspective might be appropriate for understanding the organization, such as considering the notion of the T-shaped organization (Wladawsky-Berger, 2015). T-shaped organizations focus on both the deep knowledge that exists among individuals, as represented by the vertical line, and the cross-disciplinary, often social skills, which are represented by the horizontal line. Considering a T-shaped organizational configuration seems appealing for gathering knowledge, especially to managers in high-tech organizations, and being able to use that knowledge is critical for ensuring the organization's functioning. Underlying this consideration is that competency assessment and competency development provide a means to understand what gaps might exist in the abilities that are represented by both the vertical and the horizontal lines. Needless to say, discussions about talent management, and even conceptualizing a T-shaped organization, depend to a large extent on information from a work analysis.

© The Author(s) 2019
R. L. Jacobs, *Work Analysis in the Knowledge Economy*,
https://doi.org/10.1007/978-3-319-94448-7_17

Competency Assessment

Competency assessment refers to the process of identifying to what extent individual employees, and possibly their supervisors, rate on the extent that the employee possesses the individual competencies of a job role. The primary purpose of a competency assessment is typically for providing feedback and developing employees, not for reviewing or evaluating them. In this sense, competency assessment is a diagnostic activity to identify what gaps the employee might have relative to acquiring the individual competencies.

As discussed in Chap. 16, competency assessment is largely done through the use of a graphical scale, in which employees can assess themselves, and sometimes this is accompanied by having the employee's supervisor also assess the employee. That is, the use of a 360° feedback process. Other approaches might also be used as part of a competency assessment. In this respect, competency assessment may be used as part of a performance review but, as stated, the primary purpose of a competency assessment is for employee development.

The steps of a competency assessment typically include the following:

1. Employees are given a graphical rating scale, which includes a list of the individual competencies that have been identified for their job role.
2. Employees are asked to rate themselves on each of the individual competencies, considering the behavioral anchors for the ranges of the scale.
3. Employees may become more aware of their abilities related to the individual competencies in ways other than the graphical scale, including role plays, in-basket exercises, or even customer feedback.
4. Managers may be asked to rate the employee using the same graphical scale.
5. The results for the employees and managers are calculated, often in a group sense, as a means to maintain confidentiality of the responses.
6. Managers and employees meet to review their perspectives of the employee's abilities for each of the individual competencies.
7. Managers and employees negotiate what actions might be taken, and establish learning and development goals for the employee. One of the actions may be the recommendation to participate in a competency development program.
8. The learning and development goals often become recorded in the organization's learning management system.

A competency management system is the means by which employees can plan and keep track of how they acquire the individual competencies related to their job role. Competency management systems show the knowledge, skills, and attitudes related to each individual competency and the development opportunities to acquire the behaviors of the individual competency. Competency management systems are typically developed and maintained by the human resources function of an organization as it becomes a part of the employee's personnel record.

Competency management systems typically include the following information:

- List of the employee's career goals and aspirations as developed by the employee and the manager
- List of individual competencies associated with the job roles in an organization
- Inventory of the knowledge, skills, and attitudes that support each competency
- List of development opportunities to acquire the knowledge, skills, and attitudes
- Active database showing the employee's past record of participating in development opportunities
- Development plan that identifies the learning opportunities and the schedule for a defined period of time, which may or may not be mandatory in nature for the individual to follow through on the learning opportunities

Competency Development

Competency development refers to the planned series of experiential activities from which employees can become more aware of and hopefully begin to acquire the identified individual competencies related to their job role. Competency development can be considered as a part of both the employee development and career development components of HRD practice.

Competency development programs might be considered a part of employee development because, while they focus on a job role, they also have implications for helping employees perform better in their current and future jobs. And competency development might be considered as part of career development, primarily career planning, because it provides individuals with insights into their strengths and weaknesses relative to future career opportunities in the organization. Competency development represents the commitment of the organization for institutionalizing the individual competencies identified in the job role.

When possible, HRD professionals should seek out opportunities to participate and, when possible, take a leadership role in designing competency development programs in their organizations, especially since most have had limited experience in this particular type of HRD program. Competency development programs differ markedly from most other types of HRD programs. For instance, at first glance, competency development programs may appear somewhat similar to management development programs. But most management development programs have training objectives of some kind that are stated upfront and provide planned sets of learning opportunities for trainees to follow.

By design, competency development programs do not specify what learning outcomes will occur at the end of the program, as the learning outcomes depend on the willingness of each participant to consider undertaking some level of personal change. Competency development programs focus more on providing a series of challenging experiential activities, in which participants engage, often in a small group arrangement. Whatever learning that occurs among the participants is more the result of their own individual self-reflection and response to the feedback given by others. In this sense, competency development programs are quite unique types of HRD programs.

In practice, the success of competency development programs depends on matching the most appropriate experiences with the individual competencies to be acquired. As stated, competency development programs are not designed to introduce a set of training content per se. Instead, the programs typically provide a series of challenging experiential activities for individuals to respond to, and then to be observed as they engage in the process of completing the activities. In most instances, competency development programs have program facilitators who introduce the activities to the participants and nonparticipant observers, who are assigned to carefully observe and later provide feedback to the participants relative to each activity. Structured feedback at the end of the experience is a major feature of competency development programs. The feedback should stimulate reflection on what personal changes should be undertaken and what steps might be taken to accomplish the changes.

Table 17.1 shows a competency planning matrix that was used to design a competency development program. The vertical axis lists the individual competencies to be acquired through the program, and the horizontal axis shows the various experiential learning activities that would be included. In practice, it is desirable to have at least two learning activities matched with each individual competency. The planning matrix shows the use of several challenging situations, including the following.

Table 17.1 Example of a competency planning matrix

	Group Discussion	Extemporaneous Speech	Business Case Study	Role Play #1	Role Play #2	Targeted Interview	Networking Skills Inventory
Results Focus			■			■	
Customer Orientation					■		
Interpersonal Effectiveness	■	■		■	■		
Team Leadership	■	■	■			■	
Nurturing Others				■	■		
Networking with Others						■	■

- *Group discussion.* Participants are asked to read a case study situation, from which they are given a set of performance data from their project group, which is reported to be below the targeted goals for the project. Then they are to facilitate a group meeting, attended by confederates, to present the performance data and discuss what should be done about it for the future.
- *Extemporaneous speech.* Participants are given a topic related to their work, and with just five minutes of preparation, they are asked to stand up and give a prepared presentation of at least five minutes duration.
- *Business case.* Participants are given a complete business case study related to the job role, then they are asked to respond in writing to a series of questions about the case study.
- *Role play.* Participants are told they are now the senior project manager for several projects, and that they have encountered a staff member who has apparently not performed as expected. The participant is expected to conduct a performance review session with the staff member, with the expectation that the meeting will conclude with some decisive action for remediation.

- *Targeted interview.* Each participant will undergo a structured interview, many times conducted by an external consultant to discuss the individual competencies with the participant and their relevance to the individual.
- *Networking skills instrument.* Participants are asked to complete a survey that focuses on their perceived ability to network with others in the organization. This information is gathered for the entire group of participants, and is given back as group-based results.

A review of the list confirms that these activities focus more on providing participants opportunities for engaging in a challenging activity, then providing time for formal learning. Such a series of activities may occur over a period of two to three days.

In this sense, acquiring an individual competency basically results comes from having participants engage in a set of challenging activities, that are assumed to represent the behaviors associated with the individual competency. Participants receive feedback about their level of performance demonstrated in response to the challenging activities. Participants are also asked to reflect on what the individual competency means to them in a personal sense, and finally expressing a commitment toward making a change.

Competency development may have different meanings across organizations, so the actual program design as described here may differ to some extent. Regardless of the differences in the design of the program, the underlying intent remains the same. That is, to implement some kind of planned set of experiential activities that allow individuals to become more aware of and hopefully to acquire the identified individual competencies.

Comment

As stated, many organizations invest sizeable amounts of their resources in identifying individual competencies for certain job roles, administering competency assessments by which individuals can help diagnose their gaps relative to the individual competencies, and finally designing and implementing competency development programs. Competency development programs are the logical end product of this sometimes lengthy process in organizations. These topics were discussed in this chapter and in Chaps. 11 and 12.

The primary goal of embarking on this process is to develop individuals for consideration for future promotion. Knowing about the individual competencies can also assist in selection purposes of candidates being considered to be hired into the organization. So the goals related to individual competencies are often considered to be strategic in nature, as they help ensure that the organization can achieve its long-term aspirations.

Above all else, the question that often arises is whether the investment made in the individual competency process actually results in outcomes that are more valuable than the value of the investment. The outcomes may vary, but often include questions about whether future managers perform better in their job roles, whether these future managers remain longer with the organization, and whether future managers fit into the culture and carry out the mission with greater ease.

At this time, these questions have not really been systematically addressed, partly because of the difficulty in parsing out which aspects of the process had the most influence on whatever outcomes were identified and also because of the length of time involved. The process takes time to fully implement and to determine the effects in the organization.

Regardless, most managers view competency development as a valuable outcome in itself, and that seems to be sufficient. Allowing individuals the opportunity to learn more about themselves seems valuable, in the context of performing in some challenging situations, even though the individuals fully recognize that they are in a simulated environment.

Reflection Questions

1. Do you believe that individuals will respond honestly when they complete a self-report of their abilities to perform the individual competencies?
2. What individual competencies do you believe are necessary for your current role as an employee or as a student, and how well do you think you can perform these competencies now?
3. Have you ever participated in a program similar to a competency development program, and what were your impressions of the experience?
4. Do you understand how competency development programs differ from most management development programs in organizations?
5. How difficult do you think it would be to change some aspect of your personality, as a result of feedback from a competency development program?

Reference

Wladawsky-Berger, I. (2015, December 18). The rise of the T shaped organization. *The Wall Street Journal*. Retrieved from https://blogs.wsj.com/cio/2015/12/18/the-rise-of-the-t-shaped-organization/.

Part IV

Future Perspectives

The final section of the book, Part IV, addresses the future perspectives of work, the nature of the workplace, and work analysis. The book takes the position that work analysis must be responsive to the nature of work, as it has changed from being focused mostly on physical work to knowledge work. Now, work and the workplace seem to be undergoing change again, and the future implications of these changes should be explored as well.

18

Knowledge Work and Digital Talent

A skeptic might say that anyone who purports to know what lies ahead is either just guessing or simply being foolish. Many of us find ourselves making informal conjectures about the future, while sitting with friends over coffee. How can we really say with confidence what is around the corner, predicting events that have not been seen in a concrete sense? Those sentiments being given, there seem sufficient indicators to suggest what lies ahead in terms of the future of work. For the most part, the future of work is staring most of us immediately in the face. So in this case the future may not be so difficult to predict after all, when there is so much evidence to support what direction things are headed.

Knowledge Work and Economic Development

Human resource development has long been a component of economic development considerations (Zidan, 2001). Now, with the advent of knowledge work, this relationship has become even more prominent. As mentioned in Chap. 1, Peter Drucker made some relatively accurate predictions about the future nature of work from his then perspective in the late 1950s. At the time, he wrote that work would become more complex and require greater cognitive abilities. Drucker was an especially astute observer of organizations and, even though information and communications technology had not arrived in society to any extent, that being just the beginning of sending satellites into space, he could likely interpret what changes were coming in organizations. How could any advanced society continue to prosper and be based mostly on the

© The Author(s) 2019   **245**
R. L. Jacobs, *Work Analysis in the Knowledge Economy*,
https://doi.org/10.1007/978-3-319-94448-7_18

production of things, and not ideas? That was Drucker's central point in his book with an interesting, but purposely contradictory title, *Landmarks of Tomorrow*. How can a landmark be seen, if it doesn't exist?

In truth, while Drucker was accurate on most points, he missed one key aspect when making his prediction about the emergence of knowledge work. Drucker, and most others, missed the point by stating that knowledge work would be the primary domain of those workers who were highly educated, such as professionals and scientists. In fact, we now know that knowledge work has become part of almost all jobs, regardless of the educational requirements and their level in organizations.

Drucker's point was not to devalue physical work in any way. Instead, he recognized the increasing value of knowledge work, which would eventually overcome physical work in most societies. One indicator of this today are the various reports that consistently show that the value of the service sector is growing faster than, and in some countries is now greater than, the manufacturing sector (Cappelli & Keller, 2013; *Evolution of Work and the Worker*, 2014). For economists, the service sector often serves as a proxy for knowledge work, because of its use of ideas as a product. Knowledge work now truly differentiates organizations and nations as well.

National economic and workforce development depends on the ability to move from physical work to knowledge work, over time (Jacobs & Hawley, 2009). This fact has been well illustrated when considering the progress of, say, Singapore since its independence in 1965 through today. At the beginning, Singapore was extremely poor, not anything like it is today. Led by a group of wise government officials, Singapore purposely focused on attracting employers who required employees to perform simple, repetitive, assembly-type tasks (Lee, 2000). From a work analysis perspective, most of the work involved performing simple manufacturing and assembly procedures, doing the work step-by-step.

But the government leaders did not necessarily see this type of work as being the end product for their nation, only as a means to move to the next phase of its economic development. As its educational infrastructure improved, the Singapore government changed its strategic focus to begin attracting organizations requiring more complex assembly tasks, including computer microchips and wafers, then onto information technology research and development, followed by bioengineering research and development, and now onto its current focus on advanced technologies and artificial intelligence research and development. Even though Singapore is small in stature, it often provides an illustrative benchmark for other counties to try to follow, transitioning from an economy based solely on physical work to high levels of knowledge work, across all segments of the workforce.

My own observations over the past few years while working with organizations and government agencies in Ethiopia, a now thriving developing nation in east Africa, suggests a parallel for what has occurred in Singapore. Large industrial parks have now been established near the capital of Addis Ababa, employing tens of thousands of employees, to perform simple, repetitive tasks, mostly in the clothing assembly and textile business sector. Perhaps a shirt or pair of pants that you now own, displaying a well-known designer label, was actually assembled by one of these individuals in Ethiopia. The workers all wear their assigned uniforms when they go to work, arrive for the work shift at the assigned time, and stay at their work until the shift is over.

This may sound relatively unremarkable until one understands that all of these events constitute a relatively new life and work experience for most of these individuals. In return, they receive for their efforts a living wage and benefits on a reliable basis. Only time will tell us how long Ethiopia, and other similar developing nations, will depend on this kind of work, before beginning its own climb up the economic value ladder, seeking to attract employers who require employees to perform more complex assembly work. The same pattern of advancement has been observed in many other nations over the years, including Ireland, South Korea, and Malaysia.

To declare the emergence of work knowledge in most work settings today is somewhat similar to stating that the sky is blue. To even the most casual observer, the statement is an obvious fact of contemporary life; everyone agrees about its basic truth. Interest in knowledge work has relevance for all nations and organizations, regardless of their level of development. At some point, eventually, in the near future, the future of work will impact all organizations and nations. The global economy dictates that knowledge work will have implications on an equal basis.

How to understand and plan for knowledge work has been an issue of concern for government policy makers, researchers, educators, and organization managers alike. Each group has a vested interested in helping to respond to the emerging situation. Several informative reports have recently been released by global consulting firms and nongovernmental agencies. The following is a list of some of the most helpful resources:

- Navigating the future of work: Can we point business, workers, and social institutions in the same direction? (July 2017, Issue 21). Special issue of the *Deloitte Review*.
- *Workforce of the future: The competing forces shaping 2030*. (2018). London, UK: Pricewaterhouse Coopers.
- *Technology, jobs, and the future of work*. (2017). New York: McKinsey Global Institute.

- *Inception report for the global commission on the future of work.* (2017). Geneva: International Labour Organization.
- *The future of jobs: Employment, skills and the workforce strategy for the fourth industrial revolution.* (January 2016). Geneva: World Economic Forum.

These reports, among several others, have been particularly helpful in describing what the future of work might look like, including an understanding of knowledge work. It is interesting to note that each of the resources, though independently produced, seem to converge on explaining, more or less, the same set of ideas about what the future of work will look like. As stated, there seem to be sufficient indicators all around us to allow astute observers to make informed predictions with some confidence.

In general, the following is a synthesis of information from the reports relevant to the future of work and work analysis:

- Technology will play an increasingly important role in work, through the use of digital technologies and artificial intelligence.
- In many respects, automated robots will continue to replace the physical work now being done by people, placing greater emphasis on the cognitive abilities of individuals.
- Technology will continue to make the work more complex, since it will be necessary for people to learn about the technology and the work as well, such as big data, 3D printing, robotics, and artificial intelligence.
- Communications technology will continue to disrupt the traditional work setting in which everyone comes together in one location, such that the work setting of today may evolve in totally unpredictable ways in the future.
- At the same time, human interactions are likely to become even more important, even though people may not be physically located near to each other.
- Continuous learning, on a lifelong basis, will have even more strategic importance, enabling individuals to respond to new information, with the learning occurring as a result of both formal and informal opportunities.
- Digital talent, digital fluency, and digital platforms are terms that have emerged that suggest a person's ability to work in environments in which information and communications technology have become a critical part of their jobs.
- Digital talent has become a highly valued ability, even though most resources do not provide an explicit definition of the term.
- The traditional understanding of a job, with its defined boundaries, will continue to undergo much scrutiny, leading some to question whether jobs will continue to exist in the same way as they have in the past (Slaughter, 2015).

- Given the pervasive nature of technology and automation, individuals should become more aware of the tasks they can perform and add value, which technology would have a difficult time replacing (Dewhurst, Hancock, & Ellsworth, 2013).
- Innovation will often come about in sudden spurts, often based on implementing new software or the introduction of new products or entry into new markets, requiring the ability to adapt and be flexible when confronted with new situations.
- Educational systems should begin to evolve their approaches in alignment with the new types of work and the workplace, and prepare students for a work environment in which job boundaries are increasingly uncertain and the permanence of jobs themselves will become increasingly tenuous.
- There will likely continue to be a relative disconnect between wages and educational achievement, as organizations will be subject to cost pressures from the global economy. Yet, much value will be placed on individual possessing recognized credentials based on the acquisition of both knowledge and skills.

Clearly, knowledge work and technology have become intertwined, in a broad sense. How jobs will change because of the influence of technology can already be readily seen in many workplaces. Technology has often been considered simply as a tool, or resource to use when performing the work. If the futurists are to be believed, technology may become far more integrated in assisting humans to get the work done.

Digital Talent

Perhaps no other term has encapsulated the future of work more than the emergence of the term digital talent (Kane, Palmer, Phillips, Kiron, & Buckley, 2017). Though most authors seem uncertain of its precise meaning and origin, digital talent first appeared in the popular management literature in the past few years, along with the somewhat related term of digital transformation. Digital talent has now seemingly become a catch word for the changing nature of future work. That is, the future of work is about the pervasive use of ITC, both in a broad sense, which refers to using technology across all aspects of an organization, and in a narrow sense, which refers to using technology for specific applications.

There seems no agreed-upon definition for the term digital talent. In a general sense, it suggests that technology has now become a part of most jobs, and that the next wave of employees should possess the appropriate knowledge and skills in technology to meet the emerging challenges. That prospect has become a serious area of concern for many global managers. For instance, this author serves on an advisory committee assembled by an international multinational corporation, with the specific task of recommending to the organization about how to understand and respond to the issues related to digital talent.

Jerome Buvat, in a *Wired* magazine article in 2018, declared that because of the scarcity of digital talent among the workforce, there is now a war occurring among companies to find more people who possess this ability. Numerous other resources have declared that a startling gap now exists both at the national and organizational levels, calling on policy makers, educators, and senior managers alike to view the current situation with particular alarm and that it is worthy of immediate attention. Other authors have similarly called out the need to address the apparent national skills gap (Baker, Sindone, & Roper, 2017).

Given that no common definition exists for the term, digital talent, such declarations seem to resonate with most managers as mostly being true but, at the same time, they seem to frustrate them as well. Consider that almost everyone agrees on the inferred meaning of the term digital, referring to all things related to communications technology. And everyone has a sense of the term talent, referring to what individuals possess. Yet, when the terms are combined, there remains much uncertainty about its specific meaning and, by extension, what should be done about it.

The following are some potential definitions that might be considered from a work analysis perspective:

- Digital talent refers to a set of technology-oriented knowledge and skills, based on job analyses conducted on specific jobs.
- Digital talent refers to a set of technology-oriented knowledge and skills, based on an occupational analysis conducted across job roles.
- Digital talent refers to an individual competency, based on a competency analysis conducted across multiple job roles.
- Digital talent refers to a core competency of an organization, based on a competency analysis that identifies the areas in which the organization excels.

My own view of digital talent has been influenced much by informally discussing the topic with managers from the United States, China, South Korea, Malaysia, and India, among other countries. Each of them has provided their own perspective, logically based on the context of their respective organizations. From these discussions, my belief is that, in practice, the term digital talent can refer to all of these situations at once, depending on the referent being used. That is, whether the referent is a specific job, an occupation, an individual competency, or an entire organization. Unfortunately, most authors neglect to clarify their precise referent, leaving it to the reader to make their own interpretations.

In spite of this uncertainty, what seems clear from the various definitions presented is that work analysis should play a prominent role in helping to understand the term. That is, any discussion seeking to advance an understanding of digital talent should invariably recognize the role of work analysis as part of that definition. Otherwise digital talent will remain, for most managers, a broad, sketchy, ill-defined concept.

There is no doubt that the term digital talent somehow captures the essence of the future of work. That is, broadly speaking, having an understanding of and ability to use technology will become a requirement across all jobs. Moving beyond this point requires additional information for consideration.

Comment
The future of work has been a topic of much interest, especially among government leaders, educators, and organization managers. How to know what the future holds is always a challenge, but there are numerous indicators to suggest the future of work. Work will become more dependent on technology and the ability of individuals to understand and use technology as a means to achieve new goals.

The term digital talent has emerged as a way of describing the requirements of the future workforce. There is much uncertainty about the precise meaning of this term, but it nevertheless seems to capture a common set of understandings. Work analysis should be a part of any discussions related to digital talent, because of the need to make explicit the nature of how work will undergo change.

Reflection Questions
1. Can you identify from your own experience some situations in which the work has changed?
2. Considering the given situations, what was the role of technology before the changes and after the changes?
3. What does the term digital talent mean to you, from your experience in the workplace?
4. Which definition of digital talent best fits your own understanding and experience in the workplace?
5. Can you think of some examples in which technology has become a part of doing the work?

References

Baker, E. A., Sindone, A., & Roper, C. (2017). Addressing the skills gap: A regional analysis. *Journal of Applied Business and Economics, 19*(8), 10–21.

Cappelli, P. H., & Keller, J. (2013). A Study of the extent and potential causes of alternative employment arrangements. *ILR Review, 66*(4), 874–901.

Dewhurst, M., Hancock, B., & Ellsworth, D. (2013, January–February). Redesigning knowledge work. *Harvard Business Review.* Retrieved from https://hbr. org/2013/01/redesigning-knowledge-work.

Evolution of Work and the Worker. (2014, February). New York: The Economist Intelligence Unit.

Jacobs, R. L., & Hawley, J. (2009). Emergence of workforce development: Definition, conceptual boundaries, and future perspectives. In R. MacLean & D. Wilson (Eds.), *International handbook of technical and vocational education and training.* Bonn, Germany: UNESCO-UNEVOC.

Kane, G. C., Palmer, D., Phillips, A. N., Kiron, D., & Buckley, N. (2017, Summer). *Achieving digital maturity: Adapting your company to a changing world.* MIT Management Review and Deloitte University Press Retrieved from https://www2. deloitte.com/content/dam/insights/us/articles/3678_achieving-digital-maturity/ DUP_Achieving-digital-maturity.pdf.

Lee, K. Y. (2000). *From third world to first: The Singapore story—1965–2000.* New York: Harpers.

Slaughter, S. (2015, October 25). No job title too big, or creative. *New York Times, ST2.*

Zidan, S. (2001). The role of HRD in economic development. *Human Resource Development Quarterly, 12*(4), 437–443.

19

Future Directions of Work Analysis

This book has sought to take a forward-look approach to work analysis. That is, the approach to work analysis has been to consider the area of practice in terms of today's challenges in organizations and societies. More specifically, the approach has sought to recognize the two major components of work analysis, in response to the emergence of knowledge work. In doing so, readers should realize by now that work analysis has moved well beyond the techniques associated with the Industrial Era, an economic age that began at the turn of the twentieth century. At that time, work analysis was primarily used to document simple, repetitive tasks, mostly in the form of procedures, and used primarily to identify and eliminate wasted specific actions.

With the advent of knowledge work across most jobs, work analysis has undergone much change, moving forward to meet the challenges of today's workplace. Today, work analysis has a far wider range of uses than ever before. So work analysis has progressed both in many intended purposes and the techniques used to support those intentions. What hasn't changed is the fundamental principle that documenting what people do in the workplace remains an important activity in organizations.

Now, there is a need to understand work analysis in the looming digital age, and how work analysis can be used to consider how to meet the challenges that it presents. The previous chapter summarized some additional thoughts about knowledge work. Now it seems prescient to extend that information into the future practice of work analysis. As stated, there are many indicators that suggest what will likely happen next in terms of the future of work, so those predictions are made with some level of confidence. Many authors are recognizing the digital age as being truly unique and disruptive compared to

© The Author(s) 2019
R. L. Jacobs, *Work Analysis in the Knowledge Economy*,
https://doi.org/10.1007/978-3-319-94448-7_19

past economic ages, simply because of the influence of information and communications technology and likely advances in artificial intelligence.

For one thing, it may not seem far-fetched to suggest that, in the future, automated robots will begin to replace the physical work done by humans. Currently, industrial robots are a well-established part of most manufacturing and production work settings, and the various work analyses have documented how individuals interact with and control the robots. Now there is the future possibility that the robots themselves, through some form of advanced artificial intelligence, might become independent agents in the work setting, working alongside their human counterparts.

To some extent, robots already have some limited levels of "thinking" based on inputting algorithms from known and established situations. That is, in practice, robots can differentiate by the shape of the object, which part to select next from a loading palette, and then place it in the correct position at the next station, simply because those actions are known beforehand. When robots can truly extrapolate learning from previous situations to new, unknown situations, such as with the now-experimental driverless automobiles, is when real human-like cognitive activity can be said to occur.

Many scholars identify four major economic eras:

- *Mercantile Era (1500–1900).* Mostly pursued by European countries to gain control of global trade and acquire as much wealth—gold, silver, and rare commodities—as possible. The Mercantile Era is characterized by the rise of colonial powers, and the conflicts that occurred as the countries sought dominance over each other.
- *Industrial Era (1990–2000).* The use of innovative management and production practices to produce products on a large scale, replacing the craftsman as the focus of most economies. No economy has impacted the livelihood of individuals on a global basis more than the Industrial Era.
- *Information Age (1950–2010).* The advent of the computer, the launching of communication satellites, the Internet, and communications technology have all combined to change the workplace in demonstrable ways, and all aspects of societies for that matter. The Information Age opened potential opportunities for economic activity and the use of knowledge that could not possibly be conceived of beforehand.
- *Digital Age (2010–).* Beyond the Information Age, the Digital Age has now introduced smart technologies, such as self-driving cars, which on their own suggest that another economic era may be upon us. Again, the Digital Age brings with it implications for the nature of work and the workplace of the future.

Each of the economic eras is relatively distinct from the others, though the dates are necessarily imprecise and the eras do not clearly indicate a straight line, with the option available for a return. Many developed countries are seeing many consumers show greater interest in craftsmanship, because of the perceived sameness of mass-produced products. People want something different, as can only be created by the hands of another person. Further, each economic era suggests dramatic differences in the nature of work. For instance, the Industrial Era reduced the need for workers to possess their own skill set, relying more upon the modes of production. Workers became extensions of machines.

While the economic eras have changed the nature of work, the actual patterns of the work have not really changed that much. That is, the basic sets of actions that humans use to accomplish the work. Even when performing the most complex work, people still complete the series of steps of a procedure, solve known and unknown problems, consider the various conditions to make decisions, inspect and critically analyze objects and ongoing activities, and adjust things to make them better, among other patterns of behaviors. And work processes still basically govern how things get done.

So in spite of declarations about how work has changed, how people engage in that work remains more or less the same. Of course, in today's knowledge work, the proportion of the patterns of behavior and the level of unknown situations that people are required to deal with have changed dramatically. Human behavior has not necessarily changed, but the challenges of knowledge work have certainly changed the content and the arrangement of the work in demonstrable ways.

In the face of current and future challenges, it seems appropriate to offer some recommendations relevant to documenting work, as follows:

- Even though work has become more knowledge-based and less visible, human resource development (HRD) professionals should continue to understand work as units of behavior, and to be able to visualize abstract behavior in concrete terms.
- HRD professionals should continue to keep in mind the two major components that comprise work analysis, since no other group of individuals will likely possess the same clarity about what should be done to achieve the intended goals.
- In spite of discussions about the future of work, much of the work done in organizations may not be immediately affected by these changes, requiring that HRD professionals should have a flexible perspective of work analysis, based on a well-developed professional tool kit.

- HRD professionals should be keen observers of changes in how work is done in their organizations, suggesting that even the slightest changes might in fact affect the demands on employees to perform the work.
- The increasing use of technology in the workplace should be matched by increased use of technology by HRD professionals as a means to conduct a work analysis, seeking to broaden the involvement among stakeholders and reduce the cycle time of updating information.
- HRD professionals should not be necessarily swayed by the oftentimes seductive aspects of using technology to conduct a work analysis, as the true value of the information will depend on how it will be used to address a practical problem, not the latest technique to gather the information.
- Finally, HRD professionals should be aware of the emerging role of information and communications technology, recognizing that technology as a resource will be a major part of almost all work.

For many HRD professionals, work analysis represents an area of practice requiring a specialized set of knowledge and skills. In addition, the perception exists that work analysis itself requires a set of individual competencies as well. For instance, the ability to analyze, that is, distinguishing the parts from the whole, and the ability to synthesize, that is, putting the parts back together in a new way. That work analysis may also require individual competencies, not unlike acquiring most other complex HRD professional skills. These can be developed through reflective practice.

Appendix: Example S-OJT Modules

A. Optimize process unit product yield
B. Develop the IP network preventive maintenance work plan
C. Conduct inspection of components before welding
D. Prepare IP network health check report

© The Author(s) 2019
R. L. Jacobs, *Work Analysis in the Knowledge Economy*,
https://doi.org/10.1007/978-3-319-94448-7

A-1: Optimize Process Unit Product Yield

Refinery Location: MAA/MAB/SHU

Overview: The Process Engineer must optimize each process unit's product yield in order to maximize production, revenue and profitability. This training guide presents the correct procedures for completing this task. Failure to perform this task correctly may result in inefficiency and underutilization of the process unit's production potential.

Trainee Prerequisites: Trainees must have completed the following prerequisites:

- IP-21 software information from KNPC intranet (Technical Services page)
- LIMS software information from KNPC intranet (Technical Services page)
- PRO II software or equivalent
- Oil Industries Orientation Program (PTC)
- Training Guides C-1 and F-1 for this discipline

Required Resources: Assemble the required tools, materials, equipment and documents:

- Unit Operating Manual for process units
- Process Plant P&IDs
- IP-21 software (installed on desktop)
- LIMS software access
- PRO II software access or equivalent

Expected Time to Learn: 3 Days

Step	Comment	People Involved
1. Identify the process unit(s) for which the products yield is to be optimized.	Process units are assigned to Process Engineers by the Senior Process Engineer.	Senior Process Engineer
2. Monitor the products yield of the assigned process unit(s) on a daily basis.	Monitor products yield trends by plotting yield vs. days. Refer to Training Guide C-1 to learn how to calculate the unit's products yield.	
3. Conduct simulations to determine the best achievable products yield for the process unit.	Conduct simulations using PRO II or equivalent software.	Senior Process Engineer
4. Compare the actual (calculated) products yield for the unit with the expected/design yield.	If a gap exists between the actual product yield and the expected/design yield, identify the parameter(s) which might be affecting the yield, including (but not limited to): • Pressure • Temperature • Reflux • Gas to oil ratio • Stripping steam to product ratio • Reactor inlet temperature (RIT) • Reactor outlet temperature (ROT) • Heater coil outlet temperature (COT)	

Step	Comment	People Involved

5. Identify the optimum operating parameters by performing small incremental changes at a time in one of the operating parameters and monitor the product yield difference.	To perform this step correctly:
	
	 • Check the difference between the actual product yield and the expected/design yield
	
	 • Check the values of the relevant parameters when the difference is minimal
	
	 • Check parameters that can affect the yield of the more valued products. For example, in the distillation column:
	
	    ○ Increasing the feed temperature (COT)
	
	    ○ Increasing the draw temperature
	
	    ○ Reducing operating pressure
	
	    ○ Reducing reflux
	
	 • Continue making the small changes until they start to affect product quality
	
	 • Identify the optimum values for all relevant process operating parameters
		Senior Process Engineer
		
		 Operations Department

Step	Comment	People Involved
6. Recommend to Operations the process parameters that will optimize products yield.	Recommend the optimized value for all the relevant process operating parameters to maximize the products yield.	Operations Department
7. Document the products yield optimization findings.	Summarize the findings of the products yield optimization work.	
	Update the documents/records that are maintained in both hard and soft copy.	

A-1: Review Plant Logbook/Maintenance Register

PERFORMANCE CHECK

Employee Name: _____

Directions: Observe each step in the order shown and rate as follows. **Yes** means that the employee was able to complete all steps without help. **With Help** means that help is required on some steps. **No** means that the employee required extensive help on one or more steps. Provide comments to explain why a **With Help** or **No** rating was given. A **Qualified** overall rating requires **Yes** on all steps.

Step	Ability to Complete Steps			Comments
	Yes - 3 -	With Help - 2 -	No - 1 -	
1. Review operating data for all three shifts for the previous day from the Shift Supervisor's logbook.				
2. Review important information from the Shift Controller's logbook for all three shifts of the previous day.				
3. Review information from the maintenance register for all three shifts of the previous day				
4. Arrange a meeting to discuss the plant problem(s) with the respective department and prepare a possible solution.				
Total Scores:				Overall Score:

Date of Check _____   Overall: Qualified _____   NOT Qualified _____

Checker's Signature _____   Employee's Signature _____

Discipline: Operations Engineer   Module A: Monitor Refinery Plant Performance/Maintenance   A-1: Optimize Process Units Process Yield

A-1: Develop the of IP Network Preventative Maintenance Work Plan

Training Location: Back office location

Overview: The Back Office IP Network Engineer must develop a work plan to guide preventative maintenance activities of the IP network. This training guide presents how to develop the parts of the work plan. Failure to perform this task correctly may in omitting critical parts of the IP network preventive maintenance.

Trainee Prerequisite: Trainees must have completed the following prerequisite:

   o Back Office Maintenance: Basics and Advanced

Required Resources:

   o Switch and Router Configuration Handbook
   o Fiber Cloud Network Specifications
   o IP Network Work Plan Handbook

Step	Comment	People Involved
1. Verify the back office locations and staff involved in the work plan.	Refer to Back Office Layout and Design specifications to determine location.	Unit manager should be informed that work plan is being developed.
2. Identify the recommended IP network preventative maintenance schedule.	Refer to IP Network specifications to determine schedule Schedule on the work plan must match the recommended schedule	Unit manager should approve the schedule to ensure availability of staff.
3. Identify the components of a work plan as presented in the IP Network Operations Handbook.	Work components should be listed in the Handbook Appendix. Make certain that the most recent version of the Handbook is used.	B-O engineer
4. Develop a draft of the Work Plan and submit Work Plan to unit manager.	The components of the work plan must match specifications in the Handbook.	• B-O engineer • Unit manager
5. Revise the work plan based on feedback from unit manager.	All fields of the work plan must be completed.	Contact the unit manager if there are any questions or issues.
6. Post the work plan on the internal system.	All staff must be aware of the work plan.	B-O engineer

A-1: Develop the IP Network Preventative Maintenance Work Plan

PERFORMANCE CHECK

Employee Name: _____   Date: _____

Steps	Ability to Complete Step			Comments
	Yes - 3 -	With Help - 2 -	No - 1 -	
1. Verify the back office locations and staff involved in the work plan.				
2. Verify the back office components to be included in the inspection.				
3. Identify the components of a work plan as presented in the IP Network Operations Handbook.				
4. Develop a draft of the Work Plan and submit Work Plan to unit manager.				
5. Revise the work plan based on feedback from unit manager.				
6. Post the work plan on the internal system.				
Total				

Overall: Qualified _____   NOT Qualified _____

Date of Check _____

Employee's Signature _____

Checker's Signature _____

Position: IP Network Back Office Engineer   Module A: Conducting preventive maintenance on the IP network   A-1: Develop the IP Network PM Work Plan

D-4: Conduct Inspection of Components Before Welding

Training Location: MAA/MAB/SHU

Overview: In order to conduct an inspection of components before welding, the Inspection Engineer must ensure the proper methods are used. This training guide presents the procedure for completing this Inspection. Conducting an inspection of components before welding is an important expectation of the Inspection Engineer and if not performed properly may cause equipment damage, injury to personnel, or insufficient welds.

Trainee Prerequisites: Trainees must have completed the following:

* Maximo System Training
* Methods of Equipment Cleaning
* Fundamental of Engineering Drawings
* Reading Schematic and Symbols
* Design, Fabrication and Inspection of Pressure Vessels (American Society of Mechanical Engineers (ASME) Section VIII & American Petroleum Institute (API) 510)
* Design, Fabrication and Inspection of Petroleum Pipe Lines (ASME American National Standard Institute (ANSI) B31.3 & API 570)
* Design, Fabrication and Inspection of Fired Heaters
* Design, Fabrication and Inspection of Water Tube Boilers
* Design, Fabrication and Inspection of Storage Tanks (API 620, 650 & 653)
* Design, Fabrication and Inspection of Heat Exchangers
* Design, Fabrication and Inspection of Power Piping (ASME ANSI B31.1)
* Principals of Welding and Heat Treatment

- Welding and Brazing ASME Section IX
- Principals of Metal Cutting and Machining
- Basics of Non Destructive Testing (NDT)
- Corrosion in the Refining Industry
- Material Selection and Properties
- Mechanical Failure Analysis and Prevention
- Metallurgy for Non Metallurgist

Required Resources: Assemble the required tools, materials, equipment and documents:

- Welding procedure specification (WPS)/Inspection advice ticket (IAT)
- NDT team
- Inspection tools
- Inspection Manual Chapters IC-24 and IC-25

Expected Learning Time: 5 Days

| Discipline: Inspection Engineer | Module D: Manage Welding and Heat Treatment Activities | D-4: Conduct Inspection of Components Before Welding |

Inspection Point	Criteria	Comment
1. Receive work order information.		May be received by phone, pager or Maximo system.
2. Review data and drawings of components to be welded.	Use the latest drawings. Ensure exact material to be welded.	
3. Inspect overall condition of the components.	Components must be free of oil, grease, debris, paint or any other material that might affect the weld.	Confirm materials to be welded.
4. Check the fit up between components.	Follow WPS or IAT instructions for the same. Edges must fit together with a gap for strength weld.	Use scale to measure gap if in doubt.
5. Verify the availability of welding rods/ electrodes.	Correct rods/electrodes must be used as specified in WPS/IAT. Substitute rods/electrodes may be used ONLY as specified in IC-25.	Issue IAT in case of rods/electrodes change.
6. Verify electrodes condition.	Refer to WPS or IAT for preheating temperature. Oven must be in operation at least two hours before welding.	Use TEMPILSTIKS or thermometer to confirm preheating temperature.

D-4: Conduct Inspection of Components Before Welding

PERFORMANCE CHECK

Employee Name: _____

Directions: Rate each step from the Activity Log. **Yes** means that the employee has demonstrated the complete ability to perform the step. **No** means that the employee cannot perform the step. If a **No** rating is given, the employee must go through additional training. Provide comments as necessary.

Step	Ability to Complete Steps		Comments
	Yes	No	
1. Receive work order information.			
2. Review data and drawings of components to be welded.			
3. Inspect overall condition of the components.			
4. Check the fit up between components.			
5. Verify the availability of welding rods/ electrodes.			
6. Verify electrodes condition.			

Date of Check _____   Overall: Competent _____   NOT Competent _____

Checker's Signature _____   Employee's Signature _____

C-4: Prepare IP Network Health Check Report

Training Location: Back Office Location

Overview

The Back Office IP Network Engineer is responsible for the network health check. The network health check is useful for assuring the network is stable and does not have any known problems. Without the health check, we cannot find any hidden problems.

Trainee Prerequisite

- IP network health check items

Required Resources:

- U2000 account
- Machine Room access authority
- Health check report template

Step	Comment	People Involved
1. Conduct device health checks	A. Hardware	• Senior Station Manager
	• Power cables are routed separately from service cables.	• Front Office Engineer
	• Power cables are orderly routed.	
	• Service cables are orderly routed.	
	• Cable labels are legible and accurate.	
	• Empty slots are covered with front panels.	
	• Air inlets of sub-racks are clear of dusts and ensure good heat dissipation.	
	• Redundant power input is available.	
	• Memory usage	
	• State of boards	
	• Power state	
	• Fan module state	
	• Active standby switchover function	
	B. Software	
	• Check the software versions of the VRP and BOOTROM are formal releases.	
	• Log information or log function is enabled	
	• Debugging state of the device	
	• Host name	
	• System time	
	• Configuration file	
	• Username and password account information	
	• Telnet login access	
	• NMS setting	

2. Conduct interface checks	<ul><li>Interface physical state</li><li>Interface description</li><li>Interface configuration</li><li>MAC address</li><li>ARP table</li><li>IP address</li><li>Interface statistics</li></ul>	<ul><li>Senior Station Manager</li><li>Front Office Engineer</li></ul>
3. Conduct routing checks	<ul><li>Routing table</li><li>Static routes configured</li><li>OSPF peer state</li><li>ISIS peer state</li><li>BGP peer state</li><li>Statistics of route entries</li></ul>	Front Office Engineer
4. Conduct service checks	<ul><li>Tunnels</li><li>L2VPN</li><li>L3VPN</li><li>Multicast</li></ul>	Front Office Engineer

Position: IP Network Back Office Engineer   Module C: Conducting IP Network Preventive Maintenance   C-4: Conduct IP Network Health Check and Prepare Report

5. Prepare health check report	Note: You can refer to Appendix Module C for IP Network Health Check Report template	Senior Station Manager Maintenance Manager Front Office Engineer

Position: IP Network Back Office Engineer   Module C: Conducting IP Network Preventive Maintenance   C-4: Conduct IP Network Health Check and Prepare Report

C-4: Conduct IP Network Health Check and Prepare Report   **PERFORMANCE CHECK**

Employee Name: _____   Date: _____

Steps	Ability to Complete Step			Comments
	Yes - 3 -	With Help - 2 -	No - 1 -	
3. Device health check				
4. Interface check				
5. Routing Check				
6. Service Check				
5. Prepare health check report				
Total				

Date of Check _____   Overall: Qualified _____   NOT Qualified _____

Checker's Signature _____   Employee's Signature _____

References

Allen, C. R. (1922). *The foreman and his job*. Philadelphia: J. B. Lippincott Company.

Allport, G. W. (1968). *The person in psychology*. Boston: Beacon Press.

Amadi, S., & Jacobs, R. L. (2017). A review of the literature on structured on-the-job training (S-OJT) and directions for future research. *Human Resource Development Review, 16*, 323–349.

Aron, D. (2017, October 3). How to find and hire the right digital talent for your organization. *Harvard Business Review*, pp. 1–4.

Arp, F. (2014). Emerging giants, aspiring multinationals and foreign executives: Leapfrogging, capability building, and competing with developed country multinationals. *Human Resource Management, 53*, 851–876.

Arthur, M. B., Defillippi, R. J., & Lindsay, V. J. (2008). On being a knowledge worker. *Organizational Dynamics, 37*(4), 365–377.

Baker, E. A., Sindone, A., & Roper, C. (2017). Addressing the skills gap: A regional analysis. *Journal of Applied Business and Economics, 19*(8), 10–21.

Balasa, D. A. (2015, July–August). Occupational analyses: Why such studies are important for examination and curriculum development. *CMA Today*, pp. 5–7.

Boyatzis, R. (1982). *The competent manager: A model for effective performance*. New York: John Wiley.

Boyatzis, R. E. (2008). Guest Editorial: Competencies in the 21st century. *Journal of Management Development, 27*(1), 5–12.

Brannick, M. T., & Levine, E. L. (2002). *Job analysis: Methods, research, and applications for human resource management in the new millennium*. Thousand Oaks, CA: Sage Publications, Inc.

Brobjer, T. H. (2008). *Nietzsche's philosophical context: An intellectual biography* (p. 149). Urbana, IL: University of Illinois Press.

© The Author(s) 2019
R. L. Jacobs, *Work Analysis in the Knowledge Economy*,
https://doi.org/10.1007/978-3-319-94448-7

Buckingham, M., & Clifton, D. O. (2001). *Now discover your strengths*. New York: The Free Press.

Burud, S., & Tumolo, M. (2004). *Leveraging the new human capital: Adaptive strategies, results achieved, and stories of transformation*. Palo Alton, CA: Davies-Black.

Campbell, J. P., Dunnette, M. D., Arvey, R. D., & Hellervik, L. V. (1973). The development of behaviorally based rating scales. *Journal of Applied Psychology, 57*, 15–22.

Cappelli, P., & Keller, J. R. (2013). Classifying work in the new economy. *The Academy of Management Review, 38*(4), 575–596. https://doi.org/10.5465/amr.2011.0302.

Cappelli, P. H., & Keller, J. (2013). A Study of the extent and potential causes of alternative employment arrangements. *ILR Review, 66*(4), 874–901.

Carlisle, K. E. (1986). *Analyzing jobs and tasks*. Englewood Cliffs, NJ: Educational Technology Publications.

Crandall, B., Klein, G., & Hoffman, R. (2006). *Working minds: A practitioner's guide to cognitive task analysis*. Boston: MIT Press.

Crosby, P. (1980). *Quality is free: The art of making quality certain*. New York: Signet.

Davenport, T. H. (2005). *Thinking for a living: How to get better performance and results from knowledge workers*. Boston: Harvard Business School Press.

Davenport, T. H., & Prusack, L. (2000). *Working knowledge: How organizations manage what they know*. Boston: Harvard Business School Press.

Davies, I. K. (1973). *Competency-based learning: Technology, management, and design*. New York: McGraw-Hill Book Company.

Demings, W. E. (1986). *Out of the crisis*. Boston: Massachusetts Institute of Technology, Center for Advanced Engineering Study.

Dewhurst, M., Hancock, B., & Ellsworth, D. (2013, January–February). Redesigning knowledge work. *Harvard Business Review*. Retrieved from https://hbr.org/2013/01/redesigning-knowledge-work.

Donahue, D. E. (2018). *Building leadership competence: A competency-based approach to building leadership ability*. State College, PA: Centrestar Learning.

Dooley, C. R. (1945). *The training within industry report (1940–1945): A record of the development of supervision, their use and the results*. Washington, DC: War Manpower Commission, Bureau of Training, Training within Industry Service.

Dreyfus, C. R. (2008). Identifying competencies that predict effectiveness of R&D managers. *Journal of Management Development, 27*(1), 76–91.

Drucker, P. (1957). *Landmarks of tomorrow*. New York: Harper.

Drucker, P. (1993). *Post-capitalist society*. New York: Harper Business.

Drucker, P. (1994). *Adventures of a bystander*. New York: John Wiley.

Evolution of Work and the Worker. (2014, February). New York: The Economist Intelligence Unit.

Feigenbaum, A. V. (1991). *Total quality control* (3rd ed.). New York: McGraw-Hill.

Flanagan, J. C. (1954, July). The critical incident technique. *Psychological Bulletin, 51*(4), 327–358.

Florida, R. E. (2012). *The rise of the creative class*. New York: Basic Books.

Fryklund, V. C. (1970). *Occupational analysis: Techniques and procedures*. New York: The Bruce Publishing Company.

Gael, S. (1983). *Job analysis: A guide to assessing work activities*. San Francisco, CA: Jossey-Bass.

Gawande, A. (2009). *The checklist manifesto: How to get things right*. New York: Metropolitan Books.

Gilbert, T. (2007). *Human competence: Engineering worthy performance*. San Francisco, CA: Pfeiffer.

Gilbreth, F. B. (1909). *Bricklaying system*. New York: The M.C. Clark Publishing Co.

Gilbreth, F. B., & Carey, E. G. (1948). *Cheaper by the dozen*. New York: Perennial Classics.

Gilbreth, F. B., & Gilbreth, L. M. (1917). *Applied motion study: A collection of papers on the efficient method to industrial preparedness*. New York: Sturgis & Walton Company.

Gilbreth, L. (1998). *As I remember: An autobiography*. Atlanta, GA: Institute of Industrial and Systems Engineers.

Goldratt, E. M., & Cox, J. (2004). *The goal*. New York: Routledge.

Hammer, M., & Champy, J. (1993). *Reengineering the corporation: A manifesto for business revolution*. New York: Harper Business Books.

Hartley, D. E. (1999). *Job analysis at the speed of reality*. Amherst, MA: HRD Press, Inc.

How to Hire the Best Digital Talent. (2015, October 8). Society for Human Resource Management.

Inception Report for the Global Commission on the Future of Work. (2017). Geneva: International Labour Organization.

Jacobs, R. L. (1986). Use of the critical incident technique to analyze the interpersonal skill requirements of supervisors. *Journal of Industrial Teacher Education, 23*(2), 56–61.

Jacobs, R. L. (1990). Human resource development as an interdisciplinary body of knowledge. *Human Resource Development Quarterly, 1*(1), 65–71.

Jacobs, R. L. (1994). Case studies that compare the training efficiency and product quality of unstructured and structured OJT. In J. Phillips (Ed.), *The return on investment in human resource development: cases on the economic benefits of HRD* (pp. 123–132). Alexandria, VA: American Society for Training and Development.

Jacobs, R. L. (2001). Managing employee competence and human intelligence in global organizations. In F. Richter (Ed.), *Maximizing human intelligence in Asia business: The sixth generation project* (pp. 44–54). New York: Prentice-Hall.

Jacobs, R. L. (2002). Honoring Channing Rice Dooley: Examining the man and his contributions. *Human Resource Development International, 5*(1), 131–137. https://doi.org/10.1080/13678860110057601.

Jacobs, R. L. (2003). *Structured on-the-job training: Unleashing employee expertise in the workplace*. San Francisco, CA: Berrett-Koehler Publishers.

Jacobs, R. L. (2014). System theory and human resource development. In N. Chalofsky, L. Morris, & T. Rocco (Eds.), *Handbook of human resource development*. San Francisco, CA: Jossey-Bass.

Jacobs, R. L. (2017). Knowledge work and human resource development. *Human Resource Development Review, 16*(2), 176–202.

Jacobs, R. L., & Bu-Rahmah, M. (2012). Developing employee expertise through structured on-the-job training (S-OJT): An introduction to this training approach and the KNPC experience. *Industrial and Commercial Training, 44*(2), 75–84.

Jacobs, R. L., & Hawley, J. (2009). Emergence of workforce development: Definition, conceptual boundaries, and future perspectives. In R. MacLean & D. Wilson (Eds.), *International handbook of technical and vocational education and training*. Bonn, Germany: UNESCO-UNEVOC.

Jacobs, R. L., & Wang, B. (2007). A proposed interpretation of the ISO 10015 guidelines for training: Implications for HRD theory and practice. In F. Nafuko (Ed.), *Proceedings of the annual conference of the Academy of Human Resource Development*. Bowling Green, OH: AHRD.

Jenkins, S. (2017, December 13). How to hire the best digital talent during a transformational era. *Forbes Agency Council*. Retrieved from https://www.forbes.com/sites/forbesagencycouncil/2017/12/13/how-to-hire-the-best-digital-talent-during-a-transformational-era/#171eeeaf4dd2.

Johann, B. (1995). *Designing cross-functional business processes*. San Francisco, CA: Jossey-Bass.

Juran, M. (1992). *Juran on quality by design: The new steps for planning quality into goods and services*. New York: The Free Press.

KANBAN: Just-in-time at Toyota, Management begins at the workplace. (1989). Boston: Productivity Press.

Kane, G. C., Palmer, D., Phillips, A. N., Kiron, D., & Buckley, N. (2017, Summer). *Achieving digital maturity: Adapting your company to a changing world*. MIT Management Review and Deloitte University Press Retrieved from https://www2.deloitte.com/content/dam/insights/us/articles/3678_achieving-digital-maturity/DUP_Achieving-digital-maturity.pdf.

Lacey, R. (1986). *Ford: The man and the machine*. New York: Little, Brown and Co.

Lee, K. Y. (2000). *From third world to first: The Singapore story—1965–2000*. New York: Harpers.

Liker, J. K., & Meier, D. (2006). *The Toyota way fieldbook: A practical guide for implementing Toyota's 4Ps*. New York: McGraw-Hill.

Lin, Y., & Jacobs, R. (2008). The perceptions of human resource development professionals in Taiwan regarding their working relationships with subject matter experts (SMEs) during the training design process. *Human Resource Development International, 11*(3), 237–252.

MacKenzie, L., & O'Toole, G. (Eds.). (2011). *Occupational analysis in practice*. San Francisco, CA: John Wiley.

Mager, R. F. (1982). *Troubleshooting the troubleshooting course: Or debug d'bugs*. Belmont, CA: Lake Publishing Company.

Mager, R. F. (1997). *Preparing instructional objectives: A critical tool in the development of effective instruction* (3rd ed.). Atlanta, GA: The Center for Effective Performance.

McClelland, D. (1973, January). Testing for competence rather than for "intelligence". *American Psychologist, 28*(1), 1–14.

McClelland, D. (1998). Identifying competencies with behavioral-events interviews. *Psychological Science, 9*(5), 331–338.

McCormick, E. J. (1976). Chapter 15: Job and task analysis. In M. D. Dunnette (Ed.), *Handbook of industrial and organizational psychology* (pp. 651–696). Chicago, IL: Rand McNally College Publishing Company.

McLagan, P., & Bedrick, D. (1983, June). Models for excellence: The results of the ASTD training and development competency study. *Training and Development, 37*(6), 10–12, 14, 16–20.

Merriam, S. B., Caffarella, R. S., & Baumgartner, L. M. (2007). *Learning in adulthood: A comprehensive guide*. San Francisco, CA: Jossey-Bass.

Miller, G. A. (1956). The magical number of seven, plus or minus two: Some limits on our capacity for processing information. *Psychological Review, 101*(2), 343–352.

Myers, I. B. (1995). *Gifts differing: Understanding personality type*. Mountain View, CA: Davies-Black Publishing.

Navigating the future of work: Can we point business, workers, and social institutions in the same direction?. (2017, July, Issue 21). Special issue of the *Deloitte Review*.

Norton, R. E., & Moser, J. (2007). *SCID handbook* (7th ed.). Columbus, OH: Center on Education and Training for Employment, The Ohio State University.

Norton, R. E., & Moser, J. (2008). *DACUM handbook* (3rd ed.). Columbus, OH: Center on Education and Training for Employment, The Ohio State University.

Patton, M. Q. (2015). *Qualitative research & evaluation methods: Integrating theory and practice* (4th ed.). San Francisco, CA: Sage.

Petroski, H. (1985). *To engineer is human: The role of failure in successful design*. New York: St. Martin's Press.

Prahalad, C. K., & Hamel, G. (1990). The core competence of the organization. *Harvard Business Review, 68*(3), 79–91.

Putnam, R. (2016). *Our kids: The American dream in crisis*. New York: Simon and Shuster.

Rhee, K. S. (2008). The beat and rhythm of competency development over two years. *Journal of Management Development, 27*(1), 146–160.

Rossett, A., & Schafer, L. (2007). *Job aids and performance support: Moving from knowledge in the classroom to knowledge everywhere*. San Francisco, CA: Pfeiffer.

Rothwell, W., & Gaber, J. (2010). *Competency-based training basics*. Alexandria, VA: ASTD Press.

Rummler, G., & Barche, A. (2013). *Improving performance: How to manage the white space on the organization chart.* San Francisco, CA: Jossey-Bass.

Schrock, S. A., & Coscarelli, W. C. (2007). *Criterion-referenced test development: Technical and legal guidelines for corporate training.* San Francisco, CA: Pfeiffer.

Skinner, B. F. (1965). *Science and human behavior.* New York: Free Press.

Slaughter, S. (2015, October 25). No job title too big, or creative. *New York Times,* ST2.

Sudman, S., & Bradburn, N. M. (1983). *Asking questions: A practical guide to questionnaire design.* San Francisco, CA: Jossey-Bass.

Swanson, R. A. (2007). *Analysis for improving performance: Tools for diagnosing organizations and documenting workplace expertise.* San Francisco, CA: Berrett-Koehler Publishers, Inc.

Swanson, R. A., & Gradous, D. (1986). *Performance at work: A systematic program for analyzing work behavior.* New York: John Wiley & Sons, Inc.

Swanson, R. A., & Holton, E. F. (2009). *Foundations of human resource development.* San Francisco, CA: Berrett-Koehler Publishers, Inc.

Taylor, F. (1911, 1998). *The principles of scientific management.* Unabridged Dover (1998) republication of the work published by Harper & Brothers Publishers, New York, 1911.

Technology, jobs, and the future of work. (2017). New York: McKinsey Global Institute.

The digital talent gap—Are companies doing enough? (2017, June–July). Capgemini. Retrieved from https://www.capgemini.com/wp-content/uploads/2017/10/dti_the-digital-talent-gap_20171109.pdf.

The future of jobs: Employment, skills and the workforce strategy for the fourth industrial revolution. (2016, January). Geneva: World Economic Forum.

The new tech talent you need to succeed in digital. (2016, September). McKinsey & Company. Retrieved from https://www.mckinsey.com/business-functions/digital-mckinsey/our-insights/the-new-tech-talent-you-need-to-succeed-in-digital.

Ulrich, D., Younger, J., Brockbank, W., & Ulrich, M. (2012, July). HR talent and the new HR competencies. *Strategic HR Review, 11*(4), 217–222.

Watkins, K. E., & Marsick, V. J. (1993). *Sculpting the learning organization: Lessons in the art and science systemic change.* San Francisco, CA: Jossey-Bass.

Wladawsky-Berger, I. (2015, December 18). The rise of the T shaped organization. *The Wall Street Journal.* Retrieved from https://blogs.wsj.com/cio/2015/12/18/the-rise-of-the-t-shaped-organization/.

Wood, M. C. (2003). *Frank and Lillian Gilbreth: Critical evaluations in business and management.* New York: Routledge.

Workforce of the future: The competing forces shaping 2030. (2018). London, UK: Pricewaterhouse Coopers.

Zemke, R. (1982). *Figuring things out: A trainer's guide to needs and task analysis.* Reading, MA: Addison-Wesley.

Zidan, S. (2001). The role of HRD in economic development. *Human Resource Development Quarterly, 12*(4), 437–443.

Index

© The Author(s) 2019
R. L. Jacobs, *Work Analysis in the Knowledge Economy*,
https://doi.org/10.1007/978-3-319-94448-7